Capitalism and COVID-19: Time to Make a Democratic New World Order

Studies in Critical Social Sciences

VOLUME 251

The titles published in this series are listed at *brill.com/scss*

Capitalism and COVID-19: Time to Make a Democratic New World Order

Volume II

By

Noel Chellan

BRILL

LEIDEN | BOSTON

Cover illustration: COVID-19 victims being cremated at Seemapuri crematorium, on April 23, 2021 in New Delhi, India. (Photo by Amal KS/Hindustan Times via Getty Images).

The Library of Congress Cataloging-in-Publication Data is available online at https://catalog.loc.gov
LC record available at https://lccn.loc.gov/2023004369

Typeface for the Latin, Greek, and Cyrillic scripts: "Brill". See and download: brill.com/brill-typeface.

ISSN 1573-4234
ISBN 978-90-04-53876-4 (hard back)
ISBN 978-90-04-53980-8 (e-book)

This book is printed on acid-free paper and produced in a sustainable manner.

To the many millions who lost their lives in the time of COVID-19

*To the millions of moms, dads, sons, daughters,
husbands, wives, grandmas, granddads, friends, etc.
who lost loved ones in the time of COVID-19*

To the hundreds of millions of workers on the frontline in the time of COVID-19, who have sacrificed so much – with both their lives and their energies – so that the human race can go on

To the caring states and leaders in all parts of the world – that chose lives over the profit economy in the time of COVID-19

To the many that gave little and much to the needy – in the time of COVID-19

To family, friends and colleagues who have passed on in the time of COVID-19. You will be forever remembered

To the children of the world – waiting for the adults to create a better world and a better future

The Struggle Continues

Contents

Preface

Published in two volumes viz. *F/Ailing Capitalism and the Challenge of COVID-19* (Volume I) and *Capitalism and COVID-19: Time to Make a Democratic New World Order* (Volume II), these books are about the failings of the capitalist system to effectively, and efficiently, respond to COVID-19. The two volumes present my broad analysis and understanding of the world in the time of COVID-19. Volume I deals with the failure of capitalist countries to respond effectively and efficiently to COVID-19. Volume II deals with a range of themes linked to capitalism, and in the final analysis argues for the democratic remaking of the world order. The two volumes are underpinned primarily by Karl Marx's analysis of capitalism.

If the 2008 Financial Crisis resurrected "The End of History" debate – then COVID-19 has turned up the heat on the debate quite considerably. It is hoped that these two volumes will serve as a contribution to that discussion and debate – one that will be ongoing for some time to come. I have used a kaleidoscope of views to put together these two volumes, in order to support the central thread of my argument viz. that capitalism organises society to rationalise profit over people – even during a global pandemic! I have written from a multi-disciplinary perspective. These two volumes are a combination of a broad spectrum of COVID-19 related issues, my opinions and analysis of the political-economy of COVID-19, as well as an argument for transcending to a post-capitalist society.

I attempt to make a case against the capitalist system by arguing that where citizens of a country have been infected and died, then it is in the main – due to the prevailing and stubborn capitalist ideologies – and an imperfect understanding and paradigm of liberty, freedom, democracy and human rights in the Western world. My primary aim through these two volumes is to attempt to deconstruct the prevailing and stubborn ideological beliefs of capitalism that have been in existence for many centuries. I engage with the phenomena related to COVID-19 in the capitalist era through a historical perspective as well – and within the framework of geopolitics in the globalised world. These two volumes are also a mini or micro chronicling of a vast range of views that were aired, articulated and written in all parts of the world in the time of COVID-19. For this I am indeed thankful to the many people in many parts of the world who shared their views, opinions, perspectives and criticisms in the time of COVID-19. In this regard the views of scholars, writers, journalists, opinion makers, critics etc. were left intact as quotes but integrated in a way that makes for continuous and flow of reading. Unfortunately like any book that relies on the vast array of information that is out there, all information of a similar nature could not be assimilated into these two volumes for practical reasons. I assume responsibility for any errors of one sort or another.

These two volumes are only possible because of the ample and varied views on so many aspects of the world that were available at one time in world history. This was only possible because of COVID-19. As COVID-19 unleashed the productive power of people, written material in the form of journal articles, newspaper articles, books, etc. on COVID-19 were produced thick and fast, and within the shortest possible time. COVID-19 had unleashed the ideological and the scientific human. COVID-19 had unleashed the opinionated human. COVID-19 had brought forth the critical human. These two volumes are part and parcel of the burst of information and analyses that COVID-19 had generated. The world became more informed and educated about the workings of capitalism in the one year that COVID-19 struck than it had in the hundreds of years of capitalism's existence! These two volumes are an attempt at understanding capitalism and its real workings through the lens of COVID-19. The work is a no-holds barred critique of the capitalist system – and the ideological-based economic science that keeps this historical and broken system plodding along.

In the final analysis Volume II argues for the democratic remaking of the current world order by exploring ideas and spheres of influence for a post-capitalist world. *Capitalism* and *COVID-19: Time to Make a Democratic New World Order* proposes the deepening and consolidation of freedom, democracy, human rights and privacy in a post-capitalist world. It suggests that humans should be placed back in nature and nature back in humans and argues for a global environmental movement. Volume II explores the idea of an O-shaped or use-value economy and society – and maintains that the free market should serve people and planet – instead of people and planet serving the free market. It motivates for deepening, strengthening, consolidating and trusting the state in leading the transition to a post-capitalist world. Making a democratic new world order should entail declaring war on global enemies such as gender-based violence, gun violence, poverty, racism, inequality, unemployment, classism, etc. and flattening their curves. A post-capitalist society should be one whereby planetary and peoples' well-being sit side-by-side with economic well-being. Transitioning to a post-capitalist world requires that economic science in its current ideological form be revisited in order to provide a more scientific understanding and analysis of the world economy. Exiting capitalism requires the unity of workers of all countries and the formation of a global workers movement. Ideally the transition to a post-capitalist society should be peacefully assisted and guided – instead of leaving socio-economic conditions unchanged – thereby increasing the risk for violence to enforce change for a better world. Volume II – *Capitalism and COVID-19: Time to Make a Democratic New World Order* – calls for reimagining and recreating the best of all possible worlds for present and future generations. In the final analysis, volume II both predicts and maintains that *capitalism too shall pass*!

Acknowledgements

I am extremely grateful to all of the World's Media – BBC, CGTN, RT, CNN, South African media, internet sources, the presenters, workers and professionals that appeared on TV screens, radio, Zoom, YouTube channels, etc. and shared their experiences, views and analyses on COVID-19. I acknowledge the work from all scholars that have been invaluable in my understanding of the various subject matters related to COVID-19 discussed in the two volumes. I am also grateful to family and friends who were sharing via social media in the time of COVID-19. There was a flurry of information that was churned out on a second-by-second basis on COVID-19 and its impact on all spheres of society. One simply could not keep up with the abundance of news, information and analyses. I am especially indebted to the writers and contributors in the print media that carried such large amounts and diverse range of views on COVID-19. These written media views, opinions, analyses and critique form the backbone of the two volumes relating to capitalism and COVID-19. Such views, opinions, analyses and critique provided the material and data for me to critique the capitalist system and its poor handling of a global pandemic. Without the world's print media and its many contributors – these two volumes would not have been possible. I tried to capture as many views and analyses as was practically possible – and in this burst of activity also tried to secure the sources as best as I could.

I wish to thank Kitty O'Meara for permission to use her poem, *And the People Stayed Home,* which is published in *Together in a Sudden Strangeness: America's Poets Respond to the Pandemic,* edited by Alice Quinn (NY: Alfred Knopf, 2020) and *And the People Stayed Home* by Kitty O'Meara, illustrations by Stefano Di Cristifaro and Paul Pereda (Miami, FL: Tra Publishing, 2020).

I am extremely thankful and indeed grateful to David Fasenfest, Series Editor at Brill Publishers, for facilitating the publication of the two volumes. His professional and on-the-mark suggestions on how I could go about improving the initial single manuscript has made possible the two volumes: *F/Ailing Capitalism and the Challenge of COVID-19 – Volume I* and *Capitalism* and *COVID-19: Time to Make a Democratic New World Order – Volume II.* His expert guidance and timeous feedback were pillars of strength in helping me to sustain and see my work through to completion. It was a real pleasure working with David.

My appreciation is also to Jason Prevost, Senior Acquisitions Editor at Brill Publishers, for initially accepting my book proposal and linking me up with David Fasenfest. I am indeed thankful to the reviewers for constructive feedback on the manuscripts – *volume I and volume II.* Many thanks to

Judy Pereira - Production Editor at Brill - for her skilful guidance and patience. To the entire team at Brill Publishers, thank you for agreeing to publish the two volumes titled: *F/Ailing Capitalism and the Challenge of COVID-19 – Volume I* and *Capitalism* and *COVID-19: Time to Make a Democratic New World Order – Volume II*.

To my University (The University of KwaZulu-Natal), partner and family, thank you for your continued support.

Acronyms and Abbreviations

ANC	African National Congress
BBC	British Broadcasting Corporation
BJP	Bharatiya Janata Party
CGTN	Chinese Global Television Network
CNN	Cable News Network
COVID-19	Coronavirus Disease of 2019
EU	European Union
GDP	Gross Domestic Product
PPE	Personal Protective Equipment
RT	Russia Today
UK	United Kingdom
UN	United Nations
US	United States
USA	United States of America
USSR	Union of Soviet Socialist Republics
WHO	World Health Organisation

CHAPTER 1

Capitalism – the Violent Enemy of Nature

> Man in his arrogance thinks himself a great work, worthy of the interposition of a deity. More humble, and I believe truer, to consider him created from animals.
>
> CHARLES DARWIN

•••

> Capitalism tends to destroy its two sources of wealth – Nature and Human Beings.
>
> KARL MARX

∴

1 COVID-19 and the Arrival of Nature

A virus, to most people, is an "unknown" creature of nature. Similar to economic science – it is a creature that is only studied and known by a very small section of society. But within a short space of time – between the end of 2019 and the beginning of 2020 – the entire world got to know about the existence of viruses. People learnt that viruses could be everywhere. They learnt that viruses are passed on from one person to another in ways that dumbfounded them. The scariest thing of all was that viruses are invisible to the unaided eye – they could be on our hands, and we would not even know it!

Humanity was dealing with an invisible enemy – to not only its existence but to its capitalist way of life as well. South Africa went into lockdown on 27 March 2020. A few days before, the minister of health granted permission for citizens to be allowed to go for walks or to walk one's dog – but cautioned that social distancing be maintained. The month of March is a relatively cool time of the year in Durban, South Africa. It was neither full summer nor full winter. In any event Durban has good weather almost all-year-round for one to engage in outdoor activities. On a Friday morning at about 5.30 am – the first day of the state-imposed lockdown – I got out of my home and walked and jogged for about 3km. The air was cool and clean. The sky was slowly turning blue. In

 | DOI:10.1163/9789004539808_002

all my years of living in my community, nature seemed to be at its best on that day. Well, that is except for the solid waste pollution that has become part of the natural landscape in South Africa. I noticed that the many different types of trees were not only green but different shades of green – lime green, dark green, light green, shadowy green, etc. I heard a variety of bird sounds breaking through the morning silence – a silence that was both unusual but calming. The usual noise and pollution of cars were no longer disturbing the peace, quiet and fresh air that paradoxically came with COVID-19. This was no longer the abnormal – when COVID-19 placed the capitalist way of life on pause. The temporary absence of capitalism made me more in tune with myself, with my surroundings and with nature. In many parts of the world, wildlife were seen entering urban areas and nature was in "its full glory" – when there were no people, no cars, no noise and no capitalism:

> Pollution has reduced greatly and fresh air hidden behind a persistent smog has been set free. The waters in rivers are running clean, animals are fearlessly claiming their rightful place and nature is manifesting itself in its full glory – so much so that the snow-capped peaks of the Himalayas are now clearly visible from Jalandhar in Punjab.
>
> Joint General Secretary of the RSS, 2020

With the arrival of COVID-19, the world also witnessed and experienced the wonders of nature – so long hidden beneath capitalism's domineering presence:

> Scientists and artists have used the reduction in noise pollution during the coronavirus lockdown to create the first global public sound map of the spring dawn chorus. Throughout May, people around the world have uploaded about 3,000 early-morning bird recordings made on their phones to the Dawn Chorus website, where they are being shared to help conservation and to create public art.
>
> MORSS, 2020: 19

It was the time of clear skies once again. There were other times when capitalism was failing – as in the time of the 2008 Great Crisis – that nature had been given breathing space:

> It seems planet earth breathes a sigh of relief when the capitalist economy is on a sick bed. In China carbon emissions growth had sped up

> disastrously, with the annual rate of increase reaching 3.4 percent a year for much of the decade. That rapid growth rate continues to this day, interrupted only briefly in 2009 by the world financial crisis.
>
> KLEIN, 2014: 25

The fact that economic and social life came to a standstill – and nature was temporarily rescued by COVID-19, means that our economic and social life has to now be under the analytical microscope. Will we go back to business as usual? Will the "new normal" be the abnormal again? Will nature continue to be seen as another money-making entity? Life in the time of COVID-19 showed not only that capitalism was not good for the majority of humankind – but that the capitalist way of life was also not good for nature too. Researchers at the University of East Anglia in the United Kingdom found that:

> The world's daily carbon emissions have dropped by 17%. This is a huge drop. The data covers 69 countries, accounting for 97% of all emissions. That means more than 100 other countries emit just 3% of all emissions. Published in the peer-reviewed journal Nature Climate Change, it says carbon emissions right now are at the same level as they were in 2006. Nearly half of the drop (43%) comes from people travelling on land – in cars, trains and buses – and a similar drop comes from fewer emissions from industry and energy production. A full 10% of the drop comes from flights, which normally account for 3% of global carbon emissions. In South Africa, the data shows the effect of the lockdown. On March 27, when the lockdown came into force, emissions dropped by 26 0000 tonnes a day. In the 48 days from then until the dataset ends (May 13) the country emitted 12-million tonnes less carbon than the same time last year. In a year, South Africa emits nearly 500-million tonnes. When the country moved to level four lockdown, emissions again increased by 100 000 tonnes a day. So clearly the line peddled by the fossil fuel industry – that climate action is about individual change – does not hold up. COVID-19 has provided researchers with a treasure trove of data to look at global carbon emissions. The results are showing that it is the industries and corporations of our world that do most of the polluting.
>
> KINGS, 2020: 21

The arrival of COVID-19 also symbolised the arrival of nature. It was the time of COVID-19 versus man. It was the time of nature versus capitalism.

2 Capitalism's Mad Rush for Energy – Tipping Earth's Delicate Temperature Balance

The world has never witnessed the scale and intensity at which the temperature of people in all parts of the world were taken in the time of COVID-19. Temperature is one of the key indicators as to whether a person is sick or healthy. I learnt that if my temperature was above 37.5 degrees Celsius then this type of screening would place me in the category of being potentially at risk of having COVID-19. Whatever our nationality, race, gender, qualification, wealth status, etc. we all are subjected to the same criteria pronounced by nature – we function best as human beings at a temperature of around 36.5 degrees Celsius. Like COVID-19, climate scientists can also detect the health and fitness of the planet – by observing and studying the average temperature of and on planet earth. The symptoms of COVID-19 tended to correlate with high temperatures. The many environmental disasters confronting the planet and humankind tend to correlate with increases in the average global temperature. The climate is changing and it seems irreversible. COVID-19 has provided a reference point of the negative impacts of modern humans' economic, social and cultural life on the climate. In a short space of time COVID-19 presented humankind with a global set of data, which demonstrated that the problems of global warming and climate change are also a cultural and lifestyle issue under capitalism. Modern man is living out of sync with the natural environment. Nowhere is the aberration between capitalist society and nature more pronounced than in its use and abuse of energy sources. Energy is the life-blood of any society. Human civilisation is built on the capture of energy over the millennia. But energy use in capitalist society is leading the world to the brink of ecosystems collapse because of the voracious manner in which capitalism seeks and uses energy. Capitalist man is on a high energy diet. Capitalism is on a feeding frenzy for cheap and abundant forms of energy. With lax laws and weak regulations on environmental protection guaranteed by the state, the capitalist market is aided and abetted to exploit energy both extensively and intensively in all parts of the planet. The outpouring of carbon dioxide into the planet as a result of the use of fossil fuels is leading to the formation of a blanket-like layer – a few hundred kilometers above planet earth. This in turn is fast disrupting the energy-exchange balance between the sun and the earth. The consequence of this disruption is the slow heating up of planet earth. Like a high temperature that sends one into the danger zone in the time of COVID-19, a high planetary temperature pushes the planet and all of its inhabitants into the danger zone. But it is not only the heat from the captured energy of the sun that is heating the planet – it is also the amount of heat that is generated by the capitalist system, which is contributing to global warming and subsequent climate change. Everyone knows that anything that uses energy generates heat – whether it is the human body, a mobile phone, a computer, an air conditioner, a motor vehicle, a jumbo jet, industrial and manufacturing plants, etc. Capitalism is a high energy society. Capitalist man has a large energy footprint. The energy footprint of capitalist man is thousands of times more than that of feudal-man, slave-man or the hunter-gatherer. With all of the energy that is being used – whether we call it brown or green energy, dirty or clean energy – capitalist society is emitting huge amounts of heat into the atmosphere. Fossil fuels are causing the heating up of the planet. But the heating of the planet is also due to the manner, speed and types of social and economic activities that capitalist society is subjecting fossil fuels to. The earth is not only being heated by the sun's rays trapped inside layers of greenhouse gasses, the warming of the globe is also compounded by the huge quantities of heat emitted as a result of the capitalist way of life – a way of life that has come to rely and depend on prodigious quantities of energy. It is a rat race under capitalism – and all races use up huge amounts of energy – whether it is a race to space, a race to manufacture the latest mobile phone, a race to get to work on time, a race to get economic growth going again after a pandemic, a race to develop the most sophisticated war machines, a race to get huge container ships with goods through the Suez Canal, etc. Capitalism is a system predicated on endless production – and the primary condition for this production is the continuous flow of energy: "for production to continue to stay in the race, it has to speed up the materialisation of energy" (Brennan, 1993: 139). The human cost of capitalism's greed for energy is the many lives lost as a result of the continuous wars fought over energy. The ecosystem cost – and therefore the human cost again – is the fast-changing climate: "climate change has become an existential crisis for the human species" (Klein, 2014: 21). Energy is capitalism's life-blood. Cost and potential for maximum profit are the overriding factors for capitalist society's choice of energy:

> Modern high-energy societies have preferred to develop fossil fuel resources with the highest net energy returns, and that is a major reason why we have favored crude oil in general, and the rich Middle Eastern fields in particular; oil's high energy density, and hence easy transportability, are other obvious advantages.
>
> SMIL, 2017: 16

However, it is questionable as to whether society can go through another 250 years on a high-energy diet:

> Modern civilisation has been created by the massive, and increasing, combustion of fossil fuels, but this practice is clearly limited by their crystal abundance, as well as by the environmental consequences of burning coals and hydrocarbons, and high-energy societies can ensure their survival only by an eventual transition to non-fossil sources.
>
> SMIL, 2017: 16

Capitalist society is clearly exploiting the goodness and freely-giving nature of nature as articulated by Kovel (2007: 17) in the following statement:

> That reckless expansive period driven over the past two hundred years by the assumption that nature offers an endless gift of energy to its human master.

If COVID-19 has thrown the world into disarray – whilst showing up the unequal nature of life and living under capitalism – then climate change will be far more devastating and unlike COVID-19, untreatable if countries continue on the capitalist freeway:

> The COVID-19 pandemic has confronted the world with a test that it seems to be failing. Co-operation and inclusive approaches to addressing the multifaceted consequences of the crisis have been lacking. Policymakers cannot focus only on containing the pandemic, but must also invest in the future. That includes pursuing rapid, far-reaching and unprecedented changes to limit global warming and strengthen our collective response to the threats it poses. The world may now be more receptive to such reforms. We have no choice. While we may be able to manage the COVID-19 pandemic with social distancing, new antiviral drugs and eventually, one hopes, a vaccine, climate change represents an even larger existential threat, because its effects have no defined treatment or lifespan. There may be a reset button for the post-pandemic global economy, but there is none for the planet on which it depends.
>
> MACHARIS ET AL., 2020: 21

Humans used very little energy as hunter-gatherers. In slave society, slaves were an important source of energy for the extraction of profit and capital accumulation. Feudal society got by with limited quantities and sources of energy. But capitalist society does not seem to have a limit or cap on the quantity and types of energy sources used. Activities that consume large and continued amounts of energy were also under the energy-spotlight in the time of COVID-19. We are now witnessing the planetary mayhem when a relatively young species – Homo sapiens – feels entitled to seek out and use energy as if energy is limitless – and without the thought of future generations' dependence on planet earth and energy for the next 100, 1000, 10 000, 100 000, 1000 000 years. Any apparent concern for the welfare and wellbeing of future generations is merely another rhetorical tool in capitalism's large ideological toolbox.

China decided to do away with the measurement of growth in the time of COVID-19 in 2020. It took the unusual step away from such an ideological practice for so long – to not calculate its GDP for 2020. The state went on to say that it was a price worth paying for saving lives. At the same time, we were told that countries were experiencing negative growth. When is it ever the case that growth is negative! So fixated is capitalist society on growth – that even when there is a drop in economic production, the ideological label "growth" is held onto and imprinted into global consciousness. The fascination with economic growth drives capitalist society to seek out and utilise huge amounts of energy – which in turn is driving climate change and potential ecosystems collapse. In a letter to the print media in the time of COVID-19, a writer debunks the ideology of capitalism purportedly contributing to a just and equal society – and also makes the connection with endless economic growth and environmental degradation:

> Neoliberalism has had its day. Economists like Nobel Laureate Paul Krugman say the trickle-down hypothesis has been debunked. The wealthier simply got wealthier. Climate deniers hang around discredited scientists like stale smoke from the tobacco industry. The pandemic showed cutting costs and capacity in health services leaves them overwhelmed – and kills frontline doctors. Trump and his henchmen have demonstrated that destroying not just science but rational belief in science leaves you up the creek without a paddle. And destruction of the environment in the pursuit of growth will see the creek run dry.
>
> HORNE, 2020

Capitalism prides itself on quantity. Capitalist society is fundamentally a quantitative society. Our ideologies and values have also assumed a quantitative nature under capitalism – the quantity of years we live, the quantity of years we are married, the quantity of qualifications we have, the quantity of cars we own, the quantity of places we have visited, the quantity of working hours a worker is expected to work, the quantity of dollars a business owner makes, the quantity of likes you get on your Facebook page, and the list goes on and on. Capitalism's purposes in history are growth and the accumulation of wealth: "the wealth of those societies in which the capitalist mode of production prevails, presents itself as an immense accumulation of commodities" (Marx, 1867 [2010]: 26). Capitalism is socially and culturally engineered to accumulate. It is the blind chase for accumulation – that compels capitalists to seize, capture and convert nature whenever, wherever and however. A subsequent ideology that drives capitalism to seek out more land and more energy is endless economic growth. It is why some maintain that: "growth for the sake of growth is the ideology of the cancer cell" (Edward Abbey). Like all things quantitative – it has to be measured in order to ascertain whether it is doing well or not. The pinnacle of capitalism's measurement index is the gross domestic product – GDP for short. GDP is the: "total value of all goods and services exchanged for money within a country in a year" (Kishtainy et al., 2012: 37). And the ideology that drives economic growth – which in turn drives capitalism to seek out more land and more energy – is profit or exchange-value. Economic activity takes place on planet earth. Nature is the basis for all economic activities. Humans need stuff. But how much stuff do we need? Can a post-COVID-19 society agree to use efficient and effective public transport – instead of buying a car for each adult member of the family? Can we commit to using our clothing for a minimum of 7–10 years – before going out again on a shopping spree? Can we keep our mobile phones for 10–15 years – and then get excited about the next one that comes out in the free market? Where states are allowing malls to spring up – can they instead allow natural spaces to thrive – where humans can go and connect with nature and with each other? This idea has been thought of – and practiced before:

> It was the concrete actions of the BLF and allied community members that put a stop to the overdevelopment of places like Centennial Park in Sydney. The social purpose of labour defies a narrow economism and gestures toward an expansive vision of human-nature relations that inevitably takes us beyond the workplace to the city, and ultimately to the planet as a whole. In the words of Mundey, 'what is the use of higher wages alone, if we have to live in cities devoid of parks, denuded of trees, in an atmosphere poisoned by pollution and vibrating with the noise of hundreds of thousands of units of private transport'?
>
> HEENAN and STURMAN, 2020: 196–197

In capitalist society the economy is viewed through a quantitative paradigm. Can a post-COVID-19 society view the economy through a qualitative paradigm? Can we grow the qualitative economy – an economy of happiness, an economy of well-being, an economy of safety and security, an economy of dignity and human rights, an economy of equality? Can we grow an economy where Black Lives Matter? Where Asian Lives Matter? Where Palestinian Lives Matter? Where Women's and Girls' Lives Matter? Where All Lives Matter? Can we grow the family economy – an economy where there is more family time? Can we use the human happiness indices to measure the happiness economy? Can we use the quality-of-life indices to measure the well-being economy? Can we broaden the sphere of economic science – to factor in growth of other relevant aspects of the economy – such as the growth of happiness, well-being, life and livelihood satisfaction, etc.?

3 The Ideology of Profit-Accumulation under Capitalism

There is a sculpture of a bull on Wall Street. He should ideally represent the strength and vigour of nature – but this natural wonder has been appropriated by the ruling class to symbolise capitalist greed. Maybe in a post-capitalist world he will become a museum piece on probably what was once the world's most famous capitalist street. When the capitalist economy is doing well – it is said to be bullish. When it is doing badly – it is said to be bearish. Aided and abetted by the state, the capitalist market is the social mechanism which regulates all economic activities within countries. The so-called free market, which in reality is the capitalist market, seeks to command and control both nature and labour-power. Under capitalism nature and labour-power are subjects of the free market. Free market ideology, in actual fact, means the freedom to exploit labour-power or human-energy and nature:

> Precisely because our labour is determined by production for exchange and private profit, it is often alienating and ecologically destructive.
>
> HEENAN and STURMAN, 2020: 195

It is there for all to see – since the time of the Industrial Revolution. The commodity is the means by which profit and accumulation are attained. In the same way that humans cannot be entirely separated from nature – nature cannot be separated from material wealth. Hence William Petty's insightful analysis about material wealth: "labour is its father and the earth its mother". Nature contributes to the qualitative aspect of the commodity – its shape, form, chemistry, density, purpose, etc. Nature therefore contributes to the use-value component of the commodity. Nature enables the usefulness or utility of a commodity by man. A wooden table is useful to man, so is a woolen jersey or coffee beans. Gowns and N-95 masks are extremely useful to health-care workers in the time of a global pandemic. So are ventilators for the very ill. Food is essential in everyday life and more so during a pandemic. All these examples of commodities of utility – and the trillions and trillions of other commodities that are now part of our capitalist world – are derivatives of nature. Hence if Mother Earth is being destroyed, it is because she is continually being transformed into commodities. We all need commodities for their utility. But the ideology of capitalism is not to produce commodities for utility or use – but for the accumulation of profit: "in a market system, a commodity is always produced for exchange, and has exchange-value" (Brennan, 1993: 119). Anyone of us who gets into business will have to make a profit in order for the business to survive. It is even better if it is prosperous. As shareholders in any part of the economy, we expect more than what we put in. Else, we would probably spend our monies to enjoy life today and tomorrow and the next day. One would be considered mad if one argued against the ideology of profit. After all, we expect and are constantly reminded that businesses have to make a profit. But if we are going to start labelling people as mad for calling out the profit system, then we may have to – with major discomfort – start with Jesus Christ who boldly stated: "it is easier for a camel to go through the eye of a needle than for a rich man to enter the kingdom of God". Once we call out the madness of Jesus for denouncing the madness of the rich to accumulate more riches – we can then turn to the small guy – the Pope – and call out his madness for highlighting the link between profit and greed in the time of COVID-19:

> Instead of battling the Ptolemaic model of the heavens, which described the cosmos with the Earth at the center of the universe, Francis has a much harder job: Convincing modern-day masters of the universe that greed, profit and the extraordinary concentration of wealth in the hands of a few are at the center and we revolve around it.
>
> PETRUCCI, 2021

We should then call out the maddest of them all – Karl Marx – for having the nerve to say that profit is as a result of the exploitation of the worker – and dragging nature into the picture as well. In *Capital* (1867) Marx underscores the requirement of nature in the making of a commodity:

> If we take away the useful labour expended upon them, a material substratum is always left, which is furnished by Nature without the help of man.

From this we can deduce that x% growth in the physical economy must mean x% extraction of material substratum from nature. In other words, economic growth cannot occur without the concurrent degradation and destruction of nature. The hard fact is – if the physical economy is growing then it means that nature is shrinking! If our real monies are increasing – then it means that nature is decreasing. It is therefore no surprise that capitalists who have extracted the largest quantity of diamonds or gold from Mother Earth are extremely rich people. Those who have taken out the most amount of coal and oil from the ground must have also seen their monies skyrocket. Saudi Arabia comes to mind when one thinks of oil. I am certain timber companies must have large sums of monies in their bank accounts, as a result of clearing vast swathes of forest in many parts of the world. The fishing trawlers that sweep and capture the multitude of sea creatures from the ocean floor must certainly be sitting on piles of cash. Nature diminishes as money grows. More real money equals more degradation and destruction of nature. It is why Elon Musk decided to refuse Bitcoin for his electrical vehicles – when he realised that Bitcoin mining uses large quantities of energy. Unbridled extraction from nature has been occurring for about 250 years – with the Industrial Revolution being the point at which such extraction took on gargantuan forms. Coal – nature's "ancient sunlight" – is pulled out of the earth as if there is no tomorrow. As if there is no tomorrow is the double-bind ideology of workers under capitalism – as we are reminded by Richard Smith (2011: 121):

> Given capitalism, they [workers] have little choice but to focus on the short-term, to prioritise saving their jobs in the here and now to feed their kids today – and worry about tomorrow, tomorrow.

Climate change is a far-fetched ideal for workers under capitalism. Putting food on the table and clothes on their children's backs is what matters most. Capitalist society uses nature unsustainably. Everything becomes fragmented and atomised under capitalism. Capitalism seeks to make money out of nature – even when it pretends to be acting in nature's best interest e.g., the transition to renewable energy, abstaining from eating meat, abstaining from having children, etc. without changing the fundamental relations of capitalism to nature. This is the developing ideology of the so-called green economy. It is more like green capitalism or renewable energy capitalism. It may seem difficult to make the connection between profit-accumulation and climate change. It is not difficult the make the connection that those countries that have contributed the most to climate change are also the wealthiest. The dominant paradigm of climate science focuses on the supply side of the problem – such as fossil fuels, dirty energy, inefficient technology, etc. There is hardly – or no – focus on the demand side regarding the problem of climate change. Why is there such a huge demand for oil under capitalism? Why is there such a huge demand for coal under capitalism? Why is there such a huge demand for energy under capitalism? The science of climate change needs to factor in the demand side of energy in its analyses. For many in the time of COVID-19, working from home meant that you could still get things done without using huge amounts of energy. Yes, energy-use at home would go up. But how does energy-use at home compare with the amounts of energy-use of an average of one person in one car going to and from work on a daily basis? There is evidence that the demand for energy decreased in the time of COVID-19. If humans encountered an invisible enemy since end-2019, then humans and nature have been continually exposed to the enemy of the invisible hand and capitalism for hundreds of years:

> Of course, capital has a very long way to go before it exhausts living nature, and would probably have destroyed the conditions of human survival before reaching that point. The point here is simply that in order to satisfy the demands of large-scale production, more and more of nature has to be destroyed. In this sense production under capitalism is consumption, not production; it gobbles that which is already there, and gives nothing back but waste.
>
> BRENNAN, 1993: 138

Green capitalism is not the answer to climate change and environmental degradation – as was argued in the time of COVID-19:

> Renewable energy is also based on extensive mineral and hydrocarbon extraction, much like fossil fuels. And second, environmentalism has become too corporate, implying that it has essentially 'sold out' to big capitalist interests. The distinction between so-called renewable energy and fossil fuels is false. Renewable energy infrastructure requires enormous amounts of metals. The development of this industry demands mining equipment and a proliferation of mines; processing plants to extract the metals from the ore; manufacturing facilities to assemble components; as well as transportation and operations of so-called renewable energy systems. Only celebrating green capitalism could renew the present or existing level of harm against our planet, and kill any possibility of restoring ecological balance with our environment.
>
> DUNLAP and CORREA-CABRERA, 2020

It is the innate nature of capitalism to transform nature into profit – whether such transformations are brown or green. Environmental movements subscribing to free market ideologies – instead of challenging the fundamental cause of climate change – have also come in for criticism:

> A different kind of climate movement would have tried to challenge the extreme ideology that was blocking so much sensible action, joining with other sectors to show how unfettered corporate power posed a grave threat to the habitability of the planet. Instead, large parts of the climate movement wasted precious decades attempting to make the square peg of the climate crisis fit into the round hole of deregulated capitalism, forever touting ways for the problem to be solved by the market itself.
>
> KLEIN, 2014: 25

It is now a known fact that capitalism administers violence on nature:

> There is no doubt that capitalism imposes a relentless pattern of violence on nature, Homo sapiens included. But capitalism works because violence is part of a larger repertoire of strategies that put nature to work.
>
> MOORE, 2016: 5

In other words: "our economy is at war with many forms of life on earth, including human life" (Klein, 2014: 26–27). The brutal and explicit face of capitalism's violence on nature is in the field of war. During the Vietnam War, the most capitalist country on the planet – the US – used Agent Orange in its scorched earth policy to obliterate vast tracts of forests in Vietnam – with the aim of destroying the cover of the communists. Besides the communists and the innocent women and children of the many villages that were massacred by the US state, nature was also a major casualty of capitalism's war on an innocent people. Wars wreak havoc on nature. Capitalism consumes and devours nature:

> It [capitalism] plays God and redirects nature at its own speed and from its own subject-centered standpoint. It is playing with high stakes here, because it is literally altering the physics of the world, adjusting the inbuilt logic of nature and the spatio-temporal continuum to suit itself.
>
> BRENNAN, 1993: 151

Even the scholar Fukuyama who got it wrong about capitalism's invincibility – after the fall of the Berlin Wall – conceded that capitalism has severely damaged the natural environment:

> The fantastic economic growth made possible by modern science had a dark side, for it has led to severe environmental damage to many parts of the planet, and raised the possibility of an eventual global ecological catastrophe.
>
> FUKUYAMA, 1992: 7

When and where profit thrives – nature perishes!

4 Man – Nature's Own

Through the ages, humankind has created many gods for itself. In his book *Gaia – A New Look at Life*, James Lovelock reveals that Gaia is the Greek goddess of the earth. Nature is both the known and unknown force. There are religions that view nature as God. There are also religions that speak to the importance of nature in the life of man. Nature gives life and nature is life. That nature is able to give and take life is both a wonder and a mystery. That an unseen virus can take out intelligent man in a matter of days is itself both scary, a mystery – and dare it be said – a marvel of the creatures of nature. How can it be that the tiniest of creatures could wipe out so many of us – and cause so much of heartache, pain and suffering for so many around the world! Nothing better demonstrates the inextricable link between man and nature than oxygen. A fundamental requirement for man to stay alive when tested positive for COVID-19 and hospitalised was oxygen. When India ran out of oxygen – even though it had one year to stock up on the life-saving entity – more people died. The link between George Floyd and nature was severely disrupted when a representative of the capitalist state placed his knee on George Floyd's neck for 9 minutes and 29 seconds and cut off nature's oxygen supply. The lack of oxygen into our bloodstream – for whatever reason – is a reminder of man's inextricable link to nature. Charles Darwin – by way of science – has put man squarely back into nature. It is where he belongs. It is where he has come from – and it is where he will go back to. Moore (2016: 5) states that there is an increasing awareness of human's relationship to nature:

> The notion that Homo sapiens are a part of nature, that the whole of nature makes us, is one readily accepted by a growing layer of the world's populations.

When our loved ones die we place them back into nature's soil – or we burn their bodies – and the by-products of the ash and heat also become part of nature. In Sweden, a crematorium has decided to use the heat-energy generated from the burning of dead bodies to heat up the local town. It is believed that this action does not change the nature of the ash of one's loved one. Such efficient use of heat-energy would help in the fight against climate change – even if in a very small way. Such a manner of utilising heat energy may be taboo for some cultures in other parts of the world. In the time of COVID-19, we witnessed bulldozers removing loads of earth – in order to fill the holes with thousands of dead humans. One year and four months after the world came to know about COVID-19, devastated Indians were still cremating their loved ones on pyres built on pavements – as a result of the surge in COVID-19 deaths. Whether we are alive or dead, it is evident that planet earth is our home. It is the only planet that we inhabit – there is no planet B. The metaphors heaven and hell also describe life on earth under capitalism. The belief and the ideology of heaven and earth suggest that there are other places besides earth in which man can choose or is condemned to live. This serves to justify that planet earth is a non-entity, irrelevant and therefore okay to be plundered. For the haves – life is heaven. For the have nots – life is hell. This is life under capitalism. We observed this in the time of COVID-19 – when the well-off in the main were more or less insulated from COVID-19. Karl Marx reminds us that planet earth comprises all that humans require. I do not think he has said much about heaven:

> As the earth is his original larder, so too it is his original tool house. It supplies him, for instance, with stones for throwing, grinding, pressing, cutting, &c.
>
> MARX, 1867: 125

Marx continues:

> Men can be distinguished from animals by consciousness, by religion or anything else you like. They themselves begin to distinguish themselves from animals as soon as they begin to produce their means of subsistence, a step which is conditioned by their physical organisation. By producing their means of subsistence men are indirectly producing their material life.
>
> MARX, 1845 [1998]: 37

Man is the intelligent ape. There are one hundred and ninety-three living species of monkeys and apes. One hundred and ninety-two of them are covered with hair. The exception is a naked ape self-named Homo sapiens (Morris,

1967: 9). From his teeth, his hands, his eyes and various other anatomical features, he is obviously a primate of some sort, but of a very odd kind (Morris, 1967: 15). It is said that man shares about 97% of its genes with chimpanzees. Allow me to share an anecdote of the tale of three intelligent apes: firstly, of the intelligence of one with a PhD – myself; the second – my mom – the intelligence of one with limited formal education due to the evil system of apartheid; and the third – the intelligence of curiosity – the little monkey that has an uncanny resemblance to man – in more ways than one. I had set out my work-table outdoors – left my mobile phone on my work-table – and then set off indoors to fetch a cup of tea to accompany the good winter sun and my workload for the day. Unbeknown to me – the little fellow (I'll refer to the little monkey as he) had been watching me and eying my mobile phone from high up on a tree close by. When I set-off for my cup of tea, he leapt down from the tree – grabbed my mobile phone in a lightning flash – and was back up the tree again. I caught a glimpse of this quick action, as soon as I stepped into my home. I was speechless! My instinct was to chase after the little monkey – by trying to climb the tree – hoping that I would get a chance at my mobile phone. But then I realised that evolution and ageing had drastically curtailed my tree-climbing abilities. In any event, once high up the tree, the silly monkey observed the phone for a few seconds before chewing on it. When he saw me trying to climb the tree, he leapt from the tree onto the roof of the house – and then onto another tree. The heavy animal that I was, I got down from the one tree, ran to the next and tried to do the same again – climb the tree in order to try and retrieve my main contact to the world. The clever fellow went further up – social distancing came naturally to him. By then, my mom – about 70 years of age at that time – having observed the tussle between two apes from the animal kingdom – rushed off into our home – cut up a few pieces of apple – came out and threw them at the foot of the tree. By then I had gotten wind of the plan, got down from the tree to observe the unfolding event – all the while hoping that the appeal to the stomach would lead to the desired result. The young fellow let go of the phone – came down from the tree, grabbed a few pieces of the apple – and scooted back up the tree again. The stomach rules the mind in nature! Capitalist ideology would like us to believe otherwise. Millions of stomachs go hungry under capitalism. In any event, it got me wondering – what is intelligence? One thing for sure – I was glad for the intelligence of my mom – I finally got my mobile phone back. The intelligence of the ape with a PhD did not do the trick. I joked with family and friends about the incident: "the little fellow must have been thinking – if that monkey can use a phone – why can't I"! Kowtowing to free market pressure, I have upgraded my phone at least four times since then. The ones that are no longer used will add to the mountains of e-waste that are generated each year by capitalism's never-ending treadmill of production. In the meantime, they are adding to all of the other unused stuff that I have in my home – which takes up valuable living and breathing space. It is through tens of thousands of years of material development that has delivered a society which enables man to legally own a commodity – private property – such as a mobile phone. It is a far cry from the time when property was primarily of a communal, tribal form:

> The first form of property is tribal property. It corresponds to the undeveloped stage of production, at which a people live by hunting and fishing, by cattle-raising or, at most, by agriculture.
>
> MARX, 1845 [1998]: 38

But whether as a hunter-gatherer, a feudal lord or peasant, whether as a master or a slave, or whether as a capitalist or a worker – we are all part of this great blue and beautiful planet called planet earth. Nature is in charge. We come from nature's fold and we eventually fall back into nature's fold. Western nations made it easier for people to fall back into nature's fold – in the time of COVID-19. In our modern minds we may think that we are above nature. In reality we are but another species in a planet with millions of other species. Man is nature's own: "we begin to see human organization as utterly, completely, and variably porous within the web of life" (Moore, 2016: 5). Capitalist ideology has taught us that "man is greedy by nature". It is not difficult to believe this as we witnessed how greedy businesses raised prices and how politicians – mainly if not entirely in the capitalist world – stole from the poor in the time of COVID-19. We witnessed how the price of ventilators skyrocketed in the time of COVID-19. The ideology of profit-maximisation must be the most stubborn of all ideologies under capitalism. But greed seems to be unique to the capitalist way of life – not a component of humankind's genetic code. As a species, we have roamed planet earth for about 300 000 years. For 99, 9% of our time on earth, we have been hunter-gatherers – taking only what we needed from nature. Our private property were our bows and arrows, our spears, our ostrich eggshells for carrying water, the skins on our backs, etc. Land was not part of our private property. As hunter-gatherers we did not own private land with animals or game farms. In fact, land and nature owned man. How the tables have turned since the advent of capitalism! Man now owns land and nature. And under capitalism, a few own so much – and so many own so little or nothing at all. Life is a far cry from the time that nature was for the taking – yet man took very little. Times have indeed changed since we roamed around almost naked. Capitalism has changed all of that. Capitalism has disrupted man's relationship with nature. Capitalism is fast destroying man's relationship with nature.

Private property is the hallmark of capitalism. Try taking somebody's private property – and you'll meet the full might of the state. Under capitalism, human nature has – in the main – metamorphosed into highly competitive, greedy and selfish individuals. Hence when one talks about greed in capitalist society, the knee-jerk but questionable response is almost always: "it's human nature". It is not! Dr Michael Ryan – CEO of the World Health Organisation (WHO) – when asked by a television presenter on Al Jazeera on 29 March 2020 – whether the coronavirus was man-made, replied that there is no evidence as yet that the virus was man-made. He however did say that the virus comes from nature – and in so far as man has upset the eco-system and destroyed the natural environment to the extent that it has been destroyed – then it is certainly man-made. He questioned our priorities as a civilised species. He questioned if humankind was directing resources to where they were actually needed. That capitalist societies have the wrong priorities is believable – when we see that countries have more soldiers than health care workers, more guns than gowns and face masks, more banks than hospitals, more malls and roads than spaces and playgrounds for children to play, more alcohol stores than bicycle lanes, etc. Under capitalism man has been extracted from nature – and nature has been extracted from man. For many millions of people around the world – who were once inextricably tied to nature – their land was stolen from them by the budding capitalist system – aided and abetted by powerful colonial states. By stealing his land that held man communally with his fellow men and women, capitalism began transforming natural and communal man into individualistic and selfish humans. This transformation into the ultimate selfish individual human is ongoing under capitalism. COVID-19 has shaken up humankind to tackle this reigning ideology – that man is a selfish and greedy individual – and to challenge its destructive impact on both man and nature. Since its inception, capitalism has been and is continually transforming nature into built environments, concrete jungles, skyscrapers, malls, freeways and highways, mobile phones, motor vehicles, and so forth. This is all sanctioned under the ideology of progress. Homo sapiens have a precarious relationship with nature:

> Human beings are themselves part of nature, and therefore our struggles to improve our lives and the conditions of our labour are already ecological in one sense.
>
> HEENAN and STURMAN, 2020: 195

If it does not rain for months and there is a drought, it affects the land which in turn affects all life – Homo sapiens included. If the Suez Canal is blocked by a mighty ship – as happened in the time of COVID-19, then humans cannot get their chosen commodities. Homo sapiens depend on nature – but Homo sapiens also have to continuously engage and sometimes struggle against nature in order to survive. We have to keep far from the dangerous creatures and animals like the black mambas, the lions, the tigers etc. We have to kill the mosquitoes in order not to be inconvenienced or killed-off by them – as in the case when they are carriers of malaria. We have to obliterate corona-viruses – the creatures of nature that if left unchecked will wipe out much of the human race, as it sought to do in the West – the wealthiest and most powerful part of planet earth. But as Homo sapiens, we also have to kill the chicken, the sheep, the lamb, the cow, the buck, the pig, the fish, etc. in order to feed from nature and survive as a species. As radical environmentalists, we are expected to be impartial. If we do not have an appetite for the meat variety in nature – then we "kill off" the cabbage, the carrot, the rice, etc. in order for the human race to continue living. We do this and have done this through different forms of social organisations for thousands of years: "all production is appropriation of nature by the individual within and through a definite form of society" (Marx, 1845 [1998]: 5). Capitalism is the most recent form of social organisation for the appropriation of nature – and the most devastating of all social organisations, in its relationship to nature. We challenge nature when we climb its highest peaks. There are times when we win the contest with nature and ourselves – and there are times when we lose. We have learnt how to fly by studying the birds and the sky. We have learnt how to commute under water – as in a submarine – by studying the oceans and the fish. Our relationship with nature is one of living with nature and living-off of nature. As a hunter gatherer we took from nature in order to survive and sustain livelihoods. But under capitalism we take from nature – not only for the purposes of survival and sustaining livelihoods – but mainly for the purposes of exchange-value, profit maximisation and accumulation. Under capitalism we have become creatures of accumulation as an end in and of itself. We are no longer living with nature. We are living-off of nature. We are no longer in a symbiotic relationship with nature. Under capitalism man is a parasite on nature. It is why we can poach the rhino for its horn – and then without much thought leave it to die. It is why we can slash and burn the Amazon rainforest – and not care two hoots about the variety of life that will be destroyed in the process. It is why we can continue building coal-fired power stations and leave it to our children and their children to hopefully clean up our mess. Capitalism compels the human race to devour nature: "from being the creature of nature we have become capital's puppet" (Kovel, 2007: 5). Of all the millions of creatures on planet earth, none has changed the physical and chemical structure of the earth in the way that Homo sapiens have – and continue to do so under capitalism. Man is an intelligent animal. But man is also a fearful animal under capitalism. He fears for the violence that plagues capitalist society. He fears losing his job. He fears not putting food on the table. He fears not being able to take care of his family. He fears he will go out of business if he does not make a profit. He fears that his social standing may drop. He fears the lack of protection from the state in the time of a global pandemic. Homo sapiens – wise, intelligent human – is a fearful ape under capitalism. Through this fear imposed by capitalism, we are destroying everything around us and about us. As capitalist ideologies drive us to continually devour nature, we not only destroy habitats and species – the potential for deadly viruses to enter the human world is also unleashed:

> Zoonotic diseases are responsible for 2.5 billion cases of human illness and 2.7 million deaths every year around the world. As human civilisation expands into more animal habitats, and the exploitation of the natural world continues, these infectious diseases are likely to become ever more common.
>
> LEBEDEV, 2020

As once a member of the ape species, we have broken out of the animal kingdom. But along our long journey of social evolution, we have entered the kingdom of endless accumulation: "the forest ape that became a ground ape that became a hunting ape that became a territorial ape has become a cultural ape" (Morris, 1967: 23). Fossil fuels are nature's violent enemy. So are poachers and polluters. Wars are nature's violent enemy. Profit and endless accumulation are also nature's violent enemies. Under capitalism, man has become nature's enemy. Under capitalism, man has become his own worst enemy. But man is also a becoming animal.

5 Where Do the Children Play?

Nothing better represents the wonder of nature than that of little children lost in play – oblivious to the dangers of capitalism! My youngest sister has a set of twins. She sent the following WhatsApp message amongst the many messages that we shared as family in the time of COVID-19:

> When I go to level 2 to the grocer there is emptiness where children used to scoot, run, laugh and meet friends. Interestingly so – it feels like the

> Piped Piper who took all the kids with him and the town was empty. It's amazing how it's children and their sounds which brings life to a space.
>
> GOVENDER: 2020

And with all of the capitalist development that takes place under the ideas and ideologies of progress, economic growth and profit maximisation, I am reminded of the song *Where Do the Children Play* by Cat Stevens – now known as Yusuf Islam:

> Well I think it's fine, building jumbo planes
> Or taking a ride on a cosmic train
> Switch on summer from a slot machine
> Yes, get what you want to if you want
> Cause you can get anything
> I know we've come a long way
> We're changing day to day
> But tell me, where do the children play?
> Well you roll on roads over fresh green grass
> For your lorry loads pumping petrol gas
> And you make them long, and you make them tough
> But they just go on and on, and it seems that you can't get off
> Oh, I know we've come a long way
> We're changing day to day
> But tell me, where do the children play?
> Well you've cracked the sky, scrapers fill the air
> But will you keep on building higher
> 'Til there's no more room up there?
> Will you make us laugh, will you make us cry?
> Will you tell us when to live, will you tell us when to die?
> I know we've come a long way
> We're changing day to day
> But tell me, where do the children play?

CHAPTER 2

The Ideological State

Largely Siding with the Capitalist Economy in the War with COVID-19

> It is more profitable for your Congressman to support the tobacco industry than your life.
>
> JACKIE MASON

•••

> When morality comes up against profit – it is seldom that profit loses.
>
> SHIRLEY CHISOLM

1 Declaring War on an Invisible but Known Enemy

Once the pandemic was declared by the WHO, the entire world knew that humanity was at war with COVID-19, an invisible but known enemy:

> Coronavirus pandemic is a World War like situation. It is going to change the way we live. People are frightened and dying, strict measures like lockdown or curfew is going on state by state, region by region, locality by locality. People are forced to stay at home, ensure social distancing, and abstain from eating in restaurants or bars. Restrictions have been imposed on travel. Schools, colleges and universities have been shut down. It has become very difficult to manage the on-going crisis for the states or authorities. All are fighting the enemy which is invisible. In such circumstances, international communities should come forward and cooperate with the severely affected states in combating the warlike coronavirus.
>
> JAVED, 2020

I felt safe when the South African state declared war on COVID-19 in March of 2020. The president of the country took control of the situation at the

 | DOI:10.1163/9789004539808_003

beginning – when just a few South Africans were identified as being under attack from COVID-19. When the president and all of his ministers don army uniform and address the army and the nation, then you know that the country is at war – and is serious about taking on and defeating a formidable enemy. This was a far cry from apartheid days – when the state's army was the enemy of the people. Those were really terrifying times! My view is that the entire of South Africa felt safe and protected when the president – the commander-in-chief – addressed the soldiers and told them of their important role in protecting the people of South Africa. Even political parties, which would usually demonstrate violent tendencies in the national parliament, rallied around the president and state – in the country's attempt to defeat an unseen enemy. Leaders in all countries promised to go to war – when COVID-19 was declared humankind's enemy number one. Some felt that China had declared war on the rest of the world – by releasing COVID-19 into the world to kill: "meanwhile, the Chinese government has permitted the wet markets to reopen. If another country launched a weapon that killed over 500,000 people worldwide, there would be international outrage" (*Santa Fe New Mexican*, 2020). By January 2021 the number of people made to be easily killed by an invisible enemy in the US alone was 500,000. This must surely enrage the writer regarding the US, as such an easy killing machine of its own citizens. Still, all nations promised to go to war with the zealous aim of defeating COVID-19. In holy India:

> Announcing the national lockdown to contain pandemic COVID-19, Prime Minister Narendra Modi on March 24 cautioned the people that it could take us 21 days to win the war against the virus as opposed to the 18 days the Pandavas took in the Mahabharata. On his part, Mr Modi further exhorted the people to say thanks to the medical fraternity for their service in the COVID-19 warfare; he also got the armed forces to join the thanksgiving ceremony with a floral show.
>
> *The Asian Age*, 2020

The Pandavas would have been thoroughly let-down and disappointed, if Modi was the commander-in-chief leading them on the battle field. More than 365 days later, India's war with COVID-19 was still ongoing. By April 2021, India looked like hell on earth. Capitalist ideologies in its Bharatiya Janata Party (BJP) and religious regalia failed to contain the invisible and deadly enemy. Eastern and religious philosophy was no match for COVID-19. The West – on the other hand – have centuries of experience in eliminating their perceived enemies. So, when it came to the war on COVID-19, a real enemy, it was going to be child's play, a Sunday picnic, a walk in the park, easy-peasy. Mike Pence, the then US vice-president stated on CNN: "our public health system is strong, and we are winning the fight against the invisible enemy" (*Gulf News*, 2020). As had come to be the custom, Western ideologies attempted to mask the true picture of death and mayhem in the US. All stops were pulled out – and Western propaganda went into top-gear. The West is primed and prepared for profit-making. It is also primed and prepared for war against weaker nations. It has – after all lived through two World Wars – and other well-known wars such as the Korean War, the Vietnam War and the infamous and illegal war on Iraq. The Middle East is continuously in a state of war – thanks to the West in its greed for energy resources – and strategic geo-political control of the region. For many decades the West was in a Cold War with the USSR. But as the war on COVID-19 dragged on in the West – with COVID-19 clearly winning – it seems that war fatigue set in and people needed reminding – in the war-experienced West – of the still present danger of a deadly enemy:

> The First World War lasted 52 months, the Second World War 57. This 'war' is only six months old. Using social distancing fatigue as an excuse is juvenile at best and will make a second wave à la 1918 unavoidable.
>
> GORDON, 2020

2 The Capitalist State: Siding with the Profit-Economy and Relinquishing Its Immense Power to Save Lives in the Time of War

People needed to be kept safe from the invisible enemy – and they required their basic needs to be met as well. States in the Western world in general – and in capitalist countries in particular – found themselves wanting in their efforts to both contain the invisible enemy through prolonged lockdown restrictions – whilst at the same time sustain the livelihoods of its citizens. There was pressure on the state to save lives. There was pressure on the state to save livelihoods. Most pressing of all, was the pressure on the state to save profit. When the powerful in society prefer profit over all else, then saving lives and livelihoods is always an uphill battle. Capitalist ideologies are immensely powerful. Even once usury-hating religions – such as Christianity and Islam – have become subsumed by capitalist logic and ideologies. Such religions no longer fight interest or usury – as they passionately did in the early days of capitalism's development. In the US, the state under Donald Trump saw its role from the very outset as that of saving profit. In the UK, the initial response was for there to be no state involvement to halt or slow down profit-making through its herd-immunity war model. As the bodies piled up, it then attempted to traverse the fine line between saving lives and saving profit. In other parts of the Western and capitalist world, the state – after attempting to initially save lives – gradually succumbed to the dominant ideology of profit-making. The result towards the gravitation of saving profit witnessed such states relinquishing their immense powers handed to them by their citizens and history – to save both lives and livelihoods. The debate became framed as the lives versus livelihoods debate. Keeping within the capitalist ideological framework, there was no or little mention of the lives versus profit conflict in capitalist societies. Capitalist states around the world withdrew their immense power – and left it to individual citizens to identify and fight the invisible enemy on their own. This form of individual warfare was far from successful. At least the wars on Korea, Vietnam, Iraq, etc. had the backing of powerful states. The war on COVID-19 had no such state-backing. COVID-19 was winning the battle – and the war. COVID-19 was attacking and dropping humans like flies – especially in the US – the most powerful war-machine in the world. It was becoming glaringly clear to thinking people that something was out of sync with states' decision to open up the economy in its various forms when COVID-19 was still a clear and present danger. Panel discussions titled "lives versus livelihoods" were held. Sycophants of capitalism – upon realising that people around the world were starting to question whether states valued the profit-economy over lives – took to debating platforms to quash such comparisons. Former UK prime minister Tony Blair, for example, on a BBC discussion and debate platform said it was a "false dichotomy" to speak in terms of "lives versus livelihoods". He would be correct if he was mooting for a Chinese war model against COVID-19 – a country that secured both lives and livelihoods in the war against COVID-19. Instead, he was mooting for the opening up of the profit economy – in the midst of a global pandemic. This is one of the free world leaders who bombed the Iraqi people to dust under the Western ideology and fake news of "weapons of mass destruction" – and yet he expects the world to take him seriously on his ideology of "false dichotomy" in the time of a global pandemic. The result of his recipe for citizens of the Western world in the time of COVID-19, as it was for the citizens of Iraq and the soldiers of the UK during the time of the West's illegal war on Iraq, was death and suffering on a mass scale. As the people in capitalist countries were first requested then ordered to "go back to work", it was becoming clear that it was the reality of lives versus livelihoods, and profit versus the people that were at play. If the capitalist economy really possessed the formula for saving livelihoods, then South Africa would not have an unemployment rate of about 40% – even before COVID-19 made its unexpected appearance. Unemployment was always a problem in all parts of the capitalist world before COVID-19. So, the argument that states had no choice to open up the economy in the time of war in order to save livelihoods is capitalist propaganda at its best. Among the many things that we learnt in the time of COVID-19, was that – contrary to free market ideology – forced labour is a fundamental pillar of capitalism. Capitalism would go on to have state support – and the people in the main left to deal with the invisible enemy on their own. Whereas the Chinese war model secured lives and livelihoods, the Western war model – for the most part – forced people to choose between confronting the enemy – or confronting starvation and desperation under lockdown. Whereas in China – the capitalist market economy was made to be at the service of the people, in the West – the people were forced to be at the service of the capitalist market economy.

At the beginning of the pandemic, in the Western world there was one rule for the rich and another for the poor in terms of testing – even if the poor are frontline soldiers: "as for COVID-19, the rich all got magically tested before NHS staff" (Taylor, 2020). Profit can be sweet – when people are sick and dying: "Walking Dead actor Daniel Newman doesn't know if he had the virus, but he still ended up with a bill for more than $9,000" (Werner, 2020). So good is profiteering in the US of A that his test was not processed – because if a patient does not show mild symptoms, then apparently the hospital is not allowed to send the test for processing. For its troubles, the hospital was nevertheless allowed to bill him more than $9000! In sticking to the ideology of profit before healthcare in capitalist US, Daniel Newman's health insurance company refused to pay the bill. The beauty of free market capitalism! Profit-making and profit maximisation is the central thread permeating capitalist societies – even during a deadly pandemic:

> New York Governor – Andrew Cuomo – stated that ventilators were $20 000 before COVID-19. They are now more than $50 000 dollars! He said that they did not change in two weeks in terms of technological development – 'when we started buying ventilators, they were under $20,000. The ventilators are over $50,000 if you can find them. The ventilators didn't change that much in two weeks'.
>
> WOODYATT ET AL., 2020

The governor again:

> The price of ventilators has skyrocketed – thanks to states and the federal government's furious competition to secure as many of the life-saving devices as possible.
>
> SHERMAN, 2020: 1

States in the USA were forced to compete for medical equipment. What happened to the war against COVID-19? What happened to mobilising the entire country – capitalists and workers – in the war against COVID-19? Why in the time of war against the American people were states in the United States forced to compete and become the disunited states of America – in the war against a common enemy? Peter Lavelle of the television station RT stated that the US health system is based on purely profit and not taking care of its people (22 May 2020). Amazon sold non-essential items during lockdown. Trump ordered Americans to go back to work. He shouted from the capitalist state pulpit: "we will be open for business. America was not built to be shut down". The profit-economy was dying, and it needed those in power to force workers to revive it once again. In Arizona, for instance:

> Governor Doug Ducey lifted the state's stay-at-home order on May 15 and urged constituents to immediately resume normal life. 'I want to encourage people to get out and about, to take a loved one to dinner, to go retail shopping,' he told KTAR radio Phoenix in May. 'It's safe out there'.
>
> MORROW, 2020

By 15 April 2020, the collective capitalist ideological mind swung into gear and went into full scare mode – the capitalist economy was going to tank if the system did not get back into profit-mode. The constant ideological mantra that was dished out by those in very powerful positions was that "the cure cannot be deadlier than the disease!" The race for profit – and the urge for being ahead of China in the face of overwhelming illnesses and deaths – was devoid of any moral compass:

> If we're the ones who end up in a deep recession, if not depression, for an extended period of time, and if the Chinese are somehow able to dig out faster, then a lot of countries are going to have little choice but to see the Chinese as the only game in town economically, Mr. Markey told The Washington Times.
>
> TAYLOR, 2020: 11

Another observer in the time of COVID-19 wrote:

> The president has pushed for a reopening of the economy on the grounds that the cure for COVID-19 should not be worse than the disease itself. Finally, he has sought to blame China for America's problems, because this is a lot easier than blaming himself.
>
> ELLIOT, 2020: 33

Children playing cowboys and crooks seem more determined in beating their enemy than the weak and flimsy war efforts by the Western and capitalist world on COVID-19. In a letter to the editor, the lack of seriousness and commitment of the US in its war with COVID-19 did not go unnoticed:

> When the decimated remnants of our frontline medical and essential workers call in sick because they can't endure another day, who will you turn to? Support them by wearing masks. That protects you and the economy. Front liners, like effective armies, need rest, replacements, resupply and good leaders. What leader intentionally multiplies an enemy or aids that enemy by not doing all he can to win the war? What leader foregoes the protection of helmets or kevlar vests because invisible bullets are a hoax and wearing protection projects weakness? What leader suppresses generals who plan for battle based on truth? Courageous front liners daily fight Trump's 'hands off' war knowing the enemy virus won't die out until many more of them do. They can't rest because his lies perpetuate pandemic spread upon an unknowing public while he takes no responsibility behind the lines. He callously forces his warriors to confront ever increasing community spread, whether in hospitals, created by him in meat plants, rallies, or by armed demonstration, or caused by his reckless disregard of science. With sociopathic indifference, he takes for granted front liner's assumed willingness to sacrifice and die unendingly while refusing to prioritise assets to the fight. Overwhelming force against the enemy is for protestors, but once more into the breach is for frontlines. Mattis or Kelly would have pre-emptively attacked with mandatory masks, overwhelmed early with PPE and testing made in the USA, funded deficits incurred to fight the virus, prevented supply chain bidding wars, and ensured fair allocation of supplies and medicine until a vaccine/cure existed. But Trump's concern is November, not his front liners. They (and we, including his voters) are exposed, sicken and die for naught while enforced CDC side-lining and election driven rallies inexplicably aid the enemy.
>
> MONROE ET AL., 2020

Anti-war protestors in the state of Michigan arranged protest marches against little war efforts such as the lockdown – in the name of freedom, rights and the American constitution. But lurking deep within the ideology of Western notions of freedom, rights and liberty, it seemed more a protest against the slow death of the profit-economy. Seeing through capitalist ideology, a counter-protester to opening up the capitalist economy in the US held up a placard that read: "I won't die for your economy – you can't fix stupid but you can vote it out". This was in reference to Governor Kemp of California, who decided to end the lockdown prematurely. If Eastern philosophy subscribes to the Law of Karma – meaning your lot in life is predetermined – then Western philosophy followed suit – and asked people to accept their deaths as destiny in the time of war. To mentally, psychologically and emotionally prepare the American people to accept death in the richest country on the planet, the President of the US "asked" between 100 000 and 200 000 Americans to "accept death" from COVID-19. As to which of the 100 000 to 200 000 people were to be the victims of COVID-19, it was up to individuals of American society to freely choose. The president then went on to give himself a pat on the back for allowing COVID-19 to kill off a mere 100 000 to 200 000 Americans instead of many more: "Trump says 200,000 Americans could die from coronavirus, because he's done a very good job" (Rupar, 2020: 1). He did however admit that 100 000 people dying from COVID-19 is a "horrible number" – but like so many other leaders of neoliberal capitalist countries, he made it appear that his hands were tied in the choice between saving the profit economy and saving lives. By 11 March 2021, 529 203 Americans were allowed to be killed by the invisible but known enemy. Warnings about opening up the economy prematurely were clear and timeous. About a year earlier, Dr Darough O'Caroll on CNN (12 May 2020) stated that to open up the economy when the threat is still very real is like opening up the doors of an aeroplane whilst the plane is still moving. Speaking from Hawaii, he also spoke about the strength of indigenous Hawaiian culture in dealing with COVID-19 viz. love, family, responsibility and collective action. These values were certainly missing in abundance in the Western world – where individualism is a ritual and a religion. According to Adam Brandon, CEO of FreedomWorks, citizens had to choose between being "COVID-19 patients" or "economic patients". On international television, Prof Ashish Jha was upset at the fact that US leaders would say that there is only one factory that makes testing swabs in the US. He said: "we went to the moon – I'm sure we can make more swabs!" The irony of this statement is that whilst the hospitals were running short of PPEs, the US state partnered with the private sector Space-X and sent a rocket into space. Meanwhile on planet earth, the "lives versus livelihoods" debate continued. For Sami Zeidan of the international Al Jazeera television network, the capitalist economy seemed a bigger threat to lives and livelihoods than COVID-19 itself. If citizens were forced to go back to work in the time of a global pandemic, it is because unlike the owners of the means of production and the well-off under capitalism, they are destined to perish without a people-centred state to help negotiate their survival:

> And the US's weak social-safety net, Prof. Kaufman said, has put more pressure on people to go back to work in unsafe conditions than those in Canada have experienced. 'They have greater economic inequality, a large chunk of the population without access to health care, unemployment benefits that are more stingy and harder to access, and more meagre assistance for housing and food insecurity, especially so in the Southern states,' he told The Globe and Mail.
>
> MORROW, 2020

When the dominant ideology of the capitalist market is taken to be supreme, then lives will be at risk – especially in times of disasters such as a global pandemic. Hence the liberty of choices with potentially the same result under capitalism was go out and increase the risk of dying – or stay at home and increase the risk of dying. This is Milton Friedman's inferior free to choose ideology – available to the majority of America citizens in the age of capitalism:

> 'These states are offering people the choice to endanger your life or starve,' said Damon A. Silvers, the director of policy and special counsel for the AFL-CIO.
>
> ROMM, 2020

Earlier on during the pandemic – with the invisible but present enemy knocking-off Americans in large numbers – the realisation was made that the American state prioritised the profit economy over that of its citizens. Profit was being saved, lives were being lost in the war against COVID-19:

> Still, the early threats of enforcement – at a moment when the coronavirus has killed more than 62,000 people in the United States – have left experts questioning whether some governors are prioritizing economic recovery over public health.
>
> ROMM, 2020

But the ideology of profit-making in the era of capitalism supersedes all else. Nothing is more important than profit itself:

> Top representatives for Oklahoma businesses said Wednesday they share that concern. 'In order for the Oklahoma economy to recover, we need those people back in the workforce. We need businesses opened,' said Chad Warmington, president of the State Chamber of Oklahoma.
>
> ROMM, 2020

If people were too afraid to go to work in the time of a global pandemic, then the reality of forced labour was made glaringly clear by those in power in the US of A. It is easy to trade life for profit – in the same way that it was easy to trade slaves for money. After all, it is the economy, stupid:

> A Chinese netizen commented on Sino Weibo that 'the death toll of over 100,000 cannot wake up a president who only cares about economic figures and the US government is proving its incompetence at the cost of Americans' lives'.
>
> NING, 2020

Aside from Karl Marx, it had to take a creature from nature to make intelligent man realise that the only thing that matters under capitalism is the profit economy:

> Donald Trump has all but abandoned a public health strategy of societal restrictions to tackle the coronavirus pandemic and opted instead to push for a restart of the US economy, a move that experts have warned is premature and risks handing a 'death sentence' to many Americans.
>
> MILMAN, 2020

Whatever the moralising sentiments of money by romantics, idealists and utopians – who sometimes wish to do away with it – money is king in capitalist society! COVID-19 showed us what the elites in capitalist society hold most dear:

> It is puzzling that so much effort was put into reopening bars and so little into reopening schools and keeping workers in the service sector safe. But, in America, seemingly everyone was champing at the bit to make money again, pandemic be damned. In its haste to fire up the economy, the US. seems to have instead ignited a wildfire of coronavirus and, looking ahead, the only certainty is that Americans are in for a summer of suffering.
>
> PICARD, 2020

Adam Smith's apparent invisible hand was made glaringly visible – in the time of COVID-19, as the inextricable link between the capitalist state and the free market was uncovered:

> Trump earlier this week signed an executive order forcing meat plants to remain open to avoid food supply shortages. Industry analysts say pork and beef processing has fallen 25 percent because of outbreaks, while workers say companies are not doing enough to keep them safe.
>
> GEARAN ET AL., 2020

But in a society where money is king, there are still those who believe that the king cannot rule without accountability, care and concern – by those that have made it king in the first place:

> Lawmakers, industry groups and caregivers say the death count could have been limited if states and the federal government had done more to develop an early, robust and coordinated response for nursing homes and other long-term-care facilities. Even with sufficient supplies, experts say, years of understaffing and cost-cutting have left nursing homes vulnerable to widespread outbreaks of infection. Staff turnover is particularly high among nursing aides, who often earn minimum wage and lack paid sick leave or health insurance, said Charlene Harrington, a nursing home researcher and professor at the University of California at San Francisco.
>
> MULCAHY ET AL., 2020

The following verse – linked to the book *The Rich and the Rest of US – A Poverty Manifesto* (2012) by Tavis Smiley and Cornell West – seems apt when one considers the flimsy war efforts by the US in the time of COVID-19:

> Refutable self-serving lies
> Cause misery untold.
> Dire poverty destroys the lives
> Of millions in your fold!
> America! America!
> Your dream has gone astray.
> It serves the rich and powerful
> But casts the rest away!

In capitalist UK, the war generals also performed dismally in the war against COVID-19. In this powerful, well-resourced and war-experienced country, its poor showing in the war against COVID-19 was also called out:

> We already have an inkling of how this came to pass. The government ignored Exercise Cygnus. They failed to test, trace and quarantine. They failed to procure PPE. While other governments announced lockdowns,

> our prime minister missed Cobra meetings, mused about herd immunity and boasted of shaking hands with infected patients. Less Churchill, more bumbling First World War general sending unequipped troops over the hill.
>
> OSAMA, 2020

Great Britain does have a habit of sacrificing its frontline soldiers in times of war it seems. This time the sacrifice was so easily enabled – by an ineffective and inefficient state of the First World. This is the country that built an empire through its continued wars on innocent peoples of the colonised world – but failed to declare an all-out war on a global pandemic! In capitalist Brazil, the commander-in-chief even saw his own soldiers – and the World Health Organisation – as enemies, instead of viewing COVID-19 as the singular enemy:

> With the president at war with state governors and the WHO over social distancing and lockdown measures, the virus has spread from the apartments of Brazil's jet-setting elite to deep into the Amazon.
>
> MARSHALL, 2020

In allied Canada, more finances went into vanity and profit-generating activities in the time of a global pandemic than for abused and murdered women:

> It's just mind-boggling that women have to sell baked goods in Canada to underwrite the costs of facilities that help them survive and avoid being murdered. But by all means, let's talk about possibly bailing out the Canadian Football League to the tune of tens of millions of dollars, because it's way more important.
>
> MASON, 2020: 11

Whilst the communist state in Vietnam prioritised saving lives to that of saving its profit economy, capitalist nations dependent on Vietnam for profit-making, pressurised the country to open up its economy:

> Meanwhile, the government is getting pushback from some overseas-based companies as it strives to maintain its second wave vigilance. Companies from South Korea, Vietnam's second largest foreign investors, are pressuring the government to lift mandatory two-week quarantines of their workers traveling to Vietnam, local media outlet VnExpress reported.
>
> *Business Mirror*, 2020

Like in the West, South Africa's economy is primed for profit – not for people. It is why, after 350 years of capitalist development, South Africa is a country in turmoil – even though it has the most powerful economy on the African continent. Unlike the West, South Africa under a democratic state is a newbie in the arena and affairs of war. Though wars inflicted on it as a result of colonialism and apartheid have made it the country it is today, a minority of citizens own South Africa in real terms. In capitalist South Africa:

> Our doctors and health workers are performing a heroic task. Many have become infected with the virus and some have died. They are being stretched to capacity and we must ask why, with four months to prepare, we have still been found wanting.
>
> JONAS, 2020: 19

The richest country on the continent had the state fumbling for finances to try and secure both lives and livelihoods – thanks to the private ownership of the South African economy by a tiny minority:

> We walked into this pandemic in the worst possible fiscal position, without the means to effectively respond to the health and economic storms it unleashed.
>
> MAVUSO, 2020: 19

In South Africa – what Archbishop Desmond Tutu once coined "The Miracle Nation" – the COVID-19 war response continuum went from "we'll take care of you as a caring state" – to "work places must ensure the safety of its workers" – to "it's now in your hands". Individualist ideology was dished out by all and sundry – politicians, media adverts, capitalist praise singers, etc. This happened as lobbyists of capitalism in politics, businesses, religious organisations, civil society, etc. sought to tear away the state's already constrained power under capitalism to protect the people – and revert back to an abnormal South Africa, with COVID-19 being the latest enemy of the South African people – next to crime, deaths and murder by alcohol abuse, road accidents, husbands and boyfriends, etc. Extricating the state from protecting the people in the time of a global pandemic was done in the name of "individual rights" and protecting livelihoods:

> What started off as a noble national undertaking – uniting all strata of society to combat the disease – nearly ended acrimoniously in court this

> week with disgruntled parties intent on picking holes in the lockdown rules.
>
> MTHOMBOTHI, 2020: 17

The ideology of fear was also used to effectively elbow out the state – so that capitalism could continue on its path of exploitative profiteering. In announcing the termination of the lockdown, the smiling President of South Africa made it a point to state that casinos will also be opened. Capitalism is more powerful than the state and the people in South Africa. Capitalist logic and ideology continuously made its way into the public domain:

> If the COVID-19 pandemic leads to a global economic collapse, many more lives will be lost than COVID-19 would ever be able to claim.
>
> BALLOUX cited in BRUCE, 2020: 16

The conundrum on whether to save lives or save the capitalist economy continued:

> Should we have 5 000 killed by the virus or a 100 000 killed by starvation in the future because we tried to save 5 000?
>
> LEHOHLA, 2020

China and Vietnam saved lives and livelihoods during a global pandemic. Due to the skewed ownership of the South African economy, it seemed that the South African state could not.

With the free market let loose, the people were encouraged to take on the invisible enemy pretty much on their own – without meaningful and adequate support from an economically weakened state:

> In its efforts to balance saving lives and preserving livelihoods, government has decided to allow more business sectors to open under lockdown level 3. Our optimism must never result in the propensity to recklessness. We have won small battles and the war against the COVID-19 pandemic is far from over. Fighting the virus remains everyone's responsibility. Individually and collectively, let's take aim at the invisible enemy as our lives are still under threat.
>
> *Daily Dispatch*, 2020

Capitalists also increased prices in the time of frightened people. A pharmaceutical chain in South Africa increased prices of between 43–325% in

February 2020. The television presenter questioned the spokesperson of the business about the ethical considerations of profiteering whilst many are in dire straits and many small businesses are closed. But the ideology of profit-margins was paramount. After all, we live under capitalism – not socialism! The spokesperson for the company said that they had to maintain their profit margin. When and where capitalism is in the business of saving lives, it is only because it profits handsomely – or beautifully – from such economic endeavours. We know that billions of people around the world cannot afford the expensive health care on sale under capitalism. If locking down the capitalist economy meant livelihoods were threatened, then opening up the economy witnessed lives not only being threatened by COVID-19 – but from the mad rush for alcohol as well. With life and living already a huge struggle under capitalism, alcohol appears to be an outlet for drowning one's sorrows. But alcohol-related injuries in the time of a global pandemic worsened conditions for both victims and health care workers and for those needing treatment for other health-related issues:

> A massive surge of people in hospital emergency rooms with alcohol-related injuries has put additional strain on health-care numbers and filled up ICU beds needed for COVID-19 patients. Professor Elmin Steyn, Tygerberg Hospital's head of surgery and trauma unit said alcohol plus COVID-19 'massively' reduced access to medical care for others. Whereas under lockdown, Professor Ken Boffard, trauma director of Netcare's Milpark Hospital recorded a 70% reduction in trauma cases at the hospitals.
>
> HOSKEN and NAIR, 2020: 5

Choice in South Africa is indeed a Faustian bargain. The South African state never realistically had a chance to save its citizens from infections and death. The state is part of a historical era in which the base structure (economy) and the super structure (law, religion, education, etc.) are heavily biased towards the capitalist class and its major beneficiaries. When the state attempted to step out of its capitalist mandate – with the aim of saving its citizens from mayhem and death – it was quickly disciplined, beaten and hammered back into its capitalist mould. From then onwards it stumbled – as it too began a feeding frenzy on the millions of dollars with which the capitalist class were waiting with bated breath to get their hands on. Much to the dismay of the capitalists – the capitalist state beat many of them to it. State corruption may have contributed to the COVID-19 infection and death rate in South Africa. Three months into the war with COVID-19, it seemed that the South African state needed help from the youth – that segment of South African society that are most unemployed (about 70%!) in the new democratic but still highly capitalist country:

> Health minister Dr Zweli Mkhize has paid tribute to the youth of 1976 who fought against the apartheid system and also urged today's youth to rise to the occasion and fight against the unseen enemy – COVID-19.
>
> NJILO, 2020

Meanwhile in the land of Bollywood stars and outdoor defecating:

> It is now going to be three months in a couple of days since lockdown 1.0 was announced. Far from being over, the war gets worse by the day.
>
> *The Asian Age*, 2020

Between saving the lives of its citizens and profit, the Indian state made deliberate and concerted efforts to save the profit-economy. Whilst the state gave full-backing to the saving of profit, it at the same time asked its citizens to depend on Indian mystical ideology to navigate the battle fields of COVID-19:

> The machinery of the state governments, which are fighting the war on the ground, is at the end of their tether; it could fray any moment, thanks to the lack of financial, human and knowledge resources. In between, this nation left the lakhs of guest workers to their fate, and many of them met with it while trekking their way home. Mythological recall and exhortation of yoga to win the war do no harm, but no good either; it will be as useful as the floral show and banging of the plates did for the healthcare workers. Time the Prime Minister and the government he leads get down to the real task.
>
> *The Asian Age*, 2020

In the West and capitalist countries, the leaders' and some scientists' political will to do battle with the enemy was largely fatalistic in nature – hence they were opened to the idea of a 2nd wave, a 3rd wave, a 4th wave etc. The destiny of citizens in the West were left to waves – instead of efficient and effective state planning and public health science. China did not adopt the same fatalistic war model as that of the West. It declared full-on war with COVID-19. China's population is about five times that of the US. With a capitalist economy, the communist state in China mobilised all physical, human, financial, technological and scientific resources in its war with COVID-19. The result of this commendable war plan and implementation was a relatively low casualty figure – 14,625 Chinese killed by the invisible but known enemy. At the global level, by 30 June 2022 COVID-19, the invisible enemy, had killed 6,334,351 people (Johns Hopkins Medical University, 2022). These are documented figures. With all of the underreporting going on by states in many parts of the world, we can assume that the number is much higher than that which has been documented by the Centre for Systems Science and Engineering (CSSE) at Johns Hopkins University (JHU). In fact, the article by Nolen and Singh (2022) stated that:

> An ambitious effort by the World Health Organization to calculate the global death toll from the coronavirus pandemic has found that vastly more people died than previously believed – a total of about 15 million by the end of 2021, more than double the official total of 6 million reported by countries individually.

Most of the killings by the invisible but known enemy took place in the Western world. The annual US military budget ($750 billion) is about 3 times more than China's annual military budget ($237 billion). Yet the number of American lives that were left to be decimated by the common enemy was about 70 times more than that of Chinese lives allowed to be killed. When it came to saving human lives in the war with COVID-19, the communist world has proven to be far superior to that of the capitalist world. The Chinese communist state provided for its people – whilst doing battle with an invisible but known enemy. But in the Western world, eating, drinking, shelter, etc. were left to the free market in the main. Capitalism still wanted profit in the time of war, and the capitalist state obliged by enabling this centuries' old ideological practice to continue. The losers in the war with COVID-19 were the powerless citizens of the Western world – who paid with their lives. Whereas China in the main had defeated the enemy in a matter of months, the Western world was still battling the enemy more than a year and a half later. After 20 years in Afghanistan and still having nothing to show for itself and the world, one should not be surprised with the US's tendency to prolong wars and unnecessarily lose American lives in the process.

Like it often seeks to do, capitalist ideologies of economic growth and profit-making bent the state away from saving lives – and to be at the service of the profit economy. Even when and where the state did have good intentions of saving livelihoods by opening up the profit economy, it was the road to hell for millions of people in many parts of the world. The capitalist economy is ideologically set at default position to save profit – not lives. Where the state had oversight and governance over the economy, the people were saved in large numbers. Where the free market had overwhelming control over the economy, the people died in large numbers. A straw poll conducted by Dermot Murnaghan in the television programme "After the Pandemic – Our New World" showed that the majority of people representing the globe on the programme thought that states opened the economy too soon (*Sky News*, 2020). Idealistic and emotional ideologies were plentiful in the time of a global pandemic:

> Notably the Scottish political blogger Effie Deans, who wrote that journalists had missed the public mood and should stop obsessing about things such as PPE and how other countries are doing. 'We don't want blame, we don't want argument as if this were a general election,' she wrote. 'We want a contribution to the national effort to get us out of this crisis. We want optimism and faith in our country.' Belief, not political point-scoring, was what was needed. Keeping up morale – 'which matters so much to armies' – was essential because 'morale can cause miracles, not merely in battle, but in illness'.
>
> GERARD, 2020

Yes, let's drop the real bombs on children, women and men – and mobilise optimism, faith and morale in the war against COVID-19!

3 A Synopsis of How the West Dealt with Previous Wars in Comparison to the War on COVID-19

Civilised society appears to be a barbaric society. In just the 20th century alone it went on so many killing sprees. And no one will forget the barbarism that was inflicted on the Iraqi people by the ruling and governing class in the civilised West. In the most important fields of human affairs – life and death – democracy and freedom to choose are extricated from the populace. There is no referendum to decide whether a country should go to war or not – this is decided by the capitalist state and the capitalist class in the main. There is also no or hardly any gender parity in the business of war. Men are sent to kill each other – women are to stay home and take care of the home and children. The spoils of war then go to the rich and powerful of the warring nations. The dead are celebrated as heroes as part of the ideological tool-kit of the rich and powerful. The world has witnessed two World Wars before COVID-19, World War I and World War II. One would have thought that progress also meant less – and not more – killings. It seems that profit is the main underlying factor for wars. But states also take control of the economy and take care of its people in the time of war. Simkins, et al., (2013: 39) state:

> Chauvinism and aggressive imperialism were similarly encouraged by capitalism. In April 866,000 tons of British, Allied and neutral shipping were sunk, raising the spectre of starvation in Britain. The setting up of a Food Production Department of the Board of Agriculture was more successful in boosting domestic supplies, ultimately bringing 3,000,000 additional acres under cultivation. After Lord Rhondda had replaced Devonport at the Ministry of Food in April 1917, stricter controls were introduced and 15 Divisional Food Committees were empowered to regulate prices and distribution. In February 1918 compulsory rationing of several basic commodities was instituted in London and the Home Counties and was extended throughout Britain in April. By July, thanks to rationing and the convoy system, the fear of starvation had largely vanished.
>
> SIMKINS ET AL., 2013: 271

World War I was also the war that gave the world the Spanish Flu – a pandemic that originated in the US. In Germany: "in June 1915 the Imperial Grain Office was created to oversee the purchase and distribution of grain; this was the precursor of similar bodies for other food commodities, culminating in a War Food Office in May 1916" (Simkins, et al., 2013: 154). The Western world pulled out all stops in previous wars. It did not do the same in its war on COVID-19. In previous wars prior to COVID-19:

> Once the decision to create a mass army had been taken, increased state control of industry and manpower was sure to follow. Paradoxically, an otherwise instinctively anti-interventionist government quickly armed itself with considerable powers with the passage, on 8 August 1914, of the Defence of the Realm Act – DORA. As the war went on, DORA encroached into almost every aspect of daily life and led to the abrogation of personal liberties on a scale inconceivable before August 1914. The principal need was for more efficient mobilisation and direction of military and industrial manpower.
>
> SIMKINS ET AL., 2013: 155

During World War I in Europe:

> Under the so-called Hindenburg Programme, they first created a Supreme War Office for control of the economy and then, on 5 December, pushed

> through an Auxiliary Service Law providing for the compulsory employment of all German males between 17 and 60 not already in the forces. The Munitions of War Act of July 1915 enabled the government to adopt any measures deemed necessary to expand production and helped pave the way for Britain to become a nation in arms. Many inefficient and wasteful methods were cast aside and, with trade unions generally ready, for the time being, to forego some accepted practices and privileges, the number of strikes and disputes decreased.
>
> SIMKINS ET AL., 2013: 155–156

With such vast experiences in manufacturing weapons of mass destruction, one would have thought that manufacturing PPEs, vaccines, etc. would be a walk in the park for the West. In the Western and capitalist worlds, the ideology of profit first – lives! The ideology of profit first – rules!

4 It's the Profit Economy – Stupid!

The neoliberal world order always places the economy – the capitalist economy – before all else – lives included. Lives and livelihoods are primarily planned, mediated and filtered through the neoliberal capitalist economy. In other words, lives and livelihoods are only made possible through the profit motive and the profit machinery. The free market is the ordained mechanism for profit maximisation. Socio-economic needs like the creation of employment in countries – especially in underdeveloped and developing countries – are said to only be possible through foreign direct investment – otherwise known as FDI in economic science jargon. The supremacy of the capitalist economy was made famous by a former president of the US, Bill Clinton, when he once pronounced: "it's the economy stupid!" This, after he was found-out for relishing a blow-job in the world's most powerful building: – the White House in the mighty US of A! Seemingly the buildup to the climax in this escapade was a hand-rolled cigar from socialist or communist Cuba that apparently torpedoed its way into Monica Lewinsky's innermost regions of her American anatomy. I don't know of any other time in history where material symbols of socialism, communism and capitalism were such intimate bedfellows! In any event – "it is the economy stupid"! All leaders of a country either win or lose elections based on the performance of the capitalist economy. Trump "toured a mask-making factory in Arizona last week without wearing a face covering. The Associated Press reported that he thought wearing a mask would send the wrong message and impact his re-election chances" (Pilkington, 2020: 21). If communism and socialism are criticised for sacrificing the individual in favour of the collective, then COVID-19 has demonstrated that in capitalist society, the many were on course to being sacrificed for the few owners of the capitalist economy. It was therefore hardly surprising that the UK Labour Party's slogan during its electioneering campaign was: "for the many and not for the few". In the US the Occupy Movement's slogan was 99% versus the 1%. In the time of COVID-19 the US state was willing to sacrifice the lives of hundreds of thousands of Americans, in order to save the profit-economy – which the 1% are the major beneficiaries of. The Western world chose capitalist economic ideologies over fundamental life-saving morality and pragmatism. Advertently or inadvertently, they chose profit over people! Livelihoods are incidental and not integral to the profit-only economy. With its imperative for exchange-value or profit instead of use-value and the common good, the capitalist system in its neoliberal form locked out help from effectively reaching the people when they most needed it – thereby enabling their deaths in the millions. With the millions of deaths, the families of the dead also died inside of them. Capitalist ideologies did not only kill materially – but spiritually, emotially psychologically and morally as well. COVID-19 demonstrated that capitalist society has as its single most worshippped criteria for success and progress in life – that of how much money the system makes. The profit machinery or the free market is the sacred cow in the modern world. Any interference with it – in whatever shape or form – is bound to be confronted with severe consequences. Meanwhile across the oceans, Xi Jinping of communist China had no such fatalistic ideology – about 100 000 or 200 000 Chinese being 'offered' to be 'slaughtered' by COVID-19. The way China went about its war on COVID-19 demonstrated that the Chinese were not willing to allow Chinese citizens to succumb to COVID-19. Why and how is it that China chose to kill the virus in its totality – whenever and wherever COVID-19 was detected? Why were both lives and livelihoods of people secured in China – and not in the West in general and in capitalist countries in particular? How is it that the world's richest nations were not able to save both lives and livelihoods in the war against COVID-19? How is it that the leaders of the capitalist world were confined to choosing between two evils – between possible death through COVID-19 or death through non-sustained livelihood assistance from the state? What is it about the neo-liberal capitalist state that found leaders stuck between a rock and a hard-place – in the vital areas of saving lives and providing sustainable livelihoods? It seems where profit is the dominant ideology of a society, then lives are relegated to the periphery. Naomi Klein (2014: 15) articulates the evil nature of capitalism quite aptly:

> Finding new ways to profit from disaster is what our current system is built to do; left to its own devices, it is capable of nothing else.

The Western ideology of profit over people today is the same as it was more than a century ago. On his analysis of the US – one hundred and fifteen years ago – Professor Sombart (1976 [1906]: 4–5) observed that:

> Nowhere else is acquisitiveness as clearly seen as it is there, nor are the desire for gain and the making of money for its own sake so exclusively the be-all and end-all of every economic activity. Every minute of life is filled with this striving, and only death ends the insatiable yearning for profit. Making a living from anything other than capitalism is as good as unknown in the United States, and an economic rationalism of a purity unknown in any European country serves this desire for gain. Capitalism presses forward remorselessly, even when its path is strewn with corpses. The data that provide us with information on the extent of railway accidents in the United States are merely symbolic of this. The New York Evening Post has calculated that from 1898 to 1900 the number of people killed on the American railways was 21, 847 which is equal to the number of Englishmen killed in the Boer War during the same period, including those who died of illnesses in military hospitals. In 1903 the number of people killed on the American railways was 11,006, while in Austria in the same year it was 172. If one standardises these figures per hundred kilometers and per million passengers, one finds that accidents happened in America at a rate of 3.4 per hundred kilometers, as opposed to 0.86 in Austria, and that they happened at a rate of 19 per million passengers in America, compared with one of 0.99 per million passengers in Austria. This economic and industrial system and its accompanying technology are employed relentlessly to guarantee the highest profit.

More than one hundred years after Sombart's brilliant insight into capitalism in America, the most powerful and profitable country on the planet is also the country where the most number of deaths were allowed to occur in the time of COVID-19. But when profit is the over-riding ideology in Western society, to expect a country to place lives over profit seems an inconvenient value. If Prof. Sombart made his analysis of capitalism 115 years ago, the following analysis of the capitalist system was made 250 years ago by Karl Marx:

> Use-values must therefore never be looked upon as the real aim of the capitalist; neither must the profit on any single transaction. The restless

> never-ending process of profit-making alone is what he aims at. This boundless greed after riches, this passionate chase after exchange-value, is common to the capitalist and the miser; but while the miser is merely a capitalist gone mad, the capitalist is a rational miser.
>
> MARX, 1867 [2010]: 105

Even in the face of millions dying, the ideology of profit reigns supreme in the system that has come to be celebrated as *The End of History* in the world in general and in the West in particular:

> The chief of the World Health Organization has lambasted drug makers for special deals, motivated by profit, that are getting the vaccine in greater numbers to richer nations. 'We now face the real danger that even as vaccines bring hope to some, they become another brick in the wall of inequality between the worlds of the haves and have-nots', he lamented.
>
> Editor, *Daily Camera*, 2021

Under capitalism, it has always been about the profit economy – and not the people or the natural environment: "huge vaccine divide threatens global economic recovery" (*Bloomberg*, 2021). COVID-19 has made visible current society's obsession with the capitalist economy – an obsession that is always present but hidden from view by capitalist ideologies:

> Is it good for the economy? The question illustrates the enormous sway of economic thinking, and is also an encapsulation of all that is wrong with it. Economists know, of course, that there is really no such thing as 'the economy', there are only people. Yet they have succeeded in obscuring this simple truth completely. News programs report hourly about the level of and changes in the levels of numerous stock indices. But about the quality of life of teachers, construction workers, health workers, or restaurant workers they report only very rarely. Have they more time to spend with their kids today than yesterday? And has the number of people with health insurance changed? There is little doubt that hourly reports of these indices would have spurred the government to improve them, just as reports about the stock market indices do. But the living conditions of people are not what the 'economy' is or what economics is about. Not only is 'the economy' not about the people who live in it; according to economists, 'the economy' actually requires human

> sacrifice. Food subsidies? Bad for the economy. Housing subsidies? Bad for the economy. Health insurance? Bad for the economy, too.
>
> ADLER, 2009: 113

And in the time of a global pandemic, lockdowns and restrictions of sort intended to save lives were resisted and challenged on the basis that these were bad for the economy. Service (2000: 87) tells us that for Lenin: "capitalism was bound by [its] nature to hurt most people and kill many of them". This was in relation to the hundreds of thousands of peasants that perished because of the famine that affected them in the late 19th century. For Lenin: "the famine was the product of capitalist industrialisation". Like the choice made between capitalist industrialisation and the peasants of 19th century Russia; the choice in the 21st century in the time of a global pandemic was between the capitalist economy and the people. Once again, the people lost – except where capitalism did not have a major presence. The world is extremely wealthy in terms of monies and resources, but when the people most needed these monies and resources – to meet even their basic needs – in the main such monies and resources were locked up and guarded by capitalist ideologies and private institutions. When and where willing states had to step in – to first place capitalism on a hospital bed with a ventilator – they did so by borrowing and creating fiat monies. COVID-19 has proven to the world that under capitalism – it is death by design! In the time of COVID-19 the state sided largely with the capitalist economy. The people were left to fight the war with COVID-19 more or less on their own with limited or no resources. The result was the needless deaths of millions of people in the Western world in general – and in the capitalist world in particular. The harsh reality hidden under a heap of capitalist and neoliberal ideologies is that: "when morality comes up against profit – it is seldom that profit loses" (Shirley Chisolm). What COVID-19 made painfully clear is that, under capitalism, when lives come up against profit – it is seldom that profit loses! The West gets an F – for its war on COVID-19!

CHAPTER 3

Death, Despair, Depression, Discrimination and Dogma in the Time of COVID-19

> The pandemic of mental anguish that afflicts our time cannot be properly understood, or healed, if viewed as a private problem suffered by damaged individuals.
>
> MARK FISHER

•••

> Racism is intricately linked with capitalism and I think it's a mistake to assume that we can combat racism by leaving capitalism in place.
>
> ANGELA DAVIS

1 Unpacking Aspects of the Human Condition in the Time of COVID-19

Death, despair, loneliness, anxiety, fear, discrimination, dogma, etc. were common aspects in all countries in the time of COVID-19. It was a highly confusing time for people everywhere. Whether to stay in or go out. Whether to choose lockdown or freedom and liberty. Whether to go to the gym or stay home. Whether to continue dating or abstain from any human contact and touch. Whether to hug your loved ones after a day at work or express love from a distance. Old and ingrained habits were severely challenged in the time of COVID-19. For those who could do online shopping – like myself – the risk of contracting COVID-19 was reduced. Many others without technology and internet access did not have such luxury. For those with flexibility of time in current society – like myself – I could choose the least-busiest time to do shopping. Many others had no such choice – but to be part of the rat-race under capitalism: going to work, shopping, paying bills at physical buildings, etc. I had my private car to somewhat insulate me from others in society – thereby reducing the risk of contracting COVID-19. Many – especially the black majority

 | DOI:10.1163/9789004539808_004

and working class – did not have such a luxurious option in the so-called new South Africa. They travelled scared in busses, trains and 16-seater vehicles – known as taxis in South Africa. The apartheid mobility infrastructure is still very much in place in South Africa – 28 years into democracy! Capitalism has been given a new lease on life since Mandela's ANC's time in office. Privacy also lost its traditional meaning in the time of COVID-19, as social media proliferated with pictures of the dead and the grieving. Family and friends who tested positive for COVID-19 and recovered were reluctant to disclose that they had COVID-19. Others worked through the stigma by gladly sharing their experiences of having contracted COVID-19. Some wanted to help others – by sharing information on how to prevent contracting COVID-19, and for those that were or would become infected – on how to beat COVID-19. In India a man and his wife joined a group support app after contracting and recovering from COVID-19. The husband stated:

> This was an opportunity to dispel fears surrounding the disease and rid away any stigma associated with it. I never wanted to publicise my infection as it is a personal thing to be dealt with, but I want to help people by sharing my experience. The Telegram group helps people deal with the mental and physical difficulties they face, and makes them feel strong enough to fight it.
>
> DT Next, 2020

Many were gripped by fear. People did not know who would be the next victim of COVID-19. The mass trauma of apartheid is still present with many in South Africa. Together with the rest of the world, the country will now have to deal with the aftermath of COVID-19:

> World Health Organisation (WHO) officials said that the COVID-19 pandemic has caused more 'mass trauma' than World War II and warned of its lasting consequences.
>
> *Fiji Sun*, 2021

2 Death and Despair

COVID-19 made death and dying visible. It also made death and dying untouchable. Many people died alone. To die is sad. To die alone is a human tragedy. The *Independent* had the following painful headline: "Coronavirus – Boy, 13, 'dies alone' in UK hospital after testing positive". It continued: "he died in the early hours of Monday without any family members present because of the risk of infection" (Stubley, 2020: 1). In South Africa, the sister of a renowned professor who died and who was a champion in the fight against HIV-AIDS, tweeted the following:

> The most heartbreaking thing when a friend or relative is hospitalised with COVID-19, is that they are completely alone till the end. No one to visit, take care, give them a hug or hold their hand in their hour of need. That is what is most tragic. It's the cruelest disease. I am absolutely and completely heartbroken.

Lonely hospitalisations and lonely deaths then became the norm – for the learned and the lay – in the time of COVID-19. Heartache and pain for many also became the norm for the learned and the lay. COVID-19 has really taken humanity into the depths of despair. How does one come to terms with not being present in the final hours of their loved ones passing on? The deputy president of South Africa paid a fitting tribute to the professor:

> In her honour, we should heed the call to flatten the curve by strengthening our responses to this global pandemic as well as continue the fight to achieve zero new HIV infections.

But the COVID-19 curve was not flattened in South Africa. Instead, it spiked – sometimes uncontrollably – thanks to livelihoods not being secured under capitalism – and overzealous sections of South African society pressuring the state to open up the profit-economy. In other parts of the world, citing human suffering in Ecuador in the time of COVID-19, *The Washington Post* carried the following piece:

> Every day it's getting worse: bodies of coronavirus victims are left on the streets in Ecuador's largest city. The wife of a husband who had died from COVID-19 appealed on social media to the president of the country: 'I'm only asking for you to help him die with dignity. Please! Don't leave him here, thrown on the ground'.
>
> ARMUS, 2020: 1

In many parts of the world, single parents worried what would happen to their children, if they contracted the virus and died. In the UK the somewhat comforting but sad answer given by one of the concerned leaders was that community organisations would have to be formed in order to attend to orphans whose parents may die because of COVID-19. For those with poor physical health and underlying illnesses such as asthma, HIV/AIDS, etc. the anxiety, fear and worry was that much greater. In Italy, the army was called in to enforce the lockdown – and to also take away dead bodies to cemeteries – to be given solitary burials. People were sick alone. People died alone. People were buried alone. People mourned alone. In the US, for many – especially the homeless – there were mass burials in plain wooden coffins. In many parts of the developed world – where one would least expect it – people were dying needlessly – and without dignity. The heartbreak and disappointment seemed endless in all parts of the world –but in the Western world in the main. In the UK:

> We know that the impact of this virus is far reaching, it is exposing the existing socio-economic divides and health inequalities in our societies. Every day we hear about the heart-breaking consequences of this epidemic. One British Red Cross volunteer supported a man in utter desperation, with a pregnant wife, who had not eaten for two days.
>
> ADAMSON ET AL., 2020

The grief of losing friends and family members – and not saying goodbye to them – was heart-wrenching. Some shared their heartache and pain:

> A close friend of mine died during lockdown (not due to COVID-19) and not only could I not attend the funeral, I couldn't even have a hug while I was grieving.
>
> MORRIS, 2020: 18

In a world full of people, full of things, full of money and full of capitalist ideologies – people died alone:

> People have died at home alone from COVID-19 during the pandemic and not been found for up to two weeks, doctors who have investigated such deaths have said. They have been discovered only after a relative, friend or neighbour raised the alarm and have often gone undetected for so long that their bodies have started to decompose.
>
> CAMPBELL, 2020: 1

There were so many heart-wrenching moments in the time of COVID-19:

> At a nursing home in Connecticut, a licensed practical nurse, 52, was only weeks from earning a degree as a registered nurse when she died of COVID-19. In Illinois, a registered nurse died a day later, leaving behind three children, including an infant son.
>
> MULCAHY ET AL., 2020

By December 2020, when the curve should have been flattened as promised by the state – and whilst China, New Zealand and other countries with effective and efficient states celebrated the festive season – we in South Africa were receiving many WhatsApp messages a day – about the deaths of people due to COVID-19. My mom, who was 76 years old at that time, could not attend her cousin's funeral – after he contracted COVID-19 and died within 5 days. As COVID-19 took hold in South Africa – I, like many others, lost more family and friends to COVID-19. In other parts of the world it was as if people were living through the Black Death: "families say they are digging graves in makeshift pits for their loved ones" (Javed, 2020). In a convent in the US – where 13 nuns lost their lives to COVID-19, the emotional trauma was excruciating:

> As the virus exacted a physical toll on the convent, it also levelled a crushing emotional blow to the surviving sisters, who were unable to properly mourn the sudden deaths of their friends because of the stringent restrictions still in place.
>
> CHIU, 2020

In Toronto, Canada:

> Leymo Mohammed is a rarity among teen boys – one who calls his 44-year-old mom his best friend – and three weeks later, he posted a video tribute to his favourite person. 'I really hope she gets well soon.' Then on May 9, Leymo uploaded a photo collage of his mom. 'Today, I am sad to say that my mom passed away,' he wrote. 'RIP Mom (1975–2020).' Days later, he posted a photo of himself wearing a mask and gloves, standing next to a bare wooden coffin.
>
> YANG, 2020

In Ontario, Canada, at the Forest Heights Long-Term Care Home, 51 residents had died from COVID-19:

> 'We are broken. We are sad,' Ms. Streit wrote in a letter read at the Ontario inquiry into how long-term care homes handled the pandemic. Struggling

> to describe this past spring, she called it 'hell, a bad nightmare, a war with no winners.' There was, she wrote, 'no time to cry; no time to say goodbye; no time to rest'.
>
> ANDERSSEN, 2020

As statistics of the infected and dead were gathered in all parts of the world, people were confronting the onslaught of COVID-19. In the UK:

> Before the pandemic struck, Ernest Boateng and his wife, Mary Agyeiwaa Agyapong, were planning for the future. She was expecting their second child and – after her maternity leave – wanted to become a specialist diabetes nurse; Ernest hoped to join the RAF. But as the virus tore through the UK, Mary became ill. On 7 April she was admitted to Luton and Dunstable university hospital, where she had been working as a nurse until signed off sick with shortness of breath. She tested positive for the coronavirus and was taken to theatre for an emergency caesarean section. Her baby, five weeks early, was born alive. But after five days of being treated for COVID-19 and pneumonia in intensive care, Mary, 28, died. Ernest was suddenly alone, with a premature newborn, and his two-year-old son to look after. 'I was completely lost,' he says, speaking from his home in Luton, his baby daughter, Mary, gurgling in his arms. 'I had this lovely, cute baby girl, but her mum was not around, she was gone. I had to try and pick up from where we left off and just get on with the journey'.
>
> TOPPING, 2020

Coronavirus – a creature of and from nature – pushed man into an abyss of pain and suffering:

> Family and friends bereaved by coronavirus experienced greatly increased negative experiences and showed higher grief and support needs compared to people suffering loss of loved ones from other illnesses, including cancer, researchers at Cardiff and Bristol universities found. Examining more than 500 deaths since mid-March, around half from COVID, they discovered that COVID-bereaved people were less likely to have been able to say goodbye to loved ones, less likely to have visited prior to death and less likely to have had contact with friends and family after their bereavement. One grieving daughter told the researchers: 'I caught COVID-19 from caring for my dad and was nearly not well enough to attend the funeral. This was really traumatic because I was frightened I might die'.
>
> BOOTH, 2020

If nature has stamped the seal of death on man, then capitalist society makes dying that much sooner and easier – especially for the elderly: "older people were catastrophically let down and many died before their time" (Proctor, 2020). In the country that preaches human rights to the rest of the world, the dead were managed without dignity. In Texas, US:

> A San Antonio family has sued a funeral home, claiming the facility failed to pick up their father's body from a hospital for cremation, so it was deemed abandoned and Bexar County buried him in a pauper's grave. Hoelscher said the family still doesn't know where the body is. 'We are trying to confirm location so we can secure the remains'.
>
> ZAVALA, 2021

The entire world came face-to-face with death – and the meaning of death in the time of COVID-19. For the many that died – they were gone too soon – and in the most painful of ways. For those that lost loved ones, the emotional scars will take a long time to heal – if ever it does. Whilst citizens in countries such as China, Vietnam, New Zealand, etc. had been rescued from the burden of major despair – one year on – the citizens of the Western world were still having to grapple with painful emotions of the worst kind. One year on – as COVID-19 was still winning the war in the West – death and despair continued unrelentingly on the Western landscape. Capitalism's ideological pals in the West added insult to injury and death by downplaying the severity of COVID-19: "ten times more people die of flu than COVID-19" (Gerard, 2020).

3 Mental Health, Isolation, Loneliness and Fear

Anxiety, fear and depression gripped people in all parts of the world. Mental illnesses did not discriminate on the basis of nationality, race, class, religion, gender or creed. It affected all and sundry in the time of COVID-19. Some could not take it any longer – and took their own lives. Regarding suicides in Ontario, Canada: "attempts and fatalities increased by almost a third from past years' average in eight months since Ontario declared provincial emergency" (Moore, 2020). Friends longed for each other. Families longed for one another's hugs and comforts. Social man and woman became isolated and lonely in the time of COVID-19. For those that were left only with their labour, but no place with which they could expend such labour on a planet of plenty – mental illnesses were even more severe. The link between harsh social and economic conditions of man and his mental state – was made evident in the time of COVID-19:

> People with no history of mental illness are developing serious psychological problems for the first time as a result of the lockdown, amid growing stresses over isolation, job insecurity, relationship breakdown and bereavement, the Royal College of Psychiatrists has disclosed.
>
> CAMPBELL, 2020: 1

Fear and insecurity increased manifold:

> As if the COVID-19 pandemic wasn't enough, unprecedented numbers of people are suffering emotional fallout from isolation, money worries and fear of coronavirus infection, leaving us facing a tidal wave of anxiety and depression.
>
> NASH, 2020

Being cut-off from friends and family was a major challenge for many around the world: "according to the head of the Royal College of GPs, Prof Martin Marshall the COVID-19 pandemic is also creating an epidemic of loneliness, not just for older people" (Campbell, 2020: 1). For the lonely – keeping in touch through technology was no match to real human contact:

> In the past three months, however, I have never felt lonelier. I got myself up to speed with technology and used Zoom to speak to friends and family, and virtually attend my writing group, but it's just not the same; video calls are fine for a chat, but no substitute for proper comfort.
>
> MORRIS, 2020: 18

As if the fear and anxiety of contracting COVID-19 was distressing on its own – financial and job woes compounded the mental health challenges for many:

> A separate coronavirus study from the Mental Health Foundation found that 34% of UK adults surveyed and in full-time work were concerned about losing their jobs; 20% of unemployed people surveyed said they had suicidal thoughts and feelings within the last two weeks; and 11% of unemployed people who have experienced stress during the pandemic said nothing had helped them to cope with the worry and anxiety.
>
> ELLIOT, 2020: 33

Contrary to Margaret Thatcher's fantasy ideology of human beings existing as individuals only – social man longed to belong to society:

> Equally seismic are the social repercussions. For young people, who are not only missing out on their education but also on important relationships outside the home, and who are spending more and more time in the toxic environment of cyberspace. For vulnerable people stuck at home in poor conditions; for the elderly, cut off from their families and struggling with basic things like shopping and medicines and, of course, loneliness; for the mentally ill or disabled, unable to access their usual support networks.
>
> VINE, 2020

In countries in Europe, the ideologies of Western-style individualism and economic prioritisation was also challenged:

> Belgium's prime minister, Sophie Wilmès, announced the plan last week, after being accused of prioritising the economy over people's wishes to be reunited. Allowing social bubbles to start yesterday, which was Mother's Day in Belgium and much of continental Europe, was no accident. 'The physical separation from those whom we love has in some cases become unbearable,' Wilmès said.
>
> RANKIN, 2020: 24

Health care for mental illnesses is expensive under capitalism – it is a commodity that is rarely affordable – and rarely accessible to the many. What COVID-19 revealed is that men and women do not primarily need psychoanalysis and chemicals that alter their neurological system to feel better – but other human beings, a safe and secure abode, fresh air and a society that values their skills over that of money. They needed assurances and security from a caring society and a caring state. What they got instead was fear, insecurity, worries and a constant barrage of information regarding the importance of opening up the profit-economy. Man dies in peace when he dies in the presence of his fellow-men and women. Families live in peace when their loved ones die in their presence – instead of dying alone. As in life, man is a social animal in death as well. In Ontario, Canada, at the Forest Heights Long-Term Care Home:

> When a resident's eyes showed fear, she would pull down her mask so they could see her smile, or remove a glove to touch them. It was against the rules. 'But I didn't want them to feel a plastic hand,' she says. Not when so much that was human had already been stolen away. 'No one should die alone,' she says, 'not unless it is their choice.' Ms. Streit watched COVID-19 take 49 lives –.
>
> ANDERSSEN, 2020

Ms. Streit was a care-giver at the care home.

4 Discrimination

Capitalist and Western ideologists shouted at the top of their voices: "we are all in this together!" But the empirical evidence demonstrated the direct opposite. The rich were more protected than the poor. Blacks were more affected than Whites. The elderly were thrown to the wolves. The workers were more exposed than the bosses. The masses were more impacted than the politicians. Upper and middle-class learners and students continued schooling from home – whilst the children of the poor and working classes were busy with schooling in life on how to survive in capitalist society in the midst of a global pandemic. The Italians were betrayed by the European Union (EU). And the unemployed feared both death from COVID-19 and death from starvation under capitalism. It is capitalist ideology and propaganda such as "we are all in this together" that helps to keep capitalism going. If anything – the maxim that best describes the situation in the West in the time of COVID-19 is: "all animals are equal, but some animals are more equal than others". Article 07 of the Universal Declaration of Human Rights states:

> All are equal before the law and are entitled without any discrimination to equal protection of the law. All are entitled to equal protection against any discrimination in violation of this Declaration and against any incitement to such discrimination.
>
> UN, 2015: 16

In the Western ideological world "all men are created equal". But in the real world, the inequality amongst men and between men and women was epidemic in the time of COVID-19. In the US, African-Americans were most affected by COVID-19. In the UK, ethnic minorities were also more affected than whites. This was made evident by The Public Health England (PHE) report:

> Some key findings from the report include: ethnic minorities are more likely to be diagnosed with and die from COVID-19; people of Bangladeshi origin were found to be twice as likely to die from COVID-19 than white British people; other ethnic minority groups had between a 10 and 50 per cent higher risk of death when compared to white British people.
>
> BANKOLE, 2020

Africans residing in China were discriminated against – and some were apparently treated as less than human and "thrown out onto the streets". In one of the former colonial powers, French doctors mooted the idea of first conducting vaccine experiments on Africans. Africans are known to be used as guinea pigs in scientific experiments – especially in its Western ideological forms.

Whilst vaccine trials also occurred on the African continent, the continent experienced huge obstacles in accessing vaccines from the developed world. Continental discrimination was made visible in the time of COVID-19. So was discrimination against the aged and the elderly. The elderly are clearly a non-entity in capitalist society – they matter only in so far as the capitalist system can profit hugely from their pension benefits and accumulated wealth. A senator in the US allegedly suggested that the elderly should be sacrificed for the sake of the economy. It seems that one would be labelled as being ideological, if one argued for the economy to instead serve the needs of the elderly. Such is the nature of logic in the capitalist era. Under capitalism's cost-benefit calculation, the elderly in the main are viewed as a cost to capitalist society. In the Netherlands the elderly were allegedly offered the option of euthanasia in the time of COVID-19. The ideological intention was to keep beds available for the younger generation. They apparently have a humane death policy for the elderly in the Netherlands – the state will help with seeing you off earlier than expected. It seems that planning plays a big part in the world of capitalism. In another part of the planet – where the First Nations were robbed of their land – discrimination was the order of the day in the 21st century as well:

> Despite a campaign by a local Australian government targeted at xenophobia, Chinese observers said the COVID-19 pandemic is fueling racist attacks against Chinese and Asian communities in the country, partly due to the country's deeprooted racism, which can be seen in a group of anti-China politicians who call themselves 'Wolverines'.
>
> TIANLAING, 2020: 3

In the Empire that once ruled violently and ruthlessly over much of the globe, racial discrimination continued to manifest itself in the time of COVID-19:

> During the biggest public health crisis in a generation, communities of colour are both overpoliced and underprotected. In the interests of public health, fairness and equality, as we enter the next phase of lockdown, we urge you (government) to address race disparities in the use of coronavirus powers.
>
> DEARDEN, 2020

COVID-19 showed that racial disrimination extended its tentacles not only to matters of life – but to matters of death as well:

> The mayor of London has called on the equality watchdog to urgently investigate whether the disproportionate impact of COVID-19 on people of black, Asian and minority ethnic [BAME] backgrounds could have been prevented or mitigated. Sadiq Khan's intervention comes after figures showed that black people in the UK were more than four times more likely to die from the virus than white people.
>
> SIDDIQUE, 2020: 16

In another developed country where indigenous peoples also had their land stolen for capitalist development – and thereafter subjected to mass training in Western ideologies – contradictory impacts of COVID-19 was the order of the day:

> The COVID-19 pandemic has revealed two different Canadas – one that has done better than many other countries at limiting the spread of the coronavirus in the general population; and another that allowed its seniors facilities to become killing fields. This disparity was made plain last week when the National Institute on Ageing (NIA), a Toronto-based think tank, said that 82 per cent of the COVID-19-related deaths in Canada involved residents of nursing homes and seniors residences.
>
> *The Globe and Mail*: 2020

Whilst the US was pointing fingers at China's Human Rights record regarding the treatment of the Uighurs:

> Recent data on coronavirus related deaths are opening a window into how hard the pandemic is hitting Latino communities. Across Illinois, Latino majority areas have the highest number of confirmed cases, and on average, tests in those areas come back positive 41% of the time.
>
> *COVID-19 News*, 2020: 3

Still in Illinois, US:

> More than four months into the pandemic, nursing home caregivers say they have been largely left to fend for themselves even as coronavirus outbreaks continue to overwhelm facilities across the country. In recent weeks, a growing number of lawmakers and patient advocates have blamed the homes as well as the government, saying officials have been slow to act, sending inadequate and sometimes defective supplies to facilities that are vexed by staffing shortages and ill-equipped to control

> the spread of infection. At the outset of this pandemic, it was clear that older adults and care workers were at the greatest risk, yet their needs and lives went ignored, Katie Smith Sloan, president of Leadingage, said in a written statement.
>
> MULCAHY ET AL., 2020

In Georgia in the US: "black people make up 83 percent of the coronavirus hospital patients even though they constitute one-third of the population" (Norris, 2020: 23). Neoliberal ideological narratives featured prominently in the time of COVID-19. It is bad enough that people of colour were more exposed to COVID-19, it is adding insult to injury to blame their infections and deaths on supposedly individualistic lifestyle choices:

> A survey conducted by Change Research found that a narrative of personal responsibility led some whites to conclude that underlying issues such as diabetes and hypertension were more related to poor life choices than years of systemic racism that led to failing schools, substandard housing and neighbourhoods that lack health care, steady employment or even grocery stores.
>
> NORRIS, 2020: 23

Religious propaganda of the causes of infections and deaths also featured prominently in the time of COVID-19. In the West-aligned capitalist country and biggest democracy on planet earth:

> Modi's re-election in May last year marked an escalation in the Hindu nationalist agenda. As coronavirus took hold in India in March, it was the comments of BJP politicians and public figures that helped fuel the conspiracy theory that it was a 'Muslim Virus' and that Muslims across the country were on a mission of 'corona jihad' to infect Hindus. The scapegoating of Muslims as 'super-spreaders' was followed by boycotts of Muslim businesses and refusals by hospitals to take in Muslim patients. In Telinipara, it manifested itself in an anti-Muslim riot. This week, the police filed cases against two BJP MPs for their role in triggering the violence.
>
> ELLIS-PETERSON ET AL., 2020: 27

In countries where scientific understanding was in short supply, COVID-19 elicited knee-jerk and dangerous views regarding the explanations for the causes of the coronavirus:

> In its new report on COVID-19 and human rights, the UN highlighted the use of phrases such as 'foreigner's disease' to describe the virus, saying such remarks could lead to discrimination, xenophobia, racism and violence.
>
> WINTOUR, 2020

Many Chinese living abroad were subjected to different forms of abuse – some violently. If discrimination was present amongst people – it also presented itself between and amongst countries:

> As they scrambled to respond, wealthier states busily grabbed their hands on everything they could find, slapping export bans on vital goods. According to the Centre for Economic Policy Research, these controls have increased the prices of PPE equipment such as aprons by more than 50% and masks by 40%.
>
> KAMPFNER, 2020

What COVID-19 has demonstrated is how untogether the world is under the capitalist world order. Capitalist society heavily discriminates between the rich and the poor – and this was made plain to see in the time of COVID-19: "wealthy flyers in the UK are opting for private jets to reduce COVID-19 risks and beat lockdowns, flight data shows" (Kommenda, 2021). The blind-spots to the structural foundations of discrimination in capitalist society were cast aside in the time of COVID-19. In California in the US:

> Health officials and experts say, is how COVID-19 is stalking certain groups, such as essential workers, and those in institutions including nursing homes and prisons, at much greater rates than those who have the ability to stay home.
>
> LIN ET AL., 2020

COVID-19 both exposed the systemic discrimination and amplified such discrimination of the modern world. White privilege in the main is upheld in the current world order. Class stratification determines where the resources will flow to – even in the time of a global pandemic. And even though colonialism is studied from the history books – countries were found to be still living in a highly unequal and unjust world in the time of COVID-19.

5 Domestic Violence

In South Africa – the president, in an address to the nation, referred to violence against women as the second pandemic. Under apartheid or race-based capitalism it was violence against black men, women and children by the apartheid state. There were 80 000 calls to help-lines within two weeks of the lockdown – in April 2020. COVID-19 brought focus on the real conditions of women in capitalist countries. I did not think or believe that domestic violence was at all an issue in the developed world, until COVID-19 came along! I thought that domestic violence in the West was hardly an issue. I was wrong. COVID-19 pushed aside all preconceived notions regarding the conditions of women in the civilised West. In Canada in the time of COVID-19:

> We've heard a lot about this issue during the period of isolation imposed on us by the virus, about the women and girls – at least 10 by this point – who have been killed in intimate partner homicides over the past few months. But over that period, there are thousands of others who have been beaten, bullied, harassed and generally terrified by men with whom they are either living or involved. We actually have two pandemics going on in this country; one is getting lots of attention and love by the federal government and the other is continuing to be ignored. Domestic violence is a pandemic; a deadly blight around the globe, including in this country. But we don't seem to be nearly as concerned about how we stack up against other countries in terms of the success rate of our response.
>
> MASON, 2020: 11

It certainly was not the end of history for indigenous women in Ottawa, Canada. Their misery under Canadian-style capitalism continues:

> COVID-19 has magnified the effects of systemic discrimination against Indigenous women in Canada, said Crown-Indigenous Relations Minister Carolyn Bennett at a virtual summit the federal government organized to discuss a feminist response to the pandemic. Bennett said Canada's colonial legacy has played a role in worse outcomes for Indigenous women. She said that includes more layoffs, a lack of child care and a spike in family violence.
>
> WYLD, 2021

One would have thought that a woman would be most safe in her home! However, COVID-19 blasted the myth or ideology of "home sweet home" in capitalist society. According to the charity SafeLives in the UK: "Abusers work from home" (*Daily Mail*, 2020). There were major pressures on relationships. The true picture of domestic violence emerged in the time of COVID-19. It seems that for all the decades – whilst states were primarily focused on growing the capitalist economy, the next election, more power and more corruption – women were continually beaten, bruised and murdered by men – who themselves were continually beaten and bruised by the capitalist system that extracts both surplus-value and dignity – whilst enforcing economic violence on the struggling masses. Gender-based violence is systemic in the modern world. COVID-19 also made recognisable the economic triggers for domestic violence:

> Potential victims may still face tough decisions about their situations, at a time when the pandemic is exacerbating issues such as unemployment that often trigger domestic violence while disrupting the ability of victims to get help. People who are called family annihilators, who killed not only their wives but the children are almost always unemployed, said Deborah Tucker, president of the National Center on Domestic and Sexual Violence.
>
> SWOYER ET AL., 2020: 4

In one of the biggest financial capitals of the world:

> According to the police, charges and cautions for domestic violence have risen 24 per cent since 9 March compared with last year. Hestia, a charity that provides refuges across London, said it had seen a 60 per cent increase in referrals since February.
>
> ROACH, 2020

When and where women are abused, it seems that economic insecurity under capitalism is the primary enabling force for such violence and abuse:

> We've had situations where women have left, but they are in debt and struggling to keep a roof over their head. There are a lot of people who are hungry. The risk is that they feel like they have no choice but to go back. We're making sure that people have access to food with The Felix Project.
>
> ROACH, 2020

COVID-19 swept aside the trumped-up feel-good ideology of false togetherness under capitalism – and revealed the actual conditions of women and their families:

> Constituents who've come to me for help recently include a mother trapped in temporary accommodation after fleeing domestic abuse. She shares a bedroom not just with her teenage son, but with damp, mould, leaks and electrical faults. Another regularly goes without running water. A family of five remain stuck on the council housing list in a one-bedroom flat, the father with acute health problems and a son with autism. All in it together we are most certainly not.
>
> OSAMA, 2020

COVID-19 has uncovered the ideological veil that has concealed the plight of women and children in homes in all parts of the world. Family-life encounters constant challenges in capitalist society – including in the developed Western world. When such challenges become unbearable and unmanageable – it is women and children in the main, who are victims of an uncaring economic system and an uncaring society. Capitalism has exposed itself as the uncaring and brutish system – thanks to COVID-19.

6 Religion – the Opium of the Masses in the Time of a Global Pandemic

Religious ideologies came under the spotlight in the time of COVID-19. I received many religious messages from family, friends and community members. They were from well-meaning people who wanted to provide moral support and give their fellow men and women as much hope as possible. But religion also exposed its deep and extensive ideological side in the time of COVID-19. In the UK:

> The pastors are seeking to judicially review both the Westminster government's restrictions and the Welsh government's ban on public worship services during its own 'firebreak' lockdown that recently ended. They claim that stopping believers from attending church services is a breach of Article 9 of the Human Rights Act, which guarantees the freedom to express religious beliefs.
>
> WYATT, 2020

Human Rights was a maelstrom of confusions and contests in the time of COVID-19. Article 18 of the United Nations Universal Declaration of Human Rights states:

> Everyone has the right to freedom of thought, conscience and religion; this right includes freedom to change his religion or belief, and freedom, either alone or in community with others and in public or private, to manifest his religion or belief in teaching, practice, worship and observance.
>
> UN, 2015: 18

But Article 03 of the United Nations Universal Declaration of Human Rights states: "Everyone has the right to life, liberty and security of person" (UN, 2015: 8). Surely the right to life must first be secured and protected – if a person is to practice the righ to freedom of religion? We witnessed how the issue of Human Rights in the West were argued for – devoid of an acknowledgement of other rights that required attention – the right to life being the primary right. It seems that all rights have equal weighting in capitalist society. We witnessed how human rights competed with each other – with disatrous consequences. In Delhi, India, Muslims who attended a prayer gathering in the face of a global pandemic witnessed 150 people testing positive for COVID-19. Religion – in its raw ideological form – was on a footing to worsen an already catastrophic situation – as different religions went about their ways as if all was normal. Old beliefs and old habits persist – even in the time of a global pandemic and even if these are detrimental to one's life! In Israel, the communities of orthodox Jews were the hotspots of COVID-19. Orthodox Jews have a strict belief in God over state. Regrettably there was no holy or divine intervention from above to stop COVID-19 from spreading and killing people in their millions on God's planet earth. In capitalist South Korea, the neighbour of communist North Korea, religious rituals enabled the infections and deaths of congregants as opposed to saving them:

> Church officials south of Seoul were revealed to have sprayed salt water into parishioners' mouths on the false premise it would stave off the infection. Worse, no one disinfected the bottle's nozzle, and 46 people from the congregation have already tested positive.
>
> DUDDEN and MARKS, 2020: 1

In capitalist US about 70 people were infected in a church as the priest refused to shut down services. Religious places of worship became super-spreaders of COVID-19:

> Clusters of COVID-19 transmission from Washington State to Georgia have been traced to choir sessions, with singers who lead worship or entertain communities uniquely vulnerable to the respiratory disease.

> COVID-19, the disease caused by the coronavirus, ripped through a choir in Mount Vernon, Washington, after an early March practice. Within three weeks, 45 members had been infected and two died, even though members avoided direct contact and no one seemed ill during rehearsal, according to local reports.
>
> HOWELL, 2020: 4

In capitalist South Africa, religion trumps science. Even the state chose religious ideology over that of science – in the time of a public health contagion. The writer in the print media also uncovered religions' economic and financial rationale for its existence:

> Listening to the boss telling the religious sector that it's now 'in our hands' sent a shiver down my spine, to be quite honest. Not a good move. Defiant behaviour at Easter church services sparked mini outbreaks in the Eastern Cape and Free State early on in the pandemic. Regulations or not, I see the reopening of churches and other places of collective worship as being a big mistake, one that is going to cost us lives. It could get interesting though, given the number of blag artists operating in the God industry whose tills haven't been turning over since the end of March. They must be raring to go. Holy water for R500 a bottle, guaranteed to keep COVID-19 and the devil at bay. Reopening the churches is also a serious provocation to every other business that could – and would – happily reopen with a 50-person door limit, sanitiser and masks but lacks the clout and access to government that the religious sector clearly has.
>
> HARPER, 2020: 18

Whilst the pandemic was sweeping through South Africa, a shooting at a church's headquarters resulted in:

> 5 people dead and scores injured. Maria Frahm-Arp of religious studies at the University of Johannesburg said 'succession battles that turned violent were common in new churches and money from tithes was often a key driver in battles for control'.
>
> PHETO and WICKS, 2020: 6

Money has the tendency to replace ancient gods. Blind faith in the time of COVID-19 continued unabated:

> For almost two months, people have had to worship by themselves, without the fellowship of a religious community. Some violated the level five and four regulations and gathered in secret. Police have at times made arrests. Faith leaders have the responsibility to protect those they serve.
>
> *Mail and Guardian*, 2020: 18

In the UK, religious ideological competition banged on the state's door to be given more religious rights than other religious brands and religions – and be allowed to congregate and pray in the midst of a public health crisis:

> Catholic churches should be allowed to reopen before Pentecostal churches, or mosques owing to their different styles of worship, the leader of the Catholic church in England and Wales has said. 'There's a great deal of deep spiritual sacrifice being made'.
>
> SHERWOOD, 2020: 9

In his zeal to push forward his ideological brand of religion, the good Catholic did not seem to care or take notice of the sacrifice of lives that was happening all around him. In New Orleans in the US, a preacher and blues guitarist, who succumbed to COVID-19 and died after ministering and playing at Mardi Gras, had three days before:

> Posted a meme on his Facebook page about the coronavirus, which at the time had killed about 40 people in the United States. The media, it warned, was trying to 'manipulate your life' by creating 'mass hysteria'.
>
> JAMISON, 2020: 1

Mass hysteria is what takes place in many places of worship in much of the world on a regular basis. A fellow guitarist of his, who also tested positive for COVID-19 and fortunately survived stated:

> We prayed for him and believed that we would all get better. And I got extremely better, through it all, and I believe God touched me. And I don't know the difference.
>
> JAMISON, 2020: 1

Unable to accept that there was no divine intervention to save her husband's life, the dead preacher's wife stated: "I'm not angry. I know who did it. It's the devil that comes to steal, to kill and to destroy" (Jamison, 2020: 1). Now and then we witness the devilish nature of religion – when killings are done in the name of god and religion. We saw the devilish nature of religion – when religious ideologies took priority over precious lives during COVID-19. Who will forget the Kumbh mela in India in the time of a global pandemic! Religion, in the main has had a cosy relationship with capitalism. Although religion is much older than capitalism – like so many other institutions in capitalist society – it too has become part and parcel of the overriding capitalist system. The debate on religion heightened in the time of COVID-19:

> Don't submerge yourself in ignorance, irrespective of the religion you practise, all religions still lead to the creator, don't be fooled by miracle healing. If that was so, where are those that profess about healing, when the world needs them now, this is a profitable business at the expense of followers like you.
>
> GILLITS, 2020

Religious ideology as a fundamental pillar of capitalist society was called out: "apparently, infection control, like gun control, depends on hopes and prayers, not sound public policies" (Picard, 2020). COVID-19 made us rethink the world. It pitted ideologies against each other, ideologies against science and ideologies against reality. In the war of ideas, beliefs and ideologies in the time of COVID-19, people paid with their lives. If the ideology of profit killed in the time of COVID-19, so did the ideology of religion. *Where is the sense in saving souls but losing lives!*

CHAPTER 4

Unrest, Rebellion and Revolt in the Time of COVID-19

> Those who make peaceful revolution impossible will make violent revolution inevitable.
>
> JOHN F. KENNEDY

•••

> Every generation needs a new revolution.
>
> THOMAS JEFFERSON

∴

1 Unrest, Rebellion and Revolt in the Time of COVID-19

One has to be either extremely stupid – or extremely angry – to engage in street protests, unrests and revolts in the midst of a global pandemic. Many parts of the world experienced and witnessed large numbers of unrests and protests in the time of COVID-19. Revolutions are another matter altogether! They either result in changing the status quo – as was the case with the French Revolution of 1789 – or result in the status quo remaining – as was the case with the Tunisian Revolution of 2010, also known as the Arab Spring. The Black Lives Matter movement was obviously a mass movement of very angry people in the time of COVID-19. The Black Lives Matter movement mass protests also included people of colour – many whites were part of the protests. In capitalist countries in the main, revolution seemed ripe in the time of COVID-19. At least that was the sentiment of some. In Australia:

> There is a wider political difficulty to consider in the wake of the street protests that have erupted in the United States over race and which have spread around the world, including to Australia. They show urban populations in the mood to revolt.
>
> FARRER, 2020

 DOI:10.1163/9789004539808_005

The followers of Trump also seemed very angry when they stormed Capitol Hill on 6 January 2021. Observers with the power of the pen – or rather the keyboard – analysed the protests from varied paradigms in the time of COVID-19. According to one analyst, it is the ideology of religion in general and Judeo-Christianity in particular which created the cultural conditions that enabled George Floyd's murder – which in turn triggered the Black Lives Matter mass protests first in the US, then in many parts of the world:

> Our cultures are shaped by religion. From early on, Christianity has been a weapon. It does not hate or love. It doesn't even care. It is a sanctimonious, intolerant, acquisitive and always superior compulsion, responsible for much of the greatness and also the misery in the world it has dominated for so long. Judeo-Christianity's reign is already fading, but is still capable of inflicting pain. That righteous knee on George Floyd's neck was more than 2,000 years old.
>
> BRUCE, 2020: 14

Other analysts put the Black Lives Matter global mass protests down to the history and legacy of slavery:

> People Before Profit councillors in Galway have actually demanded the removal of a memorial to Christopher Columbus because he was genocidal and the statue glorifies slavery.
>
> MCCAUSLAND, 2020

This after protestors tore down the statue of Edward Colston – a slave dealer from the 1750s – and dragged and dumped it into the river Avon. Many, except neoliberal ideologues, admit that slavery was key to the development of capitalism in Britain. In the 1750s Robert Clive got India to agree to Britain collecting revenues in India (Smart, 1996: 129). The 1750s was also a time when the Industrial Revolution picked up momentum in Britain. One television presenter mentioned that, the fact that the statue of Edward Colston was up in the public sphere meant that people had the opportunity to learn about history. It seemed that more people the world over got a lesson in slave history in the one day that the statue was torn down – than in all of the many decades that it stood tall and proud in Bristol City! Amongst the plethora of historical phenomena that COVID-19 had awoken, the French Revolution was also invoked in the time of COVID-19:

> The French Revolution of 1789 is most often depicted in terms of the dramatic and traumatic events at the national centre, and of course those killed and injured storming the Bastille on 14 July deserve such attention. But the revolution was also made in thousands of other places, where people even more hard-done by than the Parisians stood up and abolished a whole social order from below, defying a thousand years of history with the weight of their own experience and their hopes for a better future. All too often, those who took power in the name of the revolution betrayed those hopes, and in that betrayal laid the path to the tragic violence for which the 1790s are also renowned.
>
> ANDRESS, 2020

Revolutions of sorts – it seems – is one sure way of learning about history! Ideological arguments against a Marxist analysis of unrests were plentiful in the time of COVID-19. Unquestioning support for capitalism and capitalist-biased economic science was also thrown into the ideological analytical mix:

> If you have bought the Marxist package (or the faux Marxist one that now seems to be the only version available) you actually, sincerely believe that capitalism – the profit motive – is the cause of every social tragedy. Instead of seeing free market economics as a great liberator – having delivered mass prosperity, and the self-determination that follows from it, on a scale that is unprecedented in human history – you regard it as the enslavement of one class (or race) by another.
>
> DALEY, 2020

Superficial race analysis competed vigorously with that of a class analysis of capitalist society regarding the Black Lives Matter protests in the time of COVID-19:

> That doesn't mean that some locals aren't joining in on the violence; the city has its own idiots – trust-fund Trotskyites, for starters. But here as elsewhere, the worst confrontations reek of the roving radicals who rush in to turn protests into riots in some demented dream of fomenting full-on revolution.
>
> MOORE ET AL., 2020

In the country that Britain once ruled over and pillaged for centuries – India – unrests and protests erupted in the time of COVID-19. In his haste to open up India's capitalist economy and catch up with China, the holy man of Indian capitalism – Narendra Modi – decided to roll back farm laws that for many decades guaranteed state support to farmers. Modi and his band of capitalist ideologues tried their level best to open the flood gates for the capitalist market to enter and extract the farmers' profits. The farmers rebelled:

> Farmers protesting against new agriculture laws in India have broken through police barricades around the capital and entered the grounds of Delhi's historic Red Fort, in chaotic and violent scenes that overshadowed the country's Republic Day celebrations. Police hit protesters with batons and fired teargas to try to disperse the crowds after hundreds of thousands of farmers, many on tractors or horses, marched on the capital on Tuesday. One protester was confirmed to have died in the clashes and dozens were injured.
>
> ELLIS-PETERSEN, 2021

In capitalist USA, some protested in solidarity with the Indian farmers thousands of miles away:

> Hundreds of drivers made their way around downtown Detroit as snow fell Sunday in a show of solidarity with farmers in India who are protesting laws they say could devastate crop prices and reduce their earnings.
>
> TAYLOR, 2021

Capitalism has the tendency to unleash its violence on the lower classes. In this day and age – the lower classes tend to be people of colour:

> In the US, more than 100,000 people have died from COVID-19, most of them weak, elderly, poor and minorities. The death of Floyd, from another perspective, reveals the desperate inequality rampant in the US. Such inequality is all over the bottom of American society and may trigger more serious conflicts.
>
> *Global Times*, 2020

When the US state turned on its own people during protest marches in the time of COVID-19, Trump tweeted that the 75-year-old man faked his fall. In South Africa, factional battles in the ruling-ANC spilled over into major unrests in parts of the country. Whilst the jailing of former president Jacob Zuma in July 2021 triggered the unrests, the world witnessed what is possible when inequality, poverty and unemployment are prevalent in society:

> Whereas the trigger for the recent riots and widespread opportunistic looting was the arrest of the former president, Jacob Zuma, the underlying, deep structural problem is deepening inequality, which has been worsened by the Covid-19 pandemic.
>
> FIKENI, 2021

About a year later, former president Thabo Mbeki warned of South Africa's own Arab Spring:

> Former South African president Thabo Mbeki recently launched a sharp critique of the governing ANC for failure to address what it has labelled the triple challenge of poverty, unemployment and inequality. Mbeki, who led the party from 1997 to 2007, said the government seemed to have no plan to address these problems, warning rising poverty and hardship, poor governance and mounting lawlessness could see South Africa erupt into its own version of the 'Arab Spring'.
>
> Africa, 2022

Just over a week later the *Star Late Edition* carried the following headlines:

> Four killed as Tembisa burns: Death, destruction and mayhem erupts as angry residents take to the streets over service delivery, exorbitant rates, taxes and electricity bills.
>
> SADIKE, 2022

The *Citizen* stated:

> Protests over poor services occur regularly in South Africa, which is battling some of the highest unemployment and crime rates in the world. The latest bout of protests came after former president Thabo Mbeki warned the country could see an uprising similar to the Arab Spring, triggered by mounting discontent.
>
> *Citizen*, 2022

In Canada, people marched on Canada's national birthday to protest against the genocide of indigenous children in Canada's residential school system:

> The crowd chanted 'No pride in genocide' as it crossed the Portage Bridge to Wellington Street, where it was joined by more orange-shirted

> demonstrators. Placards read 'Every child matters,' 'Canada has blood on its hands,' and 'Shame'.
>
> DUFFY and GILLIS: 2021

Other protests were not that peaceful:

> Two statues, including a prominent sculpture of Queen Victoria on the front lawn of the Manitoba Legislature, were toppled by protestors demonstrating against hundreds of unmarked graves found in recent weeks at residential schools. The Queen Victoria monument was pulled off its elevated base and covered in red paint, while the base itself was littered with red handprints. A sign left at the base of the statue read, 'We were children once. Bring them home'.
>
> BILLECK ET AL., 2021

In Beirut:

> Chaotic scenes returned to Beirut last night as violent clashes broke out between police and anti-government protesters demanding revolution in the wake of Tuesday's devastating explosion that killed 158 people and destroyed the city's port.
>
> ROSE, 2020

In Columbia: "Protesters had gathered in the southwestern Colombian city of Cali late Monday, pushing for economic justice on the sixth day of anti-government demonstrations" (Grattan, 2021). Unrests and protests of various forms continued into 2022. Rising inflation also witnessed protests increase in many parts of the world. With the world preparing for a major recession together with the Russian invasion of Ukraine – capitalism would be experiencing one of its biggest failing moments ever!

2 Capitalist Society: A Society of Wealth and Poverty – but Also of Unrests and Violent Revolutions

Capitalist society is a restless society. We witnessed this in the time of COVID-19. Revolutions in feudal society finally led to its collapse. But the new society that was subsequently born – capitalism – had been a boiling cauldron of unrest and revolutions from its very beginning. To go back in time a few hundred years – Britain was in the throes of capitalist and industrial development when the French Revolution of 1789 occurred. In the 1780s, France was mostly feudal in nature – but France also comprised the building-blocks for agricultural and industrial capitalism:

> Provincial cities were often dominated by specific industries, such as textiles in Rouen and Elbeuf. Smaller, newer urban centres had sprung up around large iron foundries and coal mines, such as at Le Creusot, Niederbronn, and Anzin, where 4,000 workers were employed. However, it was particularly in the Atlantic ports where a booming colonial trade with the Caribbean colonies was developing a capitalist economic sector in shipbuilding and in processing colonial goods, as in Bordeaux, where the population expanded from 67,000 to 110,000 between 1750 and 1790.
>
> MCPHEE, 2002: 17

Thirteen years before the French Revolution of 1789 – in 1776 – Adam Smith wrote *The Wealth of Nations* – the bible of capitalism. 1776 was also the year that America gained independence from Britain. France fought on the side of the rebels against Britain. Monies for France's involvement in the United States War of Independence had to come from somewhere. King Louis XVI ruled over the lords, land, artisans, peasants and agricultural labourers in France. Like the intense taxing of the peasant class that led to the 1381 Peasant Revolt in Britain, the continued and intense taxing of the French people finally culminated in the French Revolution of 1789 and the violence that ensued. For their greed – the king and queen lost their heads. From the beginning of capitalism's time in power – the commoners have been in opposition to capitalism. In the early 1800s:

> The Luddite movement began in Nottingham in England and culminated in a region-wide rebellion that lasted from 1811 to 1816. Mill and factory owners took to shooting protesters and eventually the movement was suppressed with legal and military force.
>
> Wikipedia, 2021

The Luddites were no match for the might of capitalism:

> The original Luddites were British weavers and textile workers who objected to the increased use of mechanised looms and knitting frames. Luddites were gunned down during an attack on a mill near Huddersfield. The army had deployed several thousand troops to round up these

> dissidents in the days that followed, and dozens were hanged or transported to Australia.
>
> EVANS, 2021

But the rebellions and revolts did not stop with the violent crushing of the Luddites. Wherever and whenever man is oppressed – he finds ways and means to overcome his oppression:

> Chartism was a working-class movement, which emerged in 1836 and was most active between 1838 and 1848. The aim of the Chartists was to gain political rights and influence for the working classes. Some opponents of the movement feared that Chartists were not just interested in changing the way Parliament was elected, but really wanted to turn society upside down by starting a revolution (Web 1).

Wherever and whenever capitalism is threatened – the threats are eliminated. For example, troops representing capitalist interests killed 22 people – when on "4 November 1839, 5,000 men marched into Newport, in Monmouthshire" to protest (Web 1). 1848 must be the year when revolutions violently shook the continent of Europe – and its impacts were felt as far afield as Australia. Capitalism had by then firmly planted its profit-maximisation and accumulation flag on European soil. Marx and Engels (1848) naively believed that capitalism's days were numbered. On the eve of the revolution – they wrote in *the Communist Manifesto of February 1848*:

> A spectre is haunting Europe – the spectre of communism. All the powers of old Europe have entered into a holy alliance to exorcise this spectre: Pope and Tsar, Metternich and Guizot, French Radicals and German police-spies.

One of the heroes of the 1848 revolutions in Europe was Robert Blum – a German member-of-parliament and revolutionary captured and executed: "he was shot at 9 o'clock in the morning of November 9, 1848" (Oomkes, 2014). France seems to be the mother of revolutions. The 1848 revolutions started in France, then spread to Germany, Italy, Austria, Hungary, Denmark, Ireland, etc. The middle classes, journalists, students, small business owners, etc. were all engaged in the revolutions of 1848 – but it was the workers that were the hardcore fighters on the barricades. As fast as the revolutions happened – they were violently crushed by European states siding with capitalism:

> The triumphant progress of the European revolution in February and March 1848 had been followed by a reactionary counter-offensive. The prevention of the workers' demonstration of April 10 in London had weakened the revolutionary impetus of Chartism, and the June defeat of the French proletariat was a heavy blow for the European revolutionary movement as a whole.
>
> COHEN ET AL, 2010: xix

The middle-class component of the revolution won social and political concessions. The working class and peasant component of the 1848 revolutions – had their dreams obliterated. If the ruling classes in Europe were repressive before the 1848 revolutions – they were even more repressive after the violent crushing of the revolution. Although Britain had the Chartists to contend with – Britain escaped more or less unscathed from the impacts of the 1848 revolutions that were sweeping across Europe. However, revolutions had been taking place in Britain's colonies like Jamaica and Ceylon in India. It seemed that Britain had outsourced the 1848 revolutions to its colonies. Capitalist violence continued into the 20th century. In the US the:

> Ludlow Massacre, attack on striking coal miners and their families by the Colorado National Guard and Colorado Fuel and Iron Company guards at Ludlow, Colorado, on April 20, 1914, resulted in the deaths of 25 people, including 11 children.
>
> DEHLER, 2021

The planting of the seeds of capitalism in much of the world was not given a warm welcome. On the contrary, the indigenous peoples of the colonised lands rebelled and revolted against the coming of primitive accumulation – viz. the violent beginnings of the capitalist world order. Much blood was shed – mostly that of the indigenous peoples of the colonised lands. When the colonialists were finally forced out – they left behind the capitalist system. The biggest revolution against the beginnings of the capitalist order was that of the Russian Revolution in October of 1917. It too finally imploded in November 1989.

3 Capitalist Society: A Class Society above All Else

Slave society was a class society – it finally came to an end. Feudalism was also a class society – it too came to an end. Whilst the machinery of slave and feudal societies are a thing of the past, the class nature of such societies have not withered away. It is very much with us today in the modern world – part and parcel of our everyday lives. Slave society transformed into feudal society – with its class infrastructure still intact. Feudal society transformed into capitalist society – with its class infrastructure still intact. Many countries in many parts of the world transformed into independent countries with the fall of colonialism – but with their class infrastructure still intact. South Africa transformed from a race-based society into a democratic society in 1994 – but with its class infrastructure still intact. There are now very wealthy blacks and very many poor blacks in South Africa. Under apartheid there were only very poor blacks. In India, the caste system transformed into a class system with the departure of the British colonialists.

The Roman Empire was built on slavery – but not many of the slaves were black. The relationship between master and slave was therefore one of material exploitation. Racism and discrimination were the cultural and consequent form of material exploitation – not its cause. The British Empire was built on both slavery and worker exploitation – with many of the slaves being black and nearly all of the workers during the Industrial Revolution being white. The exploited white workers included women and children as well. The relationship between master and slave – and boss and worker – was one of material exploitation. Racism and discrimination were the cultural and consequent form of material exploitation – not its cause. The Irish were heavily prejudiced and discriminated against. Everyone knows – if he knows nothing else – that the Irish are not black. The American Empire was built on slavery and immigrant exploitation – with black being the main but amongst the 'many colours' exploited. The relationship between master and slave, boss and worker and white and black was therefore one of material exploitation. Racism and discrimination were the cultural and consequent form of material exploitation – not its cause. Racism in America is therefore not the cause for America's troubles – it is a symptom of a deeply entrenched and unequal class society – in the same way that caste in India is not the cause of India's troubles – but the consequence of a deeply entrenched and unequal class society. The country on the planet that underwent the most vicious racist policies – South Africa – could not really join their brothers and sisters en masse to proclaim that Black Lives Matter – not because black South Africans are not one of the most exploited people on the planet 28 years into non-racial democracy – but because racism as a political and legal project has been done away with. But blacks in South Africa still suffer at the hands of the police. What would have been the outcry if 36 black miners were massacred in the US – as they were in South Africa in 2012? White police officers were present – amongst many black officers – firing as if they were in the 'Wild West'. There was no such cry as Black Lives Matter in South Africa – yet all of those massacred were black! There was not even any utterance of racism against the perpetrators of such an evil act. In a world where capitalist ideologies dominate, race tends to be argued as the cause of capitalist society's troubles. Race discrimination and racism is still now and then part of life in South Africa – but class exploitation thrives and flourishes and it is legal! Race discrimination and racism still exist in the US many decades after Martin Luther King's "I Have a Dream" speech – but nothing compared to the way that class exploitation succeeds in the US! The class divide in the new South Africa shone through in the time of COVID-19, in relation to the opening of the schools debate:

> All five of SA's teacher unions are unanimous in their support for the immediate closure of schools, but school governing body associations are divided, in what amounts to a stand-off between rich and poor. An alliance of private schools and the Federation of Governing Bodies of South African Schools (Fedsas), representing mostly former Model C schools, wants pupils to stay in class. Their stance has been supported by the South African Human Rights Commission and the Anglican church.
>
> GOVENDER, 2020: 1

The well-off blacks in South Africa can now afford to send their children to private and Model C schools. If racism is the bitter fruit of the capitalist tree – then inequality, poverty, labour exploitation and unemployment are its roots. The capitalist state helps to water these roots. The class nature of capitalist society is masked by ideological labels such as Western civilisation, American values, the greatest nation on earth, etc:

> In the United States there was universal manhood suffrage almost from the very beginning. This led to the phenomenon, first brilliantly formulated by Leon Samson, of 'Americanism' as a substitute for socialism. American capitalism, Samson argued, is the socialist form of capitalism, i.e., it preaches an egalitarianism, a denial of the reality of class society, which is unlike anything one would have found in France or Britain. Therefore a worker in America could express his drive for equality in terms of, not in counter-position to, the prevailing ideology.
>
> HARRINGTON [SOMBART], 1976: X

If more of the BAME died in the time of COVID-19, then it was because they live more precarious lives under capitalism:

> He [Mayor of London] says the crisis has 'laid bare the unequal outcomes that have a negative impact on the lives of BAME Londoners', adding: 'we know that some Londoners – and particularly BAME Londoners – are more likely to live in poverty, overcrowded conditions and have less access to green space'.
>
> SIDDIQUE, 2020: 16

If BAME were the elites in 'black and Asian countries', they would more likely have been insulated from COVID-19, in the similar manner that the elites of Africa and India were insulated in the time of COVID-19 – when compared to the poor and working class of such societies. Capitalism discriminates – but fundamentally in terms of class. Racism is incidental to capitalism – not its main priority. In *The German Ideology* (1932) Marx states:

> When the crude form in which the division of labour appears with the Indians and Egyptians calls forth the caste-system in their State and religion, the historian believes that the caste-system is the power which has produced this crude social form.

It is no different for race as the apparent cause of inequality in capitalist society. In the *Communist Manifesto of 1848* Marx and Engels (1848) state:

> The history of all hitherto existing society is the history of class struggles. Freeman and slave, patrician and plebeian, lord and serf, guild-master and journeyman, in a word, oppressor and oppressed, stood in constant opposition to one another, carried on an uninterrupted, now hidden, now open fight, a fight that each time ended, either in a revolutionary reconstitution of society at large, or in the common ruin of the contending classes (14).

Revolutions are violent, messy and painful. It would have been impressive if humankind had arrived – through the ages – to capitalist society without revolutions. It would be splendid if we are able to move into a post-capitalist world – without the violence, pain and messiness of revolutions. But if history and the revolutions in the time of COVID-19 are anything to go by, then my views on peaceful revolution will or may be labelled as ideological thinking viz. utopian, dreaming and idealistic. On the issue of dreaming, John Lennon's song *Imagine* comes to mind. Utopianism, dreams and idealism aside, "oppressor and oppressed, stood in constant opposition to one another, carried on an uninterrupted, now hidden, now open fight, a fight that each time ended, either in a revolutionary reconstitution of society at large, or in the common ruin of the contending classes" are terrifying words – when one considers the protests, unrests and rebellions that have thus far characterised capitalist society – and witnessed in the time of COVID-19.

CHAPTER 5

In Search of Rights, Freedom, Democracy and Liberty in the Capitalist World

> America's support for human rights and democracy is our noblest export to the world.
>
> WILLIAM BENNETT

•••

> Humankind must first of all eat, drink, have shelter and clothing, before it can pursue politics, science, art, religion, etc.
>
> KARL MARX

1 People Protests: Terrorism in the US – but a Beautiful Sight in Hong Kong

The solitary individual with two bags in his hands blocking Chinese tanks from entering Tiananmen Square on 4 June 1989 has become the ideological symbol of the West against China. Time Magazine "later named him one of the 100 most influential people of the 20th century". Hitler and Mussolini were also on the list. The man in Tiananmen Square became known as the "Tank Man". He was protesting for democratic reforms in China. Nothing wrong with that. This was about six months before the fall of the Berlin Wall – and the subsequent break-up of the Soviet Union. Fast forward 33 years into 2021 – and the face of the 'Stop the Steal' protests on Capitol Hill in the US was that of the 'Horned Fur Hat Man'. He was part of the violent protest that sought to question the democratic processes relating to the 2020 US election. It is too early to tell whether he will make Time Magazine's top 100 list of influential persons of the 21st century. His leader Donald Trump might. What was clear about Tiananmen Square and Capitol Hill is that some people in both China and the US did not feel that they were living in the greatest countries on the planet. When such protests occur in countries, then it is a sign that there must certainly be more

 | DOI:10.1163/9789004539808_006

to life than just living in either of the two greatest economic superpowers of the world! Like so many aspects of historical events, Tiananmen Square was also invoked in the time of COVID-19:

> On this day in 1989, the Chinese military brutally crushed unarmed crowds of Chinese students who had, since April that year, been calling for political reforms and greater civil liberties. Ever since, the Chinese Communist Party has tried to airbrush the incident out of history and to discourage mention of it even in foreign media. There are several reasons why we should refuse to forget it. That was the date on which the hard-line authoritarians in China defeated the last of the more liberal-minded senior political figures. That defeat has had fateful consequences. They are writ large in the extreme authoritarianism and personality cult of Xi Jinping. Deng Xiaoping had been refusing to embrace serious reforms for a decade by then, starting with his suppression of the Democracy Wall in 1979. But the violence in 1989 was a watershed event. The Orwellian surveillance and repression we see in China under Xi are the antithesis of what the young students in Tiananmen Square were calling for in early 1989: a more open, accountable, human-rights respecting, democratic government. In the immediate wake of the bloodshed perpetrated by the so called People's Liberation Army, angry young people wrote up on their university dorms or classroom walls – before the secret police shut down dissent, arrested thousands and wiped out traces of the protests – slogans such as 'Thunder from the silent zone!', 'China is dead!', 'Where is justice?', 'The government caused the turmoil!' and 'The truth will out some day!'.
>
> PACKHAM, 2020: 10

Ever since, China has been castigated by the West – for not embracing democratic reforms, principles and processes. And since 1997, Hong Kong has become the fierce battle ground for Western and Eastern ideologies. Nothing can be more capitalist in Asia than Hong Kong. Well there's Japan, but capitalism in Japan has been struggling for a while – to keep up its appearance. It hopes to revive its capitalist image by big capitalist-driven projects like the Tokyo Olympics – whatever the science tells it about not having public events during a global pandemic. Hong Kong is a 'country' in the grip of the past and the present. Hong Kong is the place where not only democracy – but the meanings of democracy – are fought over. Hong Kongers are serious about democracy – as are many people in so many parts of the world. Hong Kongers are therefore willing to fight for it:

> The demonstrations lasted for months. In one major escalation in July, on the anniversary of the 1997 British handover, some protesters even broke into Hong Kong's legislature, shattering windows and doors. The protests continued and at times turned violent. Police used rubber bullets, water cannons and tear gas to try to dispel the crowds.
>
> O' GRADY ET AL., 2020: 12

Every year, many in Hong Kong celebrate the guts and glory of the Tank Man on the 5th of June. In 2020, the Hong Government banned any mass gatherings celebrating the Tank Man – due to COVID-19. COVID-19, arguably, was also a good excuse to prevent people protests for Western interpretations of democratic reforms. The discussions and debates on the meaning of democracy and human rights got fierce in the time of COVID-19. The Western ideological framework of human rights took a beating as well:

> The US has the highest COVID-19 death toll, and the police always abuse violence and mass shootings happen every year. But US political elites still believe such a country has the best human rights record worldwide. Now, the US human rights record is widely criticised, but the US is most interested in the national security law for Hong Kong which they believe may sabotage Hong Kong's human rights.
>
> *Global Times*, 2020

Comparisons were made between the states' responses to citizens' protests in both superpowers. Contradictory sets of values – generated in the US – for protests in the US and in Hong Kong – were highlighted by critical observers in the time of COVID-19:

> It has been about a year since riots broke out in Hong Kong, and the radical protesters' violent crimes are numerous. But Hong Kong police only shot at a rioter once since he was trying to grab the officer's gun. Hong Kong police made no more shots at the rioters and no radical protesters have been killed on the spot. However, the US government, Congress and public opinion have been accusing Hong Kong police as violent and applauded Hong Kong's riots as a 'beautiful sight' of democracy. They encouraged Hong Kong's violent protests by saying that the US stands with the people of Hong Kong. It seems that Washington has given all its care, which should have been provided to Minnesota and the lower classes, to Hong Kong's radical protesters.
>
> *Global Times*, 2020

Hong Kong is in the East but looks to the West for its self-esteem and validation. Ideological support by the West for Hong Kongers fighting for democracy was even to be translated into material forms:

> Australia is considering a British request to resettle tens of thousands of Hong Kong residents if the security situation deteriorates there, and could look at a special humanitarian intake from the Chinese territory if needed. British Foreign Secretary Dominic Raab asked his Five Eyes counterparts including Foreign Minister Marise Payne on Tuesday to consider whether they could provide residency for some of the 314,000 British National Overseas passport-holders in Hong Kong.
>
> PACKHAM, 2020: 10

No similar humanitarian offer was made to the people of Myanmar, who unlike Hong Kongers, were dying in their hundreds – fighting a military dictatorship! Whilst the Western-allied countries were going all out to welcome Hong Kongers, they were at the same time going all out to keep out migrants deserving of humanitarian help and a better life. No similar offer was made to the thousands of migrants drowning in the seas and places like the English Channel hoping to reach the lands of democracy and human rights! Western hypocrisy and double-standards were on full display in the time of COVID-19.

2 Democracy and Human Rights in the West in General and in Capitalist Countries in Particular – in the Time of COVID-19

COVID-19 shone a light on so many aspects of capitalist society. The important areas of human rights, democracy, freedom, etc. did not go undetected in the time of COVID-19. On the contrary, COVID-19 peeled away at the ideological layers hiding the real formations of human rights, democracy, freedom, etc. in the West in general – and in capitalist countries in particular. In his article "the paradox of liberty" Sircar (2020: 12) states:

> For the sake of our democracy's health, we will do well to remain extra vigilant when it comes to the state speaking of liberty's promises of progress by citing the Constitution. Because liberalism is medicine for the powerful and poison for the marginalised, it kills the anti-national and the migrant and it protects the rights of the rich. And yet, we cannot completely abandon it. That is the cruel paradox of all liberal democracies. We are condemned to live and die with it.

Human Rights mean little or nothing if it does not deliver those that it is meant to serve and protect out of their state of material suffering. COVID-19 made this inconvenient fact glaringly transparent in democratic India – the world's biggest democracy:

> India's founding fathers bequeathed a strong set of institutions of governance, with defined roles for each. The Parliament, the Judiciary, the Executive, the Election Commission, Comptroller and Auditor General, the Attorney General, are some such institutions of governance provided for in the Constitution of India. With the development of rights jurisprudence, laws were enacted to ensure and uphold implementation of fundamental rights and to give effect to the non-justiciable directive principles. These laws provided for creation of Commissions and Boards at Central and State levels, to inter-alia, protect Human Rights (1993), Women (1990), Minorities (1992), Backward Classes (1993), Safai Karamcharis (1993) and Children (2005), Unorganized Workers (2008). These Commissions and Boards were to be manned by persons who had held high public offices and embodied eminence, ability and integrity: these being the legislatively ordained preconditions for such appointments. In times of crisis, such institutions take on an enhanced importance, as members of the community seek help to navigate the chaos. In many ways, the current scenario is ripe for gauging the true mettle of our rights oriented institutions. Regrettably, what we are witnessing today is an abject failure of the public integrity system, a failure of the agencies, laws and policies that are meant to promote the welfare and interests of those they are meant to protect. These institutions and bodies have vast powers to secure well being and rights. Yet, as we see the human suffering and trauma unfolding in the aftermath of the lockdown, each of these rights oriented institutions (barring the National Human Rights Commission) can be identified by the stony silence they have maintained throughout this crisis, with no imminent signs of awakening from their slumber. From amongst the searing images and visuals that captured the heartbreak and despair of those desperate to reach the safety of their homes, the image that commanded the nation's attention: that of an exhausted child lying slumped on a suitcase being wheeled by his mother on the highway, and the news of a young 15-year-old Jyoti Kumari who cycled over 1,200 km for seven days carrying her ailing father, should have activated the National Commission for Protection of Child Rights. Unfortunately, the only response these images elicited was an invitation extended to the young lady by the Cycling Federation for trials, while

> the fate of that young child remains unknown. As regards the trauma of unorganised workers, the less about the functioning of Social Security Boards, the better.
>
> GOSWAMI and LUTHRA, 2020

The superficiality, emptiness and rhetoric of human rights and democracy in the capitalist world were exposed in the time of COVID-19:

> We have to admit that the COVID-19 pandemic has shown us examples that lack humanitarianism. This may be due to the chaos caused by the spreading threat. However, such lack of humanitarianism seems to be deep-rooted. This is because of some countries' and their ruling elites' incurable egoism. Those who proclaim themselves as moral leaders with democratic traditions did not unite all parties to seek mutual understanding. Instead, they started to act according to the law of the jungle, regardless of etiquette rules and ethical constraints. Some Western countries are politicising humanitarian issues and trying to use the pandemic to punish the governments they dislike. If not, how could we explain that these Western countries, which always talk about respecting human rights, do not want to give up their one-sided economic sanctions on developing countries (at least before the global pandemic situation is eased)? Indeed, such sanctions have weakened ordinary people's ability to exercise their social and economic rights, causing serious difficulties in protecting residents' health and hitting the most unprotected people.
>
> LAVROV, 2020: 7

The fake news about the ideals of democracy and freedom in the capitalist West was made evident in the time of COVID-19, but none so much as in the fake news that workers have freedom to choose under capitalism. Under capitalism coercion or compulsion is a constantly present and greater force than the freedom to choose:

> There are, however, intense contradictions that can undermine the realisation of the path that capital envisages. First, prima facie, there is no evidence that labour is in a rush to get back to work. Mortal fear has pushed workers, most of them migrants, to return home. This yearning for home and familiarity in times of a pandemic, though apparently inconsistent with the crude logic of cost benefit analysis, is a powerful driving force in the mass reverse migration of workers since the partial easing of the lockdown. This withdrawal from the labour market is an exercise in the

> formal freedom that capitalism supposedly grants, but which it obstructs with might. Rather than provisioning for safety measures and immediate financial support that would reassure workers, employers have resorted to coercion. The restraint on workers' physical mobility in Karnataka reflects this intent.
>
> DEEPAK, 2020

It appears that the much cherished values of liberty, democracy and freedom to choose are not applicable in the workplaces of capitalist countries: "debates are raging over whether workers may reasonably refuse to be inoculated, and if employers can discipline them for refusing" (Hosken, 2020). Those that could not stomach the hypocrisy regarding free speech in the US left their lucrative positions in powerful corporations:

> Tim Bray, a top engineer and vice-president at Amazon, announced on Monday he is resigning 'in dismay' over the company's firing of employee activists who criticised working conditions amid the coronavirus pandemic.
>
> KARI, 2020: 3

The meaning of human rights – when life or death were the only available choices in the West – was intensely interrogated and criticsed in the time of COVID-19:

> So when I read that the likes of Matrix Chambers, the leading human rights barristers, pronounce that the app is an 'interference with fundamental rights and would require significantly greater justification to be lawful' I am not just angry – I am despairing. And what a depressing irony that their ideology, that everything must bend before so-called human rights, poses a direct challenge to my human right, and that of 1.5 million others, to be able to live something resembling a life again.
>
> POLLARD, 2020

Countries that used the track and tracing app ensured that lives were saved. The right to life could now enable the right to free speech, the right to practice one's religion, etc. COVID-19 revealed that there are ideological constraints to free speech in the Western world. Doctors in the United States of America were threatened with dismissal if they complained to the media about the lack of resources:

> Hospitals are threatening to fire medical staff that talk to the media about working conditions or a lack of equipment during the coronavirus pandemic. In actual fact – it went beyond mere threats – an emergency room doctor and physician at Washington State University was fired after speaking with the media as to how the lack of medical equipment were putting the lives of both staff and patients in danger. He was told a few days later that he 'no longer had a job'. A nurse in Chicago was also fired after emailing colleagues that she wanted to wear more protective equipment while on duty. The nurse 'has asthma and cares for her father who has a respiratory disease'.
>
> O'CONNELL, 2020: 1

The captain of a navy ship was also fired for raising the alarm of the status of COVID-19 on the ship. He said that his sailors did not have to die. One would have thought that this is only what happens in North Korea or China or any other socialist or communist country for that matter. But such despicable war crimes against their own frontline soldiers were taking place in the United States of America – the land of life, liberty and where the pursuit of happiness is apparently guaranteed. I do not think that the doctor, nurse and captain would consider being fired for practising the First Amendment – "the pursuit of happiness". Jimmy Cliff's song – "*The American Dream*" – now starts to make sense. In it he sings: "*the American dream –is not what it seems"!* And what labour protection do these medical workers have in the world's most powerful economy – that they could be fired for wanting to be safe and to save lives? COVID-19 highlighted the utter lie of democracy, freedom and human rights in capitalist America. COVID-19 gave credence to Lennin's view on democracy in capitalist society: "democracy for an insignificant minority, democracy for the rich – that is the democracy of capitalist society".

3 The Free Market and Censoring the President of the Free World

The West had always prided itself on being the bastion of democracy, freedom, liberty and free speech. Such cherishing of these values was evident when more than 40 world leaders landed in Paris in 2015 – to join the massive rally in defence of the right to freedom of expression. The backdrop to the rally was the right to express onself on the apparent characteristic traits of a religious and revered leader and prophet. The freedom to express onself stood unshaken in the West – even though followers were angered and lives were lost. That was one year before Donald Trump was democratically voted into the White House in the US. The freedom to express oneself continued – maybe with little or no thought to the consequences of such freedom and expression. In 2020 another French citizen was killed – beheaded after he sought to teach his class about the freedom of expression, in relation to the religious and revered leader and prophet. We must be clear that no amount of violence is justifiable for any disagreement of what is and how it is said. When hundreds of Trump's supporters stormed Capitol Hill after Trump's freedom of speech at a rally, Twitter censored Trump indefinitely from freely expressing himself. The 40 leaders who flew to Paris in 2015 to uphold free speech did not make their way to the US to do the same. It was understandable given that COVID-19 was worse in the US than anywhere else in the world. But they had the option of upholding the cherished ideal of free speech on Zoom. They chose not to. The freedom to express oneself in the West did not stand the test of time. The censorship move by Twitter laid bare the myth and illusion of free speech in the West – and set off a flurry of heated views on free speech in the world in general – and in the Western world in particular. The president of Mexico stated:

> I don't like anybody being censored or taking away from the right to post a message on Twitter or Face(book). I don't agree with that, I don't accept that. Written media carried the following headlines: Does it violate President Trump's right to free speech?
>
> HANNA, 2021

As Western ideology was rolled out, free speech seemd no longer a cherished Western ideal but a matter of the First Amendment – which apparently allows private companies but not the state to censure citizens of the US. It is even in the important area of free speech that the free market has been given such immense power – to censure the freedom of Americans to speak! Where the private sector is given carte blanche to govern material and economic life, it is also given carte blanche to decide over political life as well. In the US, it is in the crucial area of free speech. It appeared that because the storming of Capitol Hill occurred in the US – and not in the Third World or China – some called for free speech to be severly curtailed in the Land of the Free:

> Wednesday's pro-Trump protests in Washington, which morphed into a mob attack on the US Capitol, is the most blatant wake-up call of many recent incidents that the limits of free speech and protests may need to be reconsidered.
>
> BOB, 2021

So we learn that there are limits to free speech! Who would have imagined! Who decides what these limits are? In the world that we currently inhabit, it seems it is the Big Tech companies like Twitter. Will these same limits be lobbied for – and applied in the life and death sphere of satirising religious figures – freedom of expression acts that have the tendency to trigger barbaric forms of violence and death? Context is important. But contexts for all – not only for the Western world. As if the American citizenry were suckers for information from perceived rival countries – the writer continued:

> But we already know that Russia, China, Iran and others are trying to systematically fool and inflame Americans into hating each other with sophisticated disinformation and doctored media.
>
> Ibid.

Americans were already killing each other with battle-field styled guns, decades before Russia, China, Iran and others supposedly got Americans to hate each other. It did not occur to the writer that the hate in the US was generated from within – not from without. The writer's more accurate conclusion to his analysis of the unfolding situation in the US emerged later on in his writing: "we may need to protect ourselves from ourselves" (Ibid.). Still the shock on the censorship of free speech to American society, the Western world – and then the rest of us – found its way into the headlines of mainstream media: "leader of the free world silenced online" (Meaker, 2021). The censorship by Twitter appeared to have further divided an already deeply fractured US:

> Twitter's decision to permanently suspend Donald Trump's account in the wake of the storming of Capitol Hill has stoked fierce debate, with supporters and critics split on partisan lines as they contest what the ban means for a cherished American tradition – freedom of speech.
>
> ARATANI, 2021

Some felt that capitalist US was not dissimilar to communist China or North Korea. COVID-19 threw up a slew of comparisons: "Big Tech censoring [Trump] and the free speech of American citizens is on par with communist countries like China and North Korea," tweeted Steve Daines, a senator from Montana (Aratani, 2021). It seemed inconceivable that the Western idea of free speech could one day occupy a similar platform as that of free speech of the Chinese and North Korean variety! Whilst some chose to divert blame to the Russians, Chinese and North Koreans, others in the US blamed it on the socialist and communist-inclined citizens in the US itself – the troublesome left: "the president's son Donald Trump Jr said that free speech is dead and controlled by leftist overlords" (Aratani, 2021). Tiffany Trump also wondered about free speech in free America: "whatever happened to freedom of speech?" (Ibid.). Family dynasties – and not democracy – tend to inform the political economy of the US. If your free speech does not fit the dominant ideological mould of the Western world, then you will be censored – and at times hounded and locked up for life. US citizens Edward Snowden and Chelsie Manning learnt this the hard way. Even Alexei Navalny – the opposition voice in Russia and adored by the Western world – stated that Twitter's action amounted to "censorship" (Dawson, 2021). It seemed free speech was being attacked by big corporations in the world's oldest democracy:

> It should concern everyone when companies like Facebook and Twitter wield the unchecked power to remove people from platforms that have become indispensable for the speech of billions, argued American Civil Liberties Union senior legislative counsel Kate Ruane in a media statement last week.
>
> DAWSON, 2021

2020 is the year that free speech was either killed in the US – or exposed as merely an ideological tool in the Western world. Untrammeled capitalism in the US killed scores of people in the time of COVID-19. Untrammeled corporations in the US killed free speech in the time of COVID-19.

4 United States: The Country Where Liberty Is a Statue

It is an open secret that the US's covert foreign policy is to destabilise countries that do not embrace the capitalist way of life. Most times the justification given for the invasion of countries is that of exporting democracy to other parts of the world – or securing humanitarian aid for citizens of countries in times of conflict – conflict most times often enabled and intensified by the US itself. Usually, the end game of the masked invasion is to trigger and force regime change – as was the case in Libya in 2011. Rewind back to 1972, when the socialist government of Salvador Allende in Chile came under murderous pressure from the United States, the poet Nicanor Parra wrote: "United States – the country where liberty is a statue" (Prashad, 2021). The United States' double and hypocritical standards in the important affairs of democracy and human rights is known the world over – except maybe in the United States itself. The United States got a stark reminder of its double standards when American citizens stormed their own Capitol Hill – the apparent citadel of world democracy. An official in China

> recalled in a press briefing in Beijing how US figures like House Speaker Nancy Pelosi had described a temporary occupation of Hong Kong's regional legislature by protesters as a 'beautiful sight to behold'. 'If you still remember how some US officials, lawmakers and media described what's happened in Hong Kong, you can compare that with the words they've used to describe the scenes in Capitol Hill,' Ms. Hua said. They all condemned it as 'a violent incident' and the people involved as 'rioters,' 'extremists' and 'thugs' who brought 'disgrace'.
>
> TAYLOR, 2021

Others such as Mohamad Safa, Lebanon's permanent representative to the United Nations tweeted:

> If the United States saw what the United States is doing in the United States, the United States would invade the United States to liberate the United States from the tyranny of the United States.
>
> TAYLOR, 2021

It was a time when the democratic, freedom and liberty chickens in the US had come home to roost. With all of its posturing on democracy, human rights and liberty, evidence is growing that the USA needs to first get its own house in order – before preaching and lecturing to the world on the very important matters of democracy, liberty, freedom and free speech. Democracy is an important component of the level of human development in the modern world – but it is not the only component. For example:

> The 2013 Pew Survey of Global Attitudes showed that 85 per cent of Chinese were 'very satisfied' with their country's direction, compared with 31 per cent of Americans.
>
> DELAIBATIKI, 2021

Some even referred to events on Capitol Hill as the mini "Storming of the Bastille in America" (Hazra, 2021). It seems America's democracy has always been far from the ideal it pretends and portrays it to be: "even today, Republicans try their level best to deny voting rights to Black voters, who tend to prefer Democrats" (Hazra, 2021). The events on Capitol Hill have thrown the spotlight on democracy, rights, free speech and liberty in the world in general and in the West in particular. People the world over were concerned about the implications that the events on Capitol Hill – and the censoring of the president's free speech would have for the world going forward. It raises many questions around the state of democracy in the world currently – the meaning of democracy, the practices of democracy, the strengths and weaknesses of democracy, the intensity and extent of democracy, etc. For example, does voting in elections every four or five years qualify a country to be a fully democratic country? Why is democracy a cherished ideal in politics but not in religion? Why is one allowed to have a discussion and debate in parliament – but not in mosques, churches, temples, synagogues, etc? Is the soldier in the US or UK army at liberty to place on the agenda an item on whether to bomb the life out of Iraq – or whether to drop an atom bomb on the people of Japan? Or should such societies be qualified as quasi or pseudo democratic societies? In capitalist countries much emphasis is placed on the quantitative nature of democracy – and very little or no emphasis on its qualitative nature. That a country has elections every four or five years – and that persons or political parties with the majority votes win – speaks to the quantitative nature of democracy. There has been much written and spoken on the weaknesses of the quality of America's democracy – since big money often determines the outcome of elections. Also the flawed nature of qualitative democracy in the US informs the outcome of quantitative democracy. In 2016 for example, Hillary Clinton garnered the most number of popular votes – but yet Donald Trump was sworn in as the 45th president of the United States of America! It seems that the electoral system of voting in the US seeks to dilute democracy – instead of strengthening and consolidating democracy in the world's oldest democracy. The nature of Western styled democracies have long been lacking in substance, depth and range. According to Bowles and Gintis (1985: 5):

> Democratic institutions have often been mere ornaments in the social life of the advanced capitalist nations; proudly displayed to visitors, and admired by all, but used sparingly. The places where things really get done – in such core institutions as families, armies, factories, and offices – have been anything but democratic.

In 1867 Marx alerted humankind about the empty shell of democracy and human rights in capitalist society in general – and in the private sector in particular. In *Capital* (1867), Marx states:

> This sphere that we are deserting, within whose boundaries the sale and purchase of labour-power goes on, is in fact a very Eden of the

> innate rights of man. There alone rule Freedom, Equality, Property and Bentham. On leaving this sphere of simple circulation or of exchange of commodities, which furnishes the 'Free-trader Vulgaris' with his views and ideas, and with the standard by which he judges a society based on capital and wages, we think we can perceive a change in the physiognomy of our dramatis personae. He, who before was the money-owner, now strides in front as capitalist; the possessor of labour-power follows as his labourer. The one with an air of importance, smirking, intent on business; the other, timid and holding back, like one who is bringing his own hide to market and has nothing to expect but a hiding.
>
> MARX, 1867 [2011]: 121

In other words, in capitalist society, democracy is practised albeit debatably in the political sphere – but different forms of tyranny reign supreme in the private sphere. Power-relations determine the nature and quality of democracy in capitalist society. Democracy does not determine the nature of power-relations. As part of the Western ideological narrative, we often hear: "Russia's notorious interference in the last United States presidential election, and its attempts to influence online opinion, are a case in point" (Alden, 2020). That Russia would prefer certain candidates in the White House cannot be disputed. That Russia would tend to influence the elections in one small way or another is probable. But to pin the outcome of an entire US election on the power of Russian influence thousands of kilometres away must be fantasy at its best – even if Hollywood is in the US! I believe the Americans voted on ballots with American English – not in the Russian language. After all, it was the American Barack Obama – the Leader of the Free World – that tried to influence the democratic process in the EU during the 2016 referendum: "Mr Obama was criticised by pro-Brexit campaigners after he warned of the consequences of the UK leaving the EU" (BBC, 2016). It is an open secret that one of the primary role-functions of the CIA is to influence the outcome of elections in other countries. Too often in the capitalist world, democracy is imagined and shaped to fit the mould of the interests of those in power. That all men are born equal? That is part of the ideological toolbox of the capitalist West. In reality it is far from the truth. Let us take just one example in the time of COVID-19 – the fuss around vaccines:

> The me and my people first attitude mushrooming in parts of the world is immoral and short-sighted because no one country will be safe from COVID-19 until every country is safe. No continent will be safe until every continent is safe.
>
> DLAMINI, 2021

The two most powerful and supposedly freest countries in the world – the US and the UK – supported and upheld apartheid in South Africa. Apartheid was declared a crime against humanity. The US and UK – under Reagan and Thatcher – did not support sanctions against the apartheid, undemocratic, fascist regime that was a killing machine of black people. In fact, they branded Nelson Mandela – who was fighting for freedom, human rights, democracy, etc. – a terrorist! The US and the UK did not support freedom, democracy and human rights for the majority of South Africa's peoples. Democratic and human rights values are extremely important – but they appear to be used merely as neo-colonial tools in the foreign policy of the West. Transparency is one of the hallmarks of a democratic country. One would expect this to be a non-negotiable value in the West. However, COVID-19 exposed this myth. In the UK for example:

> The government is declining to release a full list, despite its guidelines which state any contract awarded using emergency powers should be published within 30 days.
>
> EVANS ET AL., 2020

Opposing and dissenting voices are also the hallmarks of a mature democracy. But COVID-19 dented the image of the US as a country tolerant and encouraging of divergent views:

> Voice of America is a government-funded but independent news agency that has lately been the object of White House criticism. The Trump administration accused VOA this month of promoting Chinese government propaganda in its reporting about the coronavirus. The VOA's director, Amanda Bennett, has defended its independence.
>
> FARHI, 2020

Allies of the powerful believe manufacturing reality is one of their main job-functions. The extremely observant are able to tell the difference between fiction and fact:

> Here, our billionaire-owned newspapers fawn over the miracle of Boris Johnson's Easter recovery, directing us to look anywhere except at the facts. But outside the UK, the press understands we are among the worst hit countries and that something has gone terribly wrong. The world points at us in the way we once did Wuhan.
>
> OSAMA, 2020

Many believed for a long time that the emperor's new clothes looked splendid. But COVID-19 made keen-eyed observers of many. The hollowness of human rights in the US was made apparent. The US emperor was exposed in the time of COVID-19:

> For most US observers, the botched US response to the epidemic is jaw-dropping. The novel coronavirus exposes the hypocrisy of the US – the self-proclaimed greatest defender of human rights. Why has the country, which often points a finger at others over human rights affairs, done a much poorer job in protecting lives of its own people than countries that it often reproaches?
>
> NING, 2020

Western-allied democracies – who apparently long to be like North Korea, China and Saudi Arabia – seized the opportunity to do so in the time of COVID-19:

> The Brazilian government has been accused of totalitarianism and censorship after it stopped releasing its total numbers of COVID-19 cases and deaths and wiped an official site clean of swathes of data.
>
> PHILLIPS, 2020

Capitalist market, neoliberal and Western ideologies have made us numb to the real workings of the world we live in – a world that has been made for us by those in and with immense amounts of power:

> In the real world, away from human rights lawyers' chambers, most of us blithely allow a host of other apps to invade our privacy, such as letting 'location services', track our movements, etc. If we use public transport we swipe our travel passes which can be tracked. And we happily sign away our privacy in using Amazon's Alexa, for example, or through online shopping, Google searches and social media posts, allowing private firms access to reams of information about us.
>
> POLLARD, 2020

Good thing we have scientists among us who are concerned about the very important issues of democracy, human rights, privacy and liberty. For example:

> Professor Ronald Deibert and his team based in Toronto, Canada, have used their novel research methods to help expose how dozens of

> journalists, human rights activists and senior government officials, allegedly have been targeted by governments using NSO software to hack phones.
>
> KIRCHGAESSNER, 2020

When and where profit and human rights compete for the West's attention – human rights hardly ever win:

> I am sure that you will agree that the UK's recovery from the COVID-19 pandemic must not be built on the backs of slave labour, and that the UK must remain committed to human rights throughout the whole supply chain, he added. Mr Esterson told The Independent: 'The government must make sure it isn't buying PPE made with slave labour. Otherwise, they are just confirming that the Conservatives will always put commercial interests ahead of human rights'.
>
> LOVETT, 2021

If democracy and free choice are non-existent in China, Saudi Arabia and North Korea, these cherished ideals are pretending to be thriving in the West. In a part of the world that lectures to the world about the virtues of freedom and human rights – and in a new world where workers can work from home – the prime minister ordered civil servants back to the office: "a Cabinet Office source said there had been reinvigorated efforts to get people back in" (Norton et al., 2020). One must be forgiven for thinking that the defenders of freedom, democracy, human rights and human dignity do not need reminding in these very valuable areas of life. But reality under capitalism provides little or no alternative:

> 'Romanian seasonal workers are not slaves. Human dignity and health are not negotiable,' said Victor Negrescu, a Romanian MEP who with colleagues submitted a letter to the European ombudsman requesting protection of seasonal workers after a spate of incidents.
>
> CARROLL ET AL., 2020

Just as liberty is a statue in the US, the blindfold on Lady Justice prevents her from seeing the injustices in the capitalist world. COVID-19 opened our eyes to this unjust world called capitalism.

5 Rights, Liberty, Democracy and Freedom: Born Out of Blood, Sweat and Tears

We have rights as a species because history has a tendency of preventing sections of society from enjoying their nature-given gifts of freedom, liberty and the bountiful supply of nature. It is difficult to say or know what freedom means or is in the Western world. Ask Prince Harry and Meghan Markle, who left one free country for another free country. Rights and freedoms are important. In fact they are so important that men and women have died trying to attain them. Many had to give up whatever little freedom they did have – even if it meant being a little freer in capitalist society. Men like Nelson Mandela served 27 years in prison – after the apartheid state that oversaw the most ruthless and violent form of racist capitalism in the world severely curtailed the freedom of the black majority. Mandela was lucky; many thousands of other South Africans were murdered by the apartheid state, which favoured white privilege, white supremacy and white power over human rights, democracy, liberty and freedom for the black majority. After centuries of bitter and painful struggle against colonialism and apartheid, blacks in South Africa first tasted democracy, freedom, liberty and human rights in 1994 – just after the fall of the Berlin Wall – and the collapse of communism in the USSR. The most sophisticated and most developed country on the African continent is also the last country to have achieved democracy, freedom, liberty and human rights for all. Whereas China's authoritarian state favours the development of all of its people, the tyrannical apartheid state ensured the development of the white race only in South Africa. Every year since 1994, we in South Africa celebrate Freedom Day on the 27 April with much fanfare and political rhetoric. The next day, however, news in the print and visual media reminds one of the wretchedness of life and living for millions of black South Africans under capitalism. Our version of the Rights of Man is the Freedom Charter – that was put together in 1955. The opening lines of the Freedom Charter state:

> We, the People of South Africa, declare for all our country and the world to know: that South Africa belongs to all who live in it, black and white, and that no government can justly claim authority unless it is based on the will of all the people.

Sixty-five years since the Freedom Charter was conceptualised and 28 years of democracy and political rights, a small white minority still own approximately 80% of land and nature in South Africa. Human rights, freedom, democracy and liberty are much cherished values that all people should have – but it seems that human rights, freedom, democracy and liberty are insufficient social and legal tools for the good life in capitalist society. We now have rights in South Africa as black people not because it was innate to us or god-given – but because we fought for our rights. It took blood, sweat, tears and death to ensure that we have rights from the last decade of the 20th century. I recall being in countless protest marches fighting for a free, democratic and non-racial South Africa. I also had the unfortunate experience of being shot with live ammunition by the apartheid police – whilst fighting for rights, democracy and freedom. Such ideals are worth fighting for – and if need be – they are also worth dying for. Many in South Africa were killed, murdered or hanged whilst fighting for human rights, democracy and freedom – they paid the highest price for the political freedom and democracy that we now enjoy. Upon the possibility of being hanged for his unwavering belief in democracy, freedom, justice and non-racialism, Nelson Mandela had this to say in the presence of apartheid judges upholding unjust and inhumane laws:

> During my lifetime I have dedicated myself to the struggle of the African people. I have fought against white domination, and I have fought against black domination. I have cherished the ideal of a democratic and free society in which all persons live together in harmony and with equal opportunities. It is an ideal which I hope to live for and to achieve. But if needs be, it is an ideal for which I am prepared to die.

Many died fighting for a free and democratic South Africa. But 28 long years into our democracy, we are still the most unequal country in the world! Many of Mandela's friends, comrades and families are now wealthy citizens in the new democratic South Africa – whilst millions of black South Africans have still not benefitted materially from our 1994 democratic breakthrough. Blacks in South Africa now have rights – but many still go to bed hungry at night. They have liberty – but many still live in makeshift tin homes. They have freedom – but they are still killed, raped and robbed in the dozens like in no other country in the world. They have democracy – but they are still under the command and control of the capitalist economy. They have free speech – but hardly a voice to request that the land and wealth of the country be shared amongst all who live in it. In the US, many protestors who went out during COVID-19 held up placards that read "Stop the Tyranny", "Don't Use Fear to Steal our Freedom", "Don't Tread on my Rights", "Pro Common Sense", "America – The Land of the Free", "Let my People Go", "Those who would give up essential Liberty to purchase a little temporary Safety, deserve neither Liberty nor Safety – Benjamin Franklin". Like in South Africa, the many rights that US citizens were demanding be respected and upheld in the time of COVID-19, were attained through centuries of struggle and sacrifice. The capitalist ideology that rights are god-given and innate are just that – capitalist ideology:

> The rights of citizens (or of persons generally), far from being God-given as the US. Declaration of Independence asserts, have been won through the collective struggles of the dispossessed, women, racial minorities and others.
>
> BOWLES and GINTIS, 1985: ix

Whereas the famous line of "all men are created equal" was written in 1776 in the US Declaration of Independence, African Americans would only taste equality in the political sphere about 200 years later. COVID-19 and the Black Lives Matter protests unleashed hidden history:

> When America was founded, its 4.4 million or so slaves were counted as property, not citizens. This history has echoed all through its subsequent history, African Americans having to wait till the 1960s to get their civil rights.
>
> HAZRA, 2021

The Declaration of the Independence of the United States of America was conceptualised by a collective of white men who wanted to cut-off colonial ties with its mother country – Great Britain. This precious document was only possible after many lost their lives in the Revolutionary War or the American War of Independence. Rights are fought for – never freely given:

> The road from the eighteenth-century Rights of Man, which excluded not only women but most people of colour as well, to the late twentieth-century civil rights movements, feminism, and the right to a job has been a tortuous one.
>
> BOWLES and GINTIS, 1985: 5

Rights according to Karl Marx:

> Is not innate in men; on the contrary, it is gained only in a struggle against the historical traditions in which hitherto man was brought up. Thus the rights of man are not a gift of nature, not a legacy from past history, but the reward of the struggle against the accident of birth and against the privileges which up to now have been handed down by history from

> generation to generation. These rights are the result of culture, and only one who has earned and deserved them can possess them (1844).

Rights are only meaningful if the person is alive. Humankind has fought long and hard to secure rights for itself. As humankind anticipates a post-COVID-19 world, it also has to grapple with the following questions: How and why did millions of people not have their right to life upheld in the time of COVID-19 especially in the Western world? Did the people of the world have the right to proper and adequate health care in the time of COVID-19? It seems that as history unfolds – rights unfold:

> Since the 1950s the world has been swept by a cascade of Rights Revolutions: civil rights, women's rights, gay rights, children's rights, and animal rights.
>
> PINKER, 2018: 60

With all of the rights that men and women have fought for – and have secured – it is clear that the right to life is a right that cannot be guaranteed under the capitalist system. The world witnessed this harsh reality in the time of COVID-19:

> We have a right to speak freely. We also have a right to life. We treat free speech as sacred, but life as negotiable.
>
> MONBIOT, 2021

The right to profit supersedes the right to life in the capitalist epoch. To overturn this historical aberration will require plenty of resolve, courage, activism and struggle – and if need be – it seems revolution as well!

CHAPTER 6

Making Sense of Science and Scientists in the Time of COVID-19

> Report good science. Let science lead the way. The only exit from COVID is science and I think that we all have our parts to play
>
> GABRIEL LEUNG

•••

> The purpose of studying economics is not to acquire a set of ready-made answers to economic questions, but to learn how to avoid being deceived by economists
>
> JOAN ROBINSON

1 States and Their Citizens – Led by Science or Capitalist Ideologies?

Did the virus originate in the laboratory in Wuhan? Did the US military import the virus into Wuhan during the military games in late 2019? Did the virus jump from bats onto wildlife and then onto humans? Did the virus exist in other European countries like Italy – before exploding in Wuhan, China? The answers to these questions reveal the fine line between science and ideology – playing itself out between the capitalist and the communist worlds – in the time of COVID-19. Was the West led by science or ideology in the time of COVID-19? Was the East led by science or ideology in the time of COVID-19? Were communist countries guided by science or ideology in the time of COVID-19? Were capitalist countries guided by science or ideology in the time of COVID-19? These are question that a fact-seeking and an evidence-based species must explore if the human species is to contribute to the conceptualisation, shaping and forming of a future that is more habitable and sustainable than the present – one that would respond with science and not ideology to a global pandemic – if or when it happens again. There were a multitude of scientists advising states in different parts of the world on how best to deal with

 | DOI:10.1163/9789004539808_007

COVID-19. It was not only the general public that were confused about what was science and what was not science – but the scientists themselves were at loggerheads with each other – as to what was scientific and what was not. It was a huge challenge trying to understand the meaning of science – and its role in the time of COVID-19. I believe that the entire world got a basic understanding of what a virus is. Studying viruses is known as virology. Whereas prior to COVID-19 the celebrities in capitalist society were singers, sport stars, actors, the Kardashians and Donald Trump; COVID-19 generated a new type of celebrity for society – the epidemiologist:

> Epidemiologists are scientists who study diseases within populations of people. In essence, these public health professionals analyse what causes disease outbreaks in order to treat existing diseases and prevent future outbreaks. Thanks to this, epidemiologists are considered 'disease detectives' of the public health world.
>
> *Public Health Online*, 2020

But the scientists of diseases and public health were themselves divided on these life and death issues:

> Ministers keep claiming to be 'following the science' over the COVID-19 outbreak, but as the crisis unfolds, it's increasingly clear there is no one 'science', but a welter of expert opinions. Look at Sweden, whose chief epidemiologist, Anders Tegnell, has backed a policy of 'social distancing-lite' – gatherings of over 50 are banned, but schools and shops stay open. Some experts are in favour, arguing it will help keep Sweden's economy afloat as it builds up herd immunity; others believe it is recklessly endangering lives.
>
> CLARK, 2020

In the UK, the contest between public health science and neoliberal ideology continued:

> Ministers and scientists are nervous about how far they will be able to ease the lockdown in England at the end of the month, as it emerged that the UK needed to more than halve its daily infection rate of about 10,000 new cases a day.
>
> MASON ET AL., 2020: 6

Schools are places of education – but they are also caretaker institutions for children whose parents are compelled to sell their labour-power in the capitalist market. Mostly being on the side of capital and big money – states the world over have hence tried their level best to force children back to school in the middle of a global pandemic. In heated debates about whether schools should open or not, public health science was also divided. In the UK:

> The British Medical Association (BMA) said there was conflicting evidence from scientific studies on the effect of reopening schools, citing the relatively small amount of research available and the uncharted territory we find ourselves in.
>
> ADAMS ET AL., 2020: 1

Based on their scientific research and assessment:

> The British Medical Association has thrown its weight behind teacher unions opposing the government's push to reopen schools in England, as the debate over millions of pupils returning to classrooms became increasingly acrimonious.
>
> ADAMS ET AL., 2020: 1

Economic scientists are forever advising states the world over. In the time of COVID-19 the newcomers that made up the pool of scientists advising the state were the epidemiologists, behavioural scientists, psychologists, psychiatrists, computer scientists, etc. I am not aware if the military and war scientists were present – as the entire world was dealing with an invisible but known enemy that was killing people in their millions. They were instead summoned to discuss lockdown measures and unrests such as the Black Lives Matter protests that engulfed the US in the time of COVID-19. Environmental scientists also do not feature amongst the inner circle of state power – as the economic scientists of capitalism do. Economic scientists are the kings, queens, lords and knights of scientists in the world of capitalism. All other scientists tend to fall within the peasant class of scientists in capitalism's world. As to what was science and what was ideology in the time of COVID-19, made one grit one's teeth with frustration:

> Experts have voiced growing frustration with the government's claim it is 'following the science', saying the refrain is being used to abdicate responsibility for political decisions. As a scientist, I hope I never again hear the phrase 'based on the best science and evidence' spoken by a politician,

> Prof Devi Sridhar, chair of global public health at the University of Edinburgh, told the Guardian. 'This phrase has become basically meaningless.' The government has repeatedly said it is 'led by the science' on decisions ranging from banning mass gatherings to the use of face masks and, most recently, the prospects of lifting the lockdown. The diversity of scientific views was apparent in March, when case numbers were rising rapidly but the government chose not to ban mass gatherings or introduce wide-reaching physical distancing.
>
> DEVLIN, 2020

It seems that capitalist economic logic forces one to conduct a cost-benefit analysis even in the time of a global pandemic. According to Prof. Mark Woolhouse, an infectious diseases epidemiologist at the University of Edinburgh:

> What we're not talking about in the same formal, quantitative way are the economic costs, the social costs, the psychological costs of being under lockdown. I understand the government is being advised by economists, psychiatrists and others, but we're not seeing what that science is telling them. I find that very puzzling.
>
> DEVLIN, 2020

In the US, public health science was heavily shackled from leading the fight against COVID-19 by White House and strong man ideologies:

> Inconsistent and sometimes incoherent messaging from a White House suspicious of science and consumed by re-election politics also doesn't help. President Donald Trump's reluctance to be seen wearing a mask – as if protecting oneself and others from viral infection was a sign of weakness.
>
> *The Philadelphia Inquirer*: 2020

Meanwhile back in Great Britain – the issue of scientific greatness was on the discussion table:

> A group of independent scientists has branded Boris Johnson's easing of the lockdown 'dangerous' and warned that further local COVID-19 epidemics are inevitable. Its report accuses the prime minister of not 'following the science' as work and society are gradually opened up again, and criticises the limited aim of flattening infections to ensure that the NHS is not 'overwhelmed'.
>
> MERRICK, 2020

Whilst capitalist states were capitulating to free or capitalist market ideologies to open up the economy, schools, pragmatic religious institutions, civil society, worker unions and concerned citizens asserted themselves and demonstrated peoples' agency to push back on the persistent ideological stance of neoliberal states in exposing its citizens to COVID-19. In the UK, which had one of the world's highest infection and death rates at the start of the pandemic:

> The head of the University and College Union praised the 'impressive public campaigning' of teachers' unions and said it could 'achieve similar victories' just two days after the Government abandoned plans to reopen all primaries before September. Kevin Courtney, the joint general secretary of the National Education Union, which led opposition to reopening, also said the move was a 'win for science and for every NEU member'.
>
> DIXON, 2020: 1

It was becoming clear in the time of COVID-19, that there was a distinct science for the elite and well-off in capitalist society – and a separate and weaker science for the masses. There was a science that sought to protect the capitalist economy – and there was a science that sought to protect public health. There was a science that sought to protect profit – and there was a science that sought to protect people. Public health science was tossed around like a prey attacked by a hungry crocodile. According to Sir David King:

> Since the start of the COVID-19 epidemic, the government has told us they are 'following the science'. However, in the weeks and months that have followed, it has become increasingly apparent that this is simply not the case.
>
> MERRICK, 2020

Like political parties that stick to their separate tribal formations – tribalism and factionalism in science assumed a more crystallised and hardened form in the time of COVID-19:

> The group was set up because of criticism that the official Scientific Advisory Group for Emergencies (Sage) was failing to fully reflect scientific opinion and was too secretive. In addition to Sir David, it boasts Professor Gabriel Scally, a pre-eminent epidemiologist; public health expert Professor Allyson Pollock; and Professor Anthony Costello, a former director of the World Health Organisation (WHO).
>
> MERRICK, 2020

Back to the greatest nation on planet earth – the appeal for public health science to inform the war on an invisible but known enemy found lone voices here and there against the onslaught of neoliberal and capitalist ideologies masquerading as 21st century science:

> But facts have a way of breaking through. Spurred by soaring numbers of new infections in Florida, the city of Jacksonville, where the Republican Party will hold its convention beginning August 25, this week made mask-wearing mandatory for large gatherings. There is clear evidence that close and sustained indoor contact among large groups of people is a frighteningly efficient way for the coronavirus to find new hosts. Scientific fact, common sense, and common decency suggest that putting on a mask is a way individuals together can help defeat our common adversary. Not doing so is an act of surrender.
>
> *The Philadelphia Inquirer*: 2020

In South Africa, where capitalism rules with an iron fist over the state, land, nature, climate, and the majority of South Africa's people:

> As the war over the ban on booze sales heats up, the alcohol industry has asked the government to suspend R5bn in sin-tax obligations until it is allowed to trade again. In a separate development, a scientist on the ministerial advisory committee (MAC) – which advises the minister of health on COVID-19 issues – criticised the science used to justify re-imposing the sales ban.

In a world where information flows with lightning speed and uninterrupted, everywhere science was under attack by an arsenal of ideological weaponry that sought to keep the capitalist economy up and running:

> Information is now at our fingertips, providing us with tools and possibilities that we could never have imagined before. At the same time, though, we paradoxically seem to be witnessing the empowerment of bogus ideas, the growing strength of conspiracy theories and an increasing denial of science and rejection of facts.
>
> ALDEN, 2020

COVID-19 upended so much of what we thought we knew about the world. It even exposed the world of science. Comparisons were also made between the science of Brexit and the science of COVID-19:

> On the face of it there is a very great difference between the two policies. In the case of Brexit the government has consistently rejected the advice of economists, including its own. In the case of COVID-19 it constantly reiterates that it is 'following the science'. But there is an underlying connection which is important. Brexiteer arguments are centred on fantasies about British scientific and inventive genius. The government has sought to address COVID-19 at least in part on this deluded basis.
>
> EDGERTON, 2020

Incorrect scientific advice did lead to needless deaths. Capitalist economic science – or rather capitalist economic ideologies killed in the time of COVID-19:

> But after repeated questions about whether better decisions could have been made, given the UK's 45,700 plus confirmed deaths, the highest in Europe, and if some scientific advice could have been incorrect, Johnson conceded errors were possible.
>
> WALKER, 2020

How many deaths did these scientific or ideological "errors" cause? For all the deaths that took place in the UK, Boris Johnson seems to suggest that it was due to incorrect scientific advice:

> If you look at the timing of every single piece of advice that we got from our advisers, from Sage, you will find that whenever they said that we needed to take a particular step, actually, we stuck to that advice like glue, Johnson said.
>
> WALKER, 2020

Others felt that the UK state was acting contrary to scientific advice given by the scientific experts:

> At the weekend, The Guardian revealed that Dominic Cummings spoke up frequently in meetings of Sage, the supposedly independent scientific advisory group. Rather than follow the science, our political leaders are interfering with it. These distortions of truth shape public discourse – down is up and back is front.
>
> OSAMA, 2020

A child at school who wants to play with his or her friends can be forgiven for thinking that social distancing is not a problem during a global pandemic. But what does one make of a so-called "top medical adviser" who thinks that social distancing during a global pandemic is all bollocks:

> Australia's top medical adviser has declared classrooms pose no risk of spreading the coronavirus, and even says there is no need for students to follow social distancing, prompting Scott Morrison to urge the states and teachers to urgently reopen schools across the nation.
>
> JOHNSTONE ET AL., 2020

With the calibre of such scientists – who needs ideologists? Science and scientists were at loggerheads with itself – and each other – in the time of COVID-19. In South Africa scientists were accused of being political ideologues instead of scientists regarding the 'dumping' of 1.5-million doses of potentially life-saving vaccine:

> If there is one thing that worries a scientist, it is when a fellow scientist turns politician and starts speaking in algorithms in a newspaper column. Reading between the lines, it would seem the government was steered towards abandoning the AstraZeneca rollout and selecting an alternative option. Choosing another option in this case was understandable (if not premature). What is illogical is effectively abandoning 1.5 million doses of potentially life-saving vaccine.
>
> SARTORIUS, 2021

Public health science won the day in countries like China, Vietnam, New Zealand, etc. Public health science was largely missing in India's response to COVID-19. Bollywood – and not public health science – is big in India. In Indonesia, authorities hired people to dress up as ghosts in order to scare people to stay at home. Instead of being scared and locked away in their homes – villagers wanted to take selfies with the make-believe ghosts! At least ideological superstition was found out in Indonesia. If South Korea had COVID-19 largely under control, it is primarily because the country used science and modern scientific technology effectively to keep an invisible enemy at bay: "at this historic juncture, there has been a general consensus to trust in and respect the advice coming from doctors and scientists" (Dudden and Marks, 2020). Public health science was sidelined in the Western world in the main. Much of the time public health science was elbowed out of state planning to tackle COVID-19. Western ideological models of might and right were preferred over scientific public health models in the time of a global pandemic. In the US:

> Bright was director of the Biomedical Advanced Research and Development Authority for nearly four years but was shifted from the role in April. In a whistle-blower complaint, Bright has claimed he was removed after resisting pressure by the administration to make potentially harmful drugs widely available, including chloroquine and hydroxychloroquine. In his testimony to Congress, Bright wrote that science, not politics or cronyism, must lead the way to combat this deadly virus.
>
> MILMAN, 2020

The country whose military might must surely be based on the best military science in the world struggled to come up with a coherent public health scientific model to tackle COVID-19: "Models can shift based on new information as public behaviours change and scientists' understanding of the virus evolves, though some have proven more reliable than others" (Ansari, 2020). Donald Trump instead chose neoliberal economic science over that of public health science: "the pandemic is a public health issue that should be tackled with science. But for the Trump administration, science is the least important thing" (Ning, 2020). In the UK, a government spokesperson said: "this is an unprecedented global pandemic and we have taken the right steps at the right time to combat it, guided by the best scientific advice" (Henley, et al., 2020). As of 3 July 2022, UK's "best scientific advice" resulted in 22,941,360 infected COVID-19 cases and 181,093 deaths! UK public health science failed its citizens in general – and its elderly citizens in particular:

> Older people were 'catastrophically let down' and many died before their time, according to the Age UK charity. It described the policy of discharging elderly people from hospitals into care settings without COVID-19 tests as a 'terrible mistake'. The British Medical Association said the government's testing and tracing capabilities at the start of the crisis fell 'far short' of what was needed and left the infection to 'spread unchecked'.
>
> PROCTOR, 2020

As the deaths were piling up in the Western world – and as politicians made people believe that the state was "following the science" – it was becoming clear that free market science – and the ideology of Western superiority – were preferred over pragmatic public health science: "politics, through the years, has sought to give science a spin that suits its own devices or scientists themselves have been too happy to give science a spin on request" (Thapar, 2020). In the US, geopolitical science, neoliberal science or ideology trumped public health science:

> The president has pointed fingers at everyone from China to the World Health Organisation, embraced everything from conspiracy theories to overhyped 'cures,' and systematically ignored the advice of epidemiologists and public-health experts in favour of that of sycophants.
>
> PICARD, 2020

By choosing Western ideologies over pragmatic public health science in the time of a global pandemic, the Western world in reality chose death over life – for their hundreds of thousands of innocent citizens!

2 Economic Science – the Dominating Science or Ideology in the Age of Capitalism and in the Time of COVID-19

Science dominated in the West in the time of COVID-19. But it was not public and pragmatic health science that dominated – it was economic science in its ideological form. If public health science was ignored or downplayed, it is because those in power felt compelled to obey the economic science or ideologies that are so pervasive and dominant in capitalist society. Economic science of the neoliberal and free market forms rules over all other sciences in capitalist society. It is why profit can be made under the banner of neoliberal science – and environmental science struggles to protect nature. It is why workers can be strong-armed to go back to work in the time of a global pandemic under the banner of free market science – and public health science struggles to get people to social distance, wear masks, get tested and use an app to track and manage a deadly virus. It is why the protection of vaccine patents can be argued with a straight face – and people enabled to die without legal, ethical and moral responsibilities. The language and nature of economic science dominated in the time of COVID-19, as it always does in capitalist society: "with any disease there is a trade-off. Public health is largely about that trade-off," (Devlin, 2020). What cost-benefit analysis and trade-offs did countries like the US and the UK make with regards to public health and lives lost? What cost-benefit analysis and trade-offs did countries like China and Vietnam make with regards to public health and lives saved? What did all of these different countries benefit from making such trade-offs with their public health? What did such countries who did not make such trade-offs with their public health benefit? What did the former countries lose in their trade-offs? What did the latter countries lose in their trade-offs? If there was contestation and conflict in society, and in the scientific community in the time of COVID-19, then it is because public health science was overpowered, overruled and bullied by a shape, form and character of economic science – as it presents itself in capitalist society. Opening up the capitalist economy during a global pandemic is the imperative of economic science favouring neoliberalism, and not public health science and the science of war against a common enemy, for that matter, favouring the saving of lives. The science of war in many countries did hold temporarily – and in the form of rhetoric at the very beginning of the pandemic– but it soon gave way to the science of the economy in its neoliberal, Western and highly capitalistic forms. Even though economics, as it is currently conceptualised and practiced, is known as the dismal science, it does provide humankind with many analytical tools by which we try to make sense of who gets what from the work and outputs of productive workers. Making a livelihood and staying alive is hard and painful work for the majority of people – especially for the working class in capitalist society. In the time of COVID-19, we got a sense of the science of employment and unemployment, the science of supply and demand of PPEs and vaccines, the science of economic growth or rather de-growth, the science of demand and supply of money, the science of profit, the science of state subsidies for the rich and the poor, etc. Economic science – in its capitalist clothing – dominated in the Western world in the time of COVID-19 at the expense of lives. But economic science has had a questionable existence from its inception:

> Thomas Carlyle labelled the science [economics] 'dismal' when writing about slavery in the West Indies. White plantation owners, he said, ought to force black plantation workers to be their servants. Economics, somewhat inconveniently for Carlyle, didn't offer a hearty defence of slavery. Instead, the rules of supply and demand argued for 'letting men alone' rather than thrashing them with whips for not being servile. Carlyle bashed political economy as 'a dreary, desolate, and indeed quite abject and distressing [science]; what we might call the dismal science'.
>
> THOMSON, 2013

Be that as it may, the dismal science – whether it reliably, convincingly and objectively explains the making of material life or not – is the pet-science of states in the capitalist world: "governments worldwide rely on economic advisors while publicly mocking scientific studies of social relationships" (Cacioppo and Patrick, 2008: 13). Economic science has in the main been subsumed by capitalist ideas and ideologies – underpinned by profit-making and profit-maximisation – and has itself transformed into economic ideologies in the service of big business and big money. Mainstream economic science in its current ideological form seeks not to explain and analyse the capitalist economic system, but rather to uphold the abhorrent system. For far too long, economic science has been the sleeping partner of capitalism – and not its analytical critic. Economic science – in the way that it has been practiced – is in crisis because capitalism is in crisis. The fault-line of capitalist economic science was exposed by the Queen of England just after the 2008 Great Crisis when she demanded answers from economic scientists about the financial crisis: "it's awful – why did nobody see it coming?" (Greenhill, 2008). It seemed that the "financial storm on the horizon" (ibid.) was missed by the expert economic scientists – due to their blind faith in capitalism as the supposedly perfect and natural system for humankind. Ideology generally leads to blind faith – one is not able to see what's "coming". Since the 2008 Great Crisis and the Queen's questioning of the relevance of economic science in the 21st century, economic science has been somewhat reflective and undergoing small changes here and there. After the Great Depression of the 1920s and 1930s, we have also seen reforms in the science of the economy with the introduction and development of Keynesian economic science. There were attempts by a small group of concerned scholars about the state of economic science in the world – to revolutionise the economic sciences. They formed themselves into a movement called the Technocracy Movement. The Technocracy Movement proposed that economic science be premised on the science of energy – and that society should be informed by the laws of energy. Through natural sciences, we have learnt that planetary and life on earth are governed by the laws of gravity. Through physics we have learnt that life and livelihoods are governed by the laws of energy. The dismal science – economic science – has up to now upheld the ideology that life and livelihoods are governed by supposed laws of an apparent free market. In other words, that the capitalist market is a force in and of its own, analogous to that of the laws of gravity and the laws of energy – and which governs the economic life of humankind. It is why economic scientists or neoliberal ideologues like Milton Friedman, Ayn Rand and followers of such science and ideologies such as Margaret Thatcher, Ronald Reagan, amongst many others, have sought to ring-fence the capitalist market from any form of state, union or civil society regulation, planning and management. Capitalist market economic scientists refer to such attempts as "interference" in the supposedly perfect functioning of the laws of the capitalist market – a rather dismal term denoting an awfulness of human intention. Capitalist or free market economic scientists have thus far pushed through the ideology that the capitalist or free market is an independent and absolute force – which ensures equilibrium in society and that the capitalist or free market would also solve the big problems of climate change and environmental exploitation. Hence the solution thus far for trying to solve the climate crisis was to invent the concept and plans of carbon trading and its subsequent implementation. The ideology being that by leaving climate change to capitalist or free market forces, it would in time resolve itself. Homo sapiens – the species that invented the slave economy, the feudal economy and the capitalist economy – should keep out and stay out of the capitalist or free market economy – except as capitalists, sellers of labour-power, consumers of infinite amounts of stuff and as the unemployed masses! The "invisible hand" is made out to be analogous to that of the laws of gravity, the laws of physics and the laws of energy: "a stone hanging by a string is displaced from its equilibrium position, the force of gravity will at once tend to bring it back to its equilibrium position" (Marshall, 2013 [1890] 288). Like the stone that would reach equilibrium, the belief is that the market would in time ensure economic equilibrium in capitalist society. Marshall (2013 [1890]: 10–11) continues:

> Economics is defined as both the science of wealth and as part of the science of man; it is basically concerned with mainly monetary incentives to action; its study by both inductive and deductive means generates economic laws more complex and less advanced than those of the physical sciences.

As a species in our quest for understanding the human condition, we must also ask the following questions about economic science as it presents itself in capitalist society: Does economic science factor in the theft of land and natural resources through colonial invasions and conquests? Does economic science factor in slavery and the slave trade when drawing its conclusions as to why and how some countries have become wealthy and others have not? Does economic science analyse the working day, and how the worker produces for society at large? Has economic science been able to determine with science and certainty as to what creates value in a commodity? Why, for example, is a 10-carat diamond more expensive than a 10kg tank of oxygen? What makes one more valuable than the other? Why is it that the owners of big businesses end up with the lion's share of the value produced in factories, firms and on farms? Can there be such an entity as a labour market – as understood and analysed by contemporary economic science? How is it that labour can exist both in the capitalist market and in the production and consumption sphere, whereas smoking, eating or drinking exists only in the consumption sphere, but not in the exchange sphere or free market? In other words, is there such a thing as an eating, drinking or smoking market – as there is a labour market? To labour is to work. Economists should rather call it a work market and then we'll see the fraud for what economic science in its current form really is. Does economic science factor in nature in its calculation of value and wealth? Does economic science speak to the all-important issues of democracy, freedom, liberty and the pursuit of happiness in the workplace? After all, management science is the key pillar of work-place management. It's why the economist Frederick Winslow Taylor's *The Principles of Scientific Management* is so worshipped by the capitalist class. Frederick Winslow Taylor is not for nothing thought to be the real guru's guru. How much of the study of the economy is science which seeks to explain capitalism – and how much of it are ideologies which seek to uphold and maintain the capitalist system? Concerns about the quality of economic science in capitalist society has been raised on previous occasions – and such concerns are gaining momentum. For example:

> In a 1982 letter to *Science* magazine, Nobel Prize economist Wassily Leontief asked, 'how long will researchers working in adjoining fields abstain from expressing serious concern about the splendid isolation within which academic economics now finds itself?' We think Leontief's question points to the heart of the matter.

According to Hall and Klitgaard (2018: vi):

> Economics, as a discipline, lives in a contrived world of its own, one connected only tangentially to what occurs in real economic systems.

The authors continue:

> Indeed, why is economics construed and taught only as a social science, since in reality economies are as much, and perhaps even principally, about the transformation and movement of all manner of biophysical stuff in a world governed by physical laws?
>
> HALL and KLITGAARD, 2018: vi

Far from facilitating equilibrium in the world, capitalist or free market ideologies – dressed as economic science – have thus far delivered disequilibrium, chaos and anarchy in global society and the natural environment. The empirical evidence is all around and for all to see. The climate change catastrophe does not denote an ecosystem and planet in equilibrium. Unequal societies such as Brazil, India, South Africa and the US are not societies in equilibrium. They are societies on the brink of moral and social collapse. States have enabled and facilitated capitalist or free market ideologies to rule over people and planet. The latest casualty of capitalist or free market ideologies – as is protected by the 1st amendment – is free speech in the country that prides itself on freedom and free speech. In the same way that economic science in its current form hobbled the state from taking effective control of the COVID-19 pandemic, it also prevents the state from providing housing, jobs, health, education etc. when there is no pandemic – but still the need for housing, jobs, health, education, etc. exists. Public Health Science attempted to face-off against neoliberal economic science, but the backlash from Trump – the neoliberal ideologue – was harsh:

> On Wednesday, the president criticised Anthony Fauci, director of the National Institute of Allergy and Infectious Diseases, for warning against restarting the economy too quickly.
>
> MILMAN, 2020

Economic scientists – and the rich that they are associated or enamoured with – have been dishing out ideologies under the veil of economic science for decades. The result is that the rich got richer and continue to do so – and the poor got poorer and continue to do so. Thus far economic ideologies have been successful in putting itself out there as economic science. But as the failings of capitalism are being exposed, so are the economic ideologies that have thus far propped up this disastrous system:

> The prescription for our economic problems is more of the same – 'leave it to the market.' There's such endless trumpeting of the free market that it assumes almost a myth-like quality. 'It'll correct the problems.' Are there any alternatives? We have to first separate ideology from practice, because to talk about a free market at this point is something of a joke. Outside of ideologues, the academy and the press, no one thinks that capitalism is a viable system, and nobody has thought that for sixty or seventy years – if ever. Herman Daly and Robert Goodland, two World Bank economists, circulated an interesting study recently. In it they point out that received economic theory – the standard theory on which decisions are supposed to be based – pictures a free market sea with tiny little islands of individual firms. These islands, of course, aren't internally free – they're centrally managed.
>
> CHOMSKY, 1992

Where economic science of the capitalist or free market and neoliberal variety dominated over public health science, more people died in the Western world in the time of COVID-19!

3 The Economic Scientists Who Rule over Nature, Humans, Society and the State in the Age of Capitalism

Public health scientists became household names in the time of COVID-19. Before that they were obscure individuals who did not even feature much in mainstream life under capitalism. They were the detectives with long white coats, big round glasses and butterfly nets, in the depths of the jungle hunting for viruses, whilst the rest of us consumed Netflix, YouTube, McDonalds and PornHub – thanks to the productive, innovative as well as the alienating capacity of capitalism! But an unseen enemy changed all of that – well not the consumption part – but the perceptions and knowledge of public health scientists. COVID-19 catapulted public health scientists into the forefront of capitalist society. Many such scientists became overnight rock-stars and celebrities in the time of COVID-19. The world and the respective countries were led by these women and men of public health science – to navigate the pandemic that was wreaking havoc on both people and the capitalist economy. These were the scientists that were attempting to stop a public health enemy that was decimating humans in all parts of the world. Many did their damnedest to advise states on the best way forward to stave off death and destruction. There were some epidemiologists who did not know whether they were public health scientists or economic ideologues mooting for the continuation of the capitalist economy in the midst of a global pandemic. Their intentions may have been good, but such good intentions showed many millions of people the road to hell. The economic science of yesteryear is what dominates the global scientific arena in the 21st century. It is the science of the economic scientists of the past that dominates life in the present. The followers and critics of these economic scientists nonetheless reminded us as to how pervasive their economic science is in our politics, our social lives and in our personal lives as well. Their economic science dominated even in the time of a global pandemic. The economic scientist Adam Smith is revered in all corners of the globe – except in countries that believe in the economic science of Karl Marx. Adam Smith is so revered in the United Kingdom that his portrait appears on the 20-pound currency note. I do not ever recall Karl Marx's portrait appearing on even a 1-rupee note! Maybe a post-capitalist society will overturn the ideological heaviness of money – so prevalent in contemporary society. Smith's economic science classic, *An Inquiry into the Nature and Causes of the Wealth of Nations* (1776), is studied in many – if not in all – universities and has influenced politicians, politics and policies the world over. His economic science forms a major portion of the scientific foundation of capitalism. One of the pillars of his economic science is that the business owner or capitalist must retrieve more than he or she puts into their business enterprise – otherwise his or her business endeavours will come to nought:

> He could have no interest to employ them, unless he expected from the sale of their work something more than what was sufficient to replace his stock to him.
>
> SMITH, 1776: 74

In other words, the capitalist must retrieve a profit. In the time of COVID-19, the believers in the economic science of Adam Smith reminded the world about this world-famous economic scientist and his attractive brand of economic science:

> The profit motive has been a catalyst to great improvements in the world, with many believing it to be a main driver of innovation and development. In fact, it is a foundational principle of economist Adam Smith's metaphorical concept of the 'invisible hand,' which postulates that profit seekers are beneficial to society in general.
>
> Editor, *Daily Camera*, 2021

The dominance of the economic science of Adam Smith in contemporary society was everywhere highlighted in the time of COVID-19:

> Adam Smith's 1776 economic opus, *The Wealth of Nations* provided the blueprint showing how market forces in a world of small businesses (the butcher, the baker and the candlestick maker) provided benefits to all consumers. We do not live in Adam Smith's world, yet we continue to be influenced by his views.
>
> MCKINNEY, 2021

The economic scientists of the past – and their dedicated followers – were generously praised in the time of COVID-19: "free enterprise is directly connected to freedom of speech. Check Tom Locke, Thomas Jefferson, Adam Smith – super-genius dead white guys" (Bay, 2021). Whilst statues of slave dealers were brought down in the time of COVID-19, the profiles of the economic scientists – whose brand of economic science also played a part in influencing slave dealers – were highlighted and enhanced:

> JS Mill defined the economic man as one 'who inevitably does that by which he may obtain the greatest amount of necessaries, conveniences

> and luxuries with the smallest quantity of labour and physical self-denial with which they can be obtained'. This idea of someone acting in his economic self-interest chimes with the works of Adam Smith and David Ricardo, both classical economists, who considered man to be a rational, self-interested economic actor, who seeks to maximise his utility.
>
> FASAN, 2021

However, critical views in the time of COVID-19 seemed to point to the ideological slant of Adam Smith's economic science:

> One of the founders of the admirable Anti-Virus site is Sam Bowman, a senior fellow at the Adam Smith Institute (ASI). This is an opaquely funded lobby group with a long history of misleading claims about science that often seem to align with its ideology or the interests of its funders.
>
> MONBIOT, 2021

Then there were those who believed that followers of Adam Smith's economic science were gullible and non-thinking persons:

> Thought slaves to Smith are unshakably enamoured to the idea that the government should not have a hand in the working of the markets.
>
> CHULU, 2021

Many 20th century economic scientists were ardent followers of Adam Smith – and continued along the mostly ideological path of this world-famous scholar. Amongst the living public health scientists, the economic scientists of the past were most remembered, it seems, in the time of a global pandemic:

> Friedrich A. Hayek, Austrian economist, warned in his book, *The Road to Serfdom*, that many countries of the world, including the United States, were drifting from a democratic government to a Socialist nation. He noted that Communism can be attractive to a liberal society because people 'apathetically take for granted the improvements achieved through democracy'.
>
> EVANS, 2021

Some followers of the economic science of Friedrich Hayek – thinking that he was British – also invoked their favourite economic scientist in their arguments about inflation in the time of COVID-19: "British economist Friedrich

August von Hayek once said: 'I do not think it is an exaggeration to say history is largely a history of inflation'" (Shukla, 2021). Invoking Friedrich Hayek in the time of COVID-19 came thick and fast:

> In September 1945, Friedrich A. Hayek's famous essay, *The Use of Knowledge in Society,* was published in the *American Economic Review*. The main lesson from Hayek's essay is that it is impossible – not just improbable, but impossible – for the government to have the economic information it would need to centrally plan and allocate economic resources wisely. This after the federal government has described its spending plan as one that would transform the economy to make it greener, fairer, and more equitable.
>
> LAU, 2020

Others saw through the economic science mask of Hayek's neoliberal ideology – and spoke out against his ideological brand of economic science:

> The coronavirus that was born in the centrally-planned economy of China is challenging the laissez-faire theories of the free-marketeers the world over. Move over Friedrich von Hayek for Ha-Joon Chang of Cambridge University is here. Hayek's Austrian economics had its day, though most of it was bad.
>
> *New Strait Times*, 2021

It seemed had Hayek been alive, many more millions would have been infected and dead in the Western world in general – and in the capitalist world in particular:

> In his pursuit of individual liberty, Hayek wrote *The Constitution of Liberty* where he identified the social institutions that he felt would most effectively achieve the goal of liberty. Only free markets – in a democratic polity, with a private sphere of individual activity that is protected by a strong constitution, with well-defined and enforced property rights, all governed by the rule of law will support the set of institutions that both permits individuals to pursue their own values and allows them to make the best use of their own localised knowledge. In *Law, Legislation and Liberty* he was not too impressed with the concept of 'social justice' pursued by the modern welfare state, since the latter could be captured by special interests.
>
> *Millennium Post*, 2021

When the Great Crisis of 2007/2008 struck, critical thinkers were already chipping away at the ideological foundation of Hayek:

> Kevin Rudd (Moving beyond Brezhnev or Hayek, Opinion, 4/8) writes that Friedrich Hayek believed society has no obligation to others who are unknown to us and that he was prepared to allow fundamental social institutions such as the family to fend entirely for themselves against unrestrained market forces.
>
> MAWSON, 2008

When Hayek's ideology is no longer able to aid and abet capitalism, then his ideological brand of economic science is conveniently set aside by his disciples. But the hypocrisy and double standards of free marketeers and state bashers and state haters were exposed in the time of COVID-19.

> The timely pleading from John Coates (Help out athletes' plea from AOC boss, 4/8) for additional public funds to maintain Australia's ranking in world sport is somewhat baffling at a time when talk of Friedrich Hayek's influence is being raised by such a world-renowned free-market expert as Ayaan Hirsi Ali. It doesn't seem that long ago that Hayek disciples such as Margaret Thatcher looked upon government funding of sports along the lines adopted by East Germany as propaganda for the socialist state. Why don't we just let the free market look after sport in true free-market style?
>
> PARK, 2021

"Pretence to knowledge" was a Nobel acceptance speech given by Friedrich Hayek more than 40 years ago. It was about how social scientists can do great harm by pretending they know more than they do (Johns, 2021). Pretence to knowledge of free markets and state functioning in the capitalist economy should have been more likely the speech of Friedrich von Hayek. If the West and its leaders chose less state in the time of COVID-19 – where and when millions died – it is owing to the dominant ideologies of the economic scientists of the past. When the West and its leaders choose to let the capitalist or free market profit shamelessly from medicine and health care, education, housing, food, etc. then it is due to the overwhelming ideologies of the economic scientists of the distant as well as recent past. This economic paradigm:

> Shaped how we think about the role of government and markets for the previous 40 years or so. The starting point of this paradigm, which is typically referred to as 'the Washington consensus,' 'neo-liberalism' or

> 'hyper-globalization', can be a bit challenging to pinpoint. Some might date it to the elections of Margaret Thatcher and Ronald Reagan in the late 1970s and early 1980s. Others attribute it to Friedrich Hayek and Milton Friedman winning the Nobel Prize in economics in the mid-1970s.
>
> SPEER, 2021

Milton Friedman died one year before his ideological trademark of economic science was left in shambles by the Great Crisis of 2008. This was the economic science prophet of neoliberal ideology. He is still worshipped in a world where capitalist or free market functioning has proven dreadful for the poor and catastrophic for nature. If greed is the creed of modern society, then Milton Friedman is the economic scientist and ideologist that has encouraged and legitimised the doctrine of greed. He received the Noble Prize for propagating greedy economic science that is the cause for so much of greed in the world today. It is the same greed that was not left at the doorway when a global pandemic struck and killed millions. In fact – like hyenas feasting on dying people – the profit-making and corruption in the time of COVID-19 has its roots in the Milton Friedman Greed Economic Doctrine:

> Milton Friedman proclaimed more than 50 years ago that the sole purpose of a corporation is to maximise returns for its shareholders – nothing more, nothing less. A corporate entity, Friedman also proclaimed, is a morally neutral legal construct that should be agnostic of the concerns of the broader society. Profit, not common good, not employees' welfare, was its single, dominant purpose. That proclamation became known in economics, of which Friedman was a towering figure, as the shareholders doctrine. Others called it the Doctrine of Greed or the Doctrine of Selfishness.
>
> RONQUILLO, 2021

The Ideology of Greed is central to our current brand of economic science and scientists. The Arab News carried a piece on Milton Friedman – the much-loved economics science ideologue: "Friedman was an American Nobel Laureate economist and public intellectual. He made major contributions to the fields of economics and statistics. He was an advocate of economic freedom" (2020). Milton Friedman's ideological brand of economic science was given lots of airtime in the time of COVID-19:

> There is a story about the famous economist Milton Friedman on a trip to China during the early days of economic reform – decades ago. The

> Chinese had taken Professor Friedman out to see a major dam they were building. Mr. Friedman asked why they were using people with shovels rather than heavy equipment. The Chinese responded, 'it is a jobs program.' Mr. Friedman then said, 'If so, why don't you give them spoons'.
>
> RAHN, 2021

One would have thought that the good professor of economic science would have known that capitalists – whether in communist China or capitalist South Africa – would not see the need to utilise heavy and expensive machinery – if there is a readily supply of cheap labour. And yes, one could use spoons to spoon sand and earth – but spades or shovels might prove to be too inconvenient to eat food with. The arch capitalist market economic scientist and his ideologies were quoted again and again in the time of COVID-19: "nothing is so permanent as a temporary government program" (Abernathy, 2021). Some referred to Milton Friedman as: "the free-market evangelist and Nobel Memorial Prize-winning economist" (Harford, 2021). If the public health scientists were the rock stars in the time of COVID-19, it seems that the economic scientists of neoliberalism and capitalist or free market fundamentalism are the gods of rock:

> Nobel economist Milton Friedman, whose famous 1970 essay, The Social Responsibility of Business is to Increase its Profits. This was to counteract Ralph Nader, consumer-activist and hero of American corporate-bashers, published *Taming the Giant Corporation*. Nader proposed a US. federal charter of major US. corporations whereby a government gives the corporate entity existence and that entity, in return, agrees to serve the public interest.
>
> CORCORAN, 2021

Like the prophets and gurus – whose teachings we are continually reminded of in capitalist society – the teachings of the economics professor of profit were advertised far and wide in the time of COVID-19: "Nobel laureate economist Milton Friedman once observed: 'no bureaucrat spends tax (rate) payers' money as carefully as those taxpayers themselves would have'" (Moffat, 2021). Friedman was right. If the taxpayer in capitalist US has a real say as to how monies should be spent, then maybe, just maybe there would have been enough public hospitals, enough PPEs, enough ventilators, enough masks, enough oxygen, etc. to save the more than one million people that lost their lives in the richest country on the planet! This is the same Nobel Prize economic scientist who believed that one of the factors for the US's history of prosperity was that it was without the First Nations. He referred to America as: "an empty continent to conquer" (Friedman et al., 1980). He freely chose to omit the existence of a people – and their economy – in his best-selling book *Free to Choose* (1980). With this poor quality of economic science, we are also at odds to decipher whether the failure of communism in the USSR is due to a planned economy or voluntary cooperation in the economy:

> Russia is the standard example of a large economy that is supposed to be organised by command – a centrally planned economy. But that is more fiction than fact. At every level of the economy, voluntary cooperation enters to supplement central planning or to offset its rigidities – sometimes legally, sometimes illegally.
>
> FRIEDMAN ET AL., 1980: 10

The learned professor has the tendency to alter facts to tailor-fit his ideological framework of economic science. His ideological fans followed suit in the time of COVID-19.

The state of the contemporary world is in the main the result of the science, ideas and ideologies of the key economic scientists mentioned – among others of a similar ideological paradigm. Their disciples in the form of scholars, politicians, presidents, prime ministers, etc. have religiously implemented their ideological brand of economic science into policy, planning and the execution of the capitalist economy. If the world is in the mess that it currently is in, then it is because the world is primarily under the spell of an ideological economic science and scientists for so long – an ideological paradigm favouring a minority of humans at the expense of the majority and the natural environment. Which aspects of their economic science does a post-COVID-19 society wish to keep – and which aspects will it wish to cancel? It seems the cat has been let out of the bag since the Great Crisis of 2008 on the economic scientists that rule our world: "Kevin Rudd took free-market economics to task by claiming that the ideas of one of its leading 20th-century proponents, Friedrich von Hayek, have been superseded" (Hogbin, 2008). In the time of COVID-19, the chaos and confusion currently characterising the world, were laid at the door of the neoliberal economic scientists who rule over people and planet with their ideas and ideologies:

> The shocking invasion of the United States Congress by an armed mob may rightly have been blamed on Donald Trump, but the roots of what happened go back to the middle of the last century. Mr Trump was undoubtedly the catalyst that prompted them to engage in direct action,

> but the story begins in a luxurious Swiss hotel in the aftermath of World War II. A group of right-wing economists, some from the University of Chicago, linked up with some extremely wealthy businessmen, some likeminded journalists and some foundation officials at the Hotel du Parc, a Belle Epoque mansion in the mountains above Lac Leman (Lake Geneva). Aggrieved by the 1930s New Deal policies of the late President FD Roosevelt, which had entailed huge injections of public money into public works programmes aimed at bringing the US out of the Depression era, they were freshly appalled by post-war plans to base the new model of government in the US and European countries on labour unionism, a welfare state and government intervention for economic security. The conference was convened by the Austrian polymath Friedrich A. Hayek, whose gracious Old World manners belied a steely determination to oppose the social democratic consensus that appeared to be emerging.
>
> SHIPTON, 2021

If Friedrich Hayek and Milton Friedman are "right wing economists", then it seems that our current economic science – that is so dominant and prevalent in capitalist society – is one of a right-wing variety.

We have witnessed the chaos, confusion, death and destruction that is real and possible – when right-wing economic science and scientists pronounce that the capitalist or free market should be left to its own functioning – without state oversight and involvement in the time of COVID-19. This is the ideology of greed and exploitation – without laws, without rules, without regulations, without restraint and without morals. When economic scientists talk about economic freedom and freedom to choose as being capitalist values – what they actually mean is the freedom to exploit, the freedom to let greed run riot and the freedom to choose profit over the lives of people. The evidence is all around. This is the brand of economic science that has been preached all along and continues to be preached for capitalist or free market solutions to environmental challenges and catastrophes. The consequence of this variety of economic science is runaway global warming and subsequent climate change. Unequal societies are now the norm in the world, as a result of the type of economic science meted out during capitalism's reign by economic scientists such as Milton Friedman, Friedrich Hayek, Ludwig von Mises, etc. thus far. It seems that it is not only the economic science of dead white men which rules over man and nature in the age of capitalism, but the economic science of dead white women as well in the form of Ayn Rand, who dished out capitalist ideologies through her novels. The state's push for corporations to extract more profits from farmers in India has its roots in the economic science of Friedman &

Co. We continued to see the chaos that was India, as farmers' protests reflected the current form of economic science, one that seeks to destroy their lives and livelihoods – whilst this same economic science favours big profit-making by large corporations. The thing with economic science in its current form is that it is not seen for its ideological intent and purposes. It is religiously accepted as good economic science in our schools, universities, states and society:

> Laissez faire is the object of a faith that is widely accepted and uncontroversial. According to this faith a pure free market system, unencumbered by government interference, must provide the best economy. But despite our unquestioning belief and despite the appearance of prosperity so confidently exuded by soaring financial markets, there is a wide range of data (that we ignore) that calls this faith into question. It is remarkable that even economists are blind to this.
>
> FRIEDMAN, 2003: 12

In his *An Inquiry into the Nature and Causes of the Wealth of Nations* (1776), Adam Smith states:

> He intends only his own gain, and he is in this, as in many other cases, led by an invisible hand to promote an end which was no part of his intention. Nor is it always the worse for the society that it was no part of it. By pursuing his own interest he frequently promotes that of the society more effectually than when he really intends to promote it. I have never known much good done by those who affected to trade for the public good.
>
> SMITH, 1776: 593

The man's economic science is praised:

> Adam Smith's flash of genius was his recognition that the prices that emerged from voluntary transactions between buyers and sellers – for short, in a free market – could coordinate the activity of millions of people, each seeking his own interest, in such a way as to make everyone better off. It was a startling idea then, and it remains one today, that economic order can emerge as the unintended consequence of the actions of many people, each seeking his own interest.
>
> FRIEDMAN ET AL., 1980: 13–14

But the developing world witnessed how Adam Smith's economic science and ideology of self-interest in the arena of vaccine distribution saw the young and youth vaccinated in the West – and the elderly unvaccinated in the South due to the self-interest demonstrated through vaccine nationalism and vaccine apartheid. Reality does seem to shake-off the ideological foundations of capitalist society – as we had learnt in the time of COVID-19. It was a similar situation in the time of the Great Crisis of 2008, when the economic ideological foundation of the capitalist world was severely disrupted. Even the Queen of England – and leader of the Commonwealth – tried to make sense of economic science in a world teeming with Nobel Laureates. The ideologies of philosophers such as Aristotle and Plato sanctioned slave society. Their philosophies were the ideological glue that kept slave society intact for many hundreds of years. The ideologies of philosophers such as Sir Robert Filmer served to keep feudal society intact for a number of years. The ideologies of economic scientists such as Adam Smith, Friedrich Hayek, Ayn Rand, Milton Friedman, etc. is the glue that serves to keep capitalism intact. Their ideologies are the glue that sought to make capitalism stick to man and nature. It did for a very long time. But the ideological glue of these capitalist or free market economic scientists are gradually becoming undone. Their ideologies are gradually being critiqued as a result of the real observations and assessments of how the capitalist economy works in the real world – and not in the fantasy worlds contrived by such economic scientists. It is time that 21st century society interrogates the standing and status awarded to these and similar economic scientists – whose brand of economic science has heaped so much of death and destruction on humankind and the natural environment for so long.

4 Science – the Roadmap to a Better World

For a very long time in the history of humans – the world was flat. This was the ideological thinking of man for a long time. The earth then changed from flat to round with the development of science. For a long time in the life of humans – the sun moved around the earth. This was the ideological thinking of man – in the time when the church took it upon itself to think for the rest of humankind. Though we still see and talk about sun-set and sun-rise, with the development of science the earth began to rotate on its axis and move around the sun. For a long time – humankind has tried to understand the world through means other than that of science. Unfortunately, large parts of humankind still attempt to understand the world of today through means other than science. We were witnesses to the conspiracy theories doing its rounds in the time of

COVID-19. There are probably a few nutcases who still believe that the earth is flat – and that the sun moves around the earth. With all of its superstitious beliefs, humankind's ability to forge a known and predictable world for itself has been steady – even though at times slow:

> Scientific thought about social affairs up to now has had to wage war primarily against established intolerance and institutionalised suppression. It has been struggling to establish itself against its external enemies, the authoritarian interest of church, state, and tribe.
>
> MANNHEIM, 1953: xiv

But science is not without its fair share of troubles as we have witnessed in the time of COVID-19. Nowhere has the role of science in society been more pronounced and contested than in the burning issue of climate change. In the same way that scientists were at loggerheads with each other in the time of COVID-19; for a long time, scientists were at loggerheads with each other in the science of climate change: "climate change deniers fail to realise the vast danger they are plunging themselves and everyone else into by insisting on their reassuring delusion" (Alden, 2020). We have learnt and continue to learn about the world through science: "the word 'science' comes from the Latin scientia, which means knowledge" (Wootton, 2015: 33). The current form of economic science has, in the main, produced the world that we live in – a world where the rich have a secure life – and the poor an insecure one. The current form of economic science leans more towards ideologies seeking to uphold the current chaotic world order. The frightful thing is that it has been presented to us for so long as truth – in the same way that men were presented as superior to women, whites as superior to blacks, Jews as less than human, etc. We are still told that there are gods living in the sky. It is why sometimes footballers – after scoring a goal – look up to the sky. The last time I travelled by Emirates Airways, I only saw the sun, the moon, bouncy clouds and – unfortunately at times – the wing of the airplane. The current form of economic science has given us the high levels of unemployment that we witness in many parts of the world. The current brand of economic science is enabling the heating of the planet as well as the rampant consumerism that is causing large scale environmental degradation – under the banners of free choice and supply and demand economics. If society is to transition to a new normal, then its economic science needs to also undergo change, transformation, a revolution and a disruption. It should not be the same defunct economic science informing a post-COVID-19 world:

> Economic conditions are constantly changing, and each generation looks at its own problems in its own way. In England, as well as on the Continent and in America, economic studies are being more vigorously pursued now than ever before; but all this activity has only shown more clearly that economic science is, and must be, one of slow and continuous growth.
>
> MARSHALL, 2013 [1890]: xix

This observation of the changing nature of economic science was made about 130 years ago! A planet and people-centred science is what the human race and the planet requires – as its analytical tools for shaping a more agreeable and liveable world. Signs are pointing that COVID-19 may start humankind to terminate the economic ideological freeway that it has been on for quite some time now. Whilst we are witnessing death, despair and economic depression, we may also be witnessing the beginning of the end of economic science in its neoliberal ideological form:

> The pandemic has once again debunked the long-held myth in the West about the 'end of history,' an all-powerful model of hyper-liberal development, based on the principles of individualism, and a firm belief in the ability to solve all problems through the market alone.
>
> LAVROV, 2020: 7

Like previous societies that have undergone great transformations – from a hunter-gatherer society, then to a slave society, then to a feudal society and now to a capitalist society – so too has there been great transformations in the scientific field as well. For example: "Darwin and Wallace made the designer unnecessary" (Pinker, 2018: 33). Ideology blinds us to the human condition – but science enlightens us of the human condition: "science is shedding new light on the human condition" (Pinker, 2018: 468). Science and scientists have developed COVID-19 vaccines in record time: "science and medicine have risen to the challenge of this historic pandemic by developing and bringing to market vaccines in record speed" (Editor, *Daily Camera*, 2021). A people-centred science has a history of eradicating diseases that have afflicted humankind in the past: "scientific knowledge eradicated smallpox, a painful and disfiguring disease which killed 300 million people in the 20th century alone" (Pinker, 2018: 469). Science can be used to kill people in their tens of thousands – as was done with the US Manhattan Atomic Bomb Project. Science can also be used to save lives – as countries like China, Vietnam, New Zealand, etc. had demonstrated in the time of COVID-19. Many of the countries that threw science at COVID-19 used scientific technology for its peoples' benefit. It used the vast powers of the internet in the interest of its citizens. It used its brand of economic science to deliver goods and services to its people and to the world. Science – and not ideology – won the day in countries like China, Vietnam, Cuba, etc.

That economic science will or should never be the same again is a view that is felt in many corners of the world. COVID-19 has reached all parts of the world. Its impacts have and is also reaching the innermost spheres of economic science – and is causing a quiet revolution in the way that economic science seeks to explain the capitalist economy:

> COVID-19 is changing many things. And economics is one of them. Although we are creatures of old habits – even of some very bad ones – we must use this time to give our economics a big rethink. For far too long we have been under the hypnosis of Hayek's *The Road to Serfdom*, a treatise on how to keep the hand of the government out of the market. It is such thinking that has made the one per cent of the world decide how the 99 per cent should live their lives.
>
> *New Straits Times*, 2020

If many voices were calling for people to wear masks, sanitise and maintain social distancing in the time of COVID-19, many voices were also calling for new forms of economic thinking:

> So Kevin Rudd will take us beyond Leonid Brezhnev and Friedrich Hayek? We simply don't have to choose between centrally planned dictatorship and the free market anymore? By removing the straitjacket of these 20th-century paradigms we can embrace new ideas, such as those of the 2020 summiteers, to solve the new challenges of the new century?
>
> MCKINNON, 2021

Through the sometimes brilliance of Adam Smith, economic science has enlightened us on the science of the division of labour:

> The greatest improvement in the productive powers of labour, and the greater part of the skill, dexterity, and judgment with which it is anywhere directed, or applied, seem to have been the effects of the division of labour.
>
> SMITH, 1776: 17

Karl Marx built on the economic science of Adam Smith, David Ricardo, etc. He has indicated that it is not labour that the worker sells but his or her labour-power. How can current economic scientists build on the economic scientists of the past? The ideology of laissez-faire policy is that the state does nothing. The reality is something else. Child labour is regulated by the state. If left to the capitalist or free market children would be in the mines, in the factories, as domestic workers, etc. Millions of people in the Eastern countries are alive today – because scientific technology was put to effective and humane use. The Western world had in their possession all of the technologies that were painstakingly built up over the centuries – to save their lives of their citizens. They failed to mobilise their technological and scientific capital to save their citizens from death and despair. Western civilisation, in its current ideological form, enabled the deaths of citizens – in the same way that Nazi ideology enabled the deaths of millions of Jews – and the ideology of greed enabled the two World Wars. COVID-19 has caused so much of pain and suffering. But overnight it has also made the entire world scientists of sorts. Epidemiologists cannot now claim that they are the only ones who know about viruses. My 78-old mom, who due to apartheid ideologies could not finish high school, now knows about viruses. So too do my 9-year-olds niece and nephew. Even economists now know about viruses! When science is shared with the entire world, the world has the potential to better itself. Man must continue to unshackle the ideological chains that keeps him imprisoned. He must continue on the path of scientific evolution and revolution – if he is to realise his full potential as the intelligent ape. That would mean leaving behind defunct economic science, outdated ideologies and recycled superstitions. COVID-19 has triggered an ideological awakening in humankind. The challenge going forward is – how do we use this ideological awakening to shape and make a new world – that is greener, better and happier than the one that we currently inhabit?

CHAPTER 7

An Ideological Awakening

A World Different to That of Capitalism Was Glimpsed

> There is no such thing as society.
>
> MARGARET THATCHER

•••

> Man is by nature a social animal.
>
> ARISTOTLE

∴

1 COVID-19 and Revealing the Real World through Ideological Unlayering

COVID-19 made us to sit-up and think about how we live our lives in contemporary times. Since its inception capitalism has gradually atomised the human race. It has transformed social animals into atomistic individuals – in its continuous quest for profit and wealth accumulation. From this atomistic space, we are in continuous search for ourselves and our happiness. We are living in a world whose ideological architecture and scaffolding were laid down by the likes of Adam Smith, Milton Freedman, Margaret Thatcher, Ronald Reagan and others belonging to the neoliberal tribe. For centuries humankind has been under the spell of capitalist ideas and ideologies – ideas and ideologies that were enforced through a myriad of ways – through textbooks, schooling, mainstream media, religious institutions, universities, politicians, the state, etc. Profit-maximisation is the over-riding ideology of capitalist society. The ideology of profit decides, in the main, who will live and who will die. It has been the guide-rule for humankind since the advent of capitalism. But COVID-19 brought a new perspective to humankind – a perspective that all the while lay buried and hidden under the weight of capitalist ideologies. These ideologies served to indoctrinate humankind into believing that we are purely individuals in an individualistic world. They hammered it into our heads that Homo

 | DOI:10.1163/9789004539808_008

sapiens – by nature – act purely for their own selfish interest. People in powerful and influential positions, like Margaret Thatcher, forced us into believing that "there is no such thing as society". COVID-19 taught us that the ideology of the Iron Lady of capitalism – "there is no such thing as society" – had come from 10 Downing Street to destroy any idea of a united opposition to capitalism – thereby enabling the building of an unfettered, harsh and brutal economy. All the while, it was not the people that benefitted from such an ideological grip on humankind, but the big corporations – and their friends in high positions in state and society. They profited handsomely and beautifully from such ideological brainwashing of the masses. The ideology of Margaret Thatcher – of individualistic man – has in the main ruled the world up until the time of COVID-19. In Margaret Thatcher's world, there can't be family as well – only individuals. It seems that her party of conservatives in government was really an illusion; they were merely individuals representing their own individualistic conservative and neoliberal self-interests. They taught us from childhood – that we can only be happy if we have more money and more things. They turned a natural, playful and curious species into a heavily worked, constantly worried, fearful and consumerist species. They drummed it into our heads that success and happiness lay only in the future, that we had to continuously work – in order to chase so-called success and happiness; and that's what we did and do until too late in our lives – when we realise that it was a wasted life of working and accumulating – and until we dropped dead. As a friend of mine once remarked: "we are continuously chasing destinations" (Naidoo, 2021). It's what we do under capitalism. Our brains and bodies have been wired with capitalist ideologies – meant to serve our boss, master and king – called capitalism. But COVID-19 gave us insights into other possible worlds – ones that we probably had an idea existed but could never quite acquire – owing to the heavy weight of capitalist ideologies masquerading as economic science and human values. COVID-19 brought us death – but it also opened our eyes to the preciousness of life. It brought us despair – but also hope. It inflicted isolation but also togetherness. COVID-19 caused stagnation – but also creativity. COVID-19 gave us insights into how divided we are – as a human race under the historical system called capitalism. We divided ourselves into nationalities, races, religions, genders, geographies, ethnicities, etc. But when the people died, when the doctors died, when the nurses died, when the teachers died, when moms and dads and grandparents and children died – a large part of the human race had died. Communist China tried everything in its power to keep its citizens alive. The capitalist West tried everything in its power to keep the capitalist economy alive. All along, the ideology of capitalist society has been that our inner world determines our outer world. This ideology shifted responsibility of agency for happiness and the good life to the desperate individual – and the desperate individual alone. If a person is poor, then she is to blame – not the unequal system that she lives in. If a person is extremely wealthy, then it is solely due to his hard work – not the state support that he had received all along – and the exploitative system that he is part and parcel of. If there are mass shootings in the US, then the person is pronounced to be mentally unstable – the shocking ease with which a person can acquire war-like firearms and ammunition apparently has nothing to do with tens and hundreds of people being murdered at one go. After such shooting, there is apparently no need to make guns difficult to access – all one has to do is pray to an imaginary god – like happens every time in the USA. But COVID-19 has taught us how important the outer world is in hugely influencing – if not determining – the make-up of our inner worlds. A society immersed in a sea of guns will experience waves of killings and murders. A man with mental health issues is of greater risk to himself and society, if he has easy access to guns and ammunition – as is the case in the USA. A man with an extreme set of ideologies is of greater risk to himself and society, if he has easy access to guns and ammunition – as is the case in parts of the world. Capitalist ideologies indoctrinated us into believing that the ideal presupposes the real, but COVID-19 has shown us first-hand how important the material world is in the lives and livelihoods of humans. It taught us that we need nature, we need fresh air and oxygen, we need PPEs, we need ventilators, we need natural and built spaces for our mental health, we need food and water, we need shelter, we need decent and secure employment, we need each other, we need a caring state with oversight and sensitivity. COVID-19 taught us, as Marx pronounced more than 150 years ago, that our "being determines our consciousness", that the way we live is – in the main – the way we think. We do not or hardly think of bows and arrows – because we do not live in a hunter-gatherer society any longer. We do not or hardly think of white cotton fields under a harsh sun – because we do not live in a slave society any longer. We do not or hardly think of bowing to the king or the noble lords – because we do not live in a feudal society any longer. But now we keep thinking of money, profit, whether we can afford medical aid, education for our children, housing, credit card, unemployment, pension fund, crime, etc.; capitalism compels us to think this way because we live in a capitalist society. Our "being determines our consciousness" – not the other way around. For centuries, capitalist ideologues fed us the dictum that "I think – therefore I am". Those who thought that they could be safe from COVID-19, if they just thought that they were safe in their minds – and not bother with social distancing, mask-wearing and hand-sanitising in the real world – received harsh lessons on the real workings of the material and natural world.

The dominant ideology of "mind over matter" has thus far served neoliberal capitalism and its beneficiaries quite well. The ideologies and propaganda – akin to fake news and lies – that were dished out all these decades about capitalism – has been exposed by the power of a micro-organism from nature. Amidst the pain of losing loved ones, the despair, the depression, discrimination, dogma, etc., in many places around the world there appeared to be a global awakening – an awakening from centuries of capitalist ideologies that have been heaped on humankind throughout the life of capitalism. In the words of Terry Eagleton even before COVID-19:

> It seemed that the destruction of the old society has given way to new forms of thinking: Rather as a bout of dengue fever makes you newly aware of your body, so a form of social life can be perceived for what it is when it begins to break down.
>
> EAGLETON, 2018: xv

COVID-19 broke through the ideological armour of capitalism – and demonstrated that the supposedly impossible can be made possible. That well-resourced and caring states can make the economy, capitalist or free market and money work for and in the interest of humankind. COVID-19 demonstrated that states and civic organisations can at least try to push for patent laws to work in the interest of lives instead of for profit – as was attempted by countries like South Africa and India. COVID-19 demonstrated that one can temporarily forgo freedoms and liberties – in order to have the freedom and liberty to live. With the immense death and destruction all around – there was also an awakening from humankind's ideological slumber for so long under capitalism.

2 COVID-19 and People-Centred State Planning and Execution

COVID-19 showed humankind most if not all things are possible, when the state is willing and able – and not wrapped and smothered with free market and neoliberal ideologies. In the capitalist era, we all depend on the functioning of capitalism in order to get by on a daily basis – whether such capitalism is mediated through the state or the free market. Even Marx – the millennium's greatest thinker – depended on capitalism to support himself and his family whilst he wrote about the evils of capitalism. On the other end of the ideological spectrum, persons like Margaret Thatcher and Ronald Reagan spoke about the evils of the state whilst occupying the apex of state power. In the final analysis, it is not about individuals per se, but about the capitalist system itself – in which such individuals find themselves. We should not only want a better world for ourselves and our children, we should want the best of all possible worlds – because Homo sapiens are intelligent, dreamers, planners and doers. In the midst of pain, suffering and chaos, we got glimpses into the potential of the human race to plan and execute a different world from the one we were accustomed to. In Germany, the state made the wearing of masks compulsory. Nearly all states around the world ensured that the livelihoods of all people were sustained – even if for a brief period of time. Imagine the worse devastation and deaths if states around the world adhered religiously to the neoliberal ideology of the likes of Milton Friedman and Ronald Reagan that "there is nothing so permanent as a temporary government program". The Western world adhered to this sick ideology for a while when the pandemic struck in the Western world. But when people died in the absence of state care and support, this bizarre ideology was gradually dropped from the capitalist state's ideological toolbox. COVID-19 demonstrated that a caring, supportive and people-centred state can make the economy work meaningfully for the people – instead of the people working religiously for the economy – as has been the case for hundreds of years. In the lower half of Korea:

> On 17 March, a temporary provision entailed a small subsidy of 454,900 South Korean won (£313) a month to cover basic living expenses. The same funding is available to those who are self-isolating, regardless of whether they test positive for the virus. It's not hugely generous, but provides subsistence for those whose lives are upended by necessary measures such as the ministry of education's closure of schools.
>
> DUDDEN and MARKS, 2020: 1

With all of its failings, the UK Prime Minister said that the state is there to take care of the people. Amazing what the state can do if they have the political will and held accountable by the people! When we remove the Western ideological layers enforced on Cuba – with a strong and caring state – we then see the humanity embedded in the state and country. Cuba has:

> Sent doctors to Italy as the doctors there are labouring under exhaustion and 24-hour restrictions on movement are just starting to stem the rise of new infections.
>
> SSEMOGERERE, 2020

The Chinese state built a hospital in 10 days when China finally acknowledged that COVID-19 was a clear and present danger. The UK state learnt from the Chinese state and converted one of its stadiums into a hospital in 9 days. Intending to gain ideological mileage over its communist nemesis, the UK state said that it built the hospital – instead of saying that it transformed a stadium in 9 days! Never mind, the state although late – acted to save lives. With all of his delays, anti-science rhetoric, love for the free market and illusory freedoms and liberties in the US, Trump finally ordered General Motors to produce ventilators – by invoking the Defence Production Act. Also, in the US, the state ordered a navy ship with many beds to serve as a mercy ship for COVID-19 patients to be stationed in Los Angeles. Some businesses did transition to forms of civic duty – even if miniscule. Amazon reported that it would build its own on-site COVID-19 testing station. In Russia, Rosatom – a nuclear company – embarked on producing ventilator equipment. Aside from some capitalist and neoliberal states going rogue and failing its people, the COVID-19 generation are witnesses to the power and benefits of states in societal planning and execution. The state has the potential to be a killing machine – as was the case with the US in its numerous wars in many parts of the globe over the many decades. But the state also has huge potential to be caring and humane – as was the case in New Zealand, China, Vietnam, etc. in the time of COVID-19. Society as a whole should decide what the nature of the state must be in the transition to a post-COVID-19 and post-capitalist world. We have, as a human race, invented democracy to help us do this. The Indian state ordered private hospitals to make 80% of beds available. As the world thinks, discusses and plans for a post-COVID-19 world, the fear heaped on generations by capitalist and neoliberal ideologues over time must be challenged by evidence, science, transparency and people-power. For too long the ideologues of capitalism have hammered it into our heads that the state is evil and should get out of the way of human affairs. When positioning the state to help transition to a post-capitalist world, the immortal words of Franklin D. Roosevelt must ring true: "there's nothing to fear but fear itself". In the time of COVID-19, the New York Governor stated that for the first time we understood what it means to share and that before, hospitals were their own private enterprises. A Company in France wanted to make vaccines available to the US first. More than 100 states objected and said that the vaccines must also be available to other countries as well. The president of South Africa spearheaded the initiative for a "people's vaccine". All wishes were not achieved, but the power of the state in saving and securing lives was well acknowledged, accepted and agreed upon by a great many people in all parts of the world. COVID-19 demonstrated that states are best placed to enable and secure the livelihoods of its citizens:

> The textbook free-market solution to unemployment is that workers can always price themselves back into a job by being willing to take a pay cut. Fortunately, no government believes this nonsense, and the story of the past couple of months has been frantic attempts to prevent a health emergency from morphing into an employment emergency. Britain's furlough scheme has been one response to this incipient crisis, but there has also been a response in the US, where Trump, keen not to become the new Herbert Hoover, has adopted a three-pronged approach. First, the administration has provided an extra $600 (£480) a week in unemployment benefits until the end of July.
>
> ELLIOT, 2020: 33

If the planet is to be saved – and humans to live healthy and happy lives – then the institution in society that is best placed to oversee these important goals and values is the state:

> In one of the biggest car-free initiatives of any city in the world, the capital's mayor announced yesterday that main streets between London Bridge and Shoreditch, Euston and Waterloo, and Old Street and Holborn, will be limited to buses, pedestrians and cyclists. 'By ensuring our city's recovery is green, we will also tackle our toxic air, which is vital to make sure we don't replace one public health crisis with another. I urge all boroughs to work with us to make this possible.' Many cities have already announced measures to improve walking and cycling and support a low-carbon, sustainable recovery from the coronavirus crisis.
>
> TAYLOR, 2020

China – with a robust and hands-on state – was the lifeline to the world after it attended to COVID-19 at home. In Thailand, the state had guaranteed low income and unemployed people the sum of 5000 baht per month for 3 months. The US state signed into law a stimulus package of 2.2 trillion dollars. This is contrary to the project of fear instituted by capitalist or free market ideologues like Ronald Reagan when he stated that the most terrifying words in the English language are: "I'm from the government and I am here to help". What Reagan failed to add is that states in capitalist countries – like the one he was leading – have mainly helped and served the rich in society. The state can and should be a force for good in society. The state must be made to recognise the harsh, brutal and unjust nature and functioning of capitalism – and help lead society to a post-capitalist world. However, whilst the state should lead current society to a post-capitalist world, it is the people in all parts of the world that must form the battering ram that knocks down the door – which keep us all locked inside the ruthless and brutal system called capitalism.

3 The Rebirth of Communal Man in the Time of COVID-19

Before COVID-19, we mostly insulated ourselves from our neighbours, communities, relatives and friends. We mostly inhabited socio-economic worlds that sought to increase our material status and career options – for those of us who are fortunate to have businesses or to be employed under capitalism. We hardly found time for connecting with other human beings. But COVID-19 seemed to have triggered changes to these alien forms of living and existing under capitalism:

> In the 10 years that he has lived in his house in Wavertree, Liverpool, Greg Schofield is not sure he has ever gone into the alleyway behind his rear garden, an unlovely strip of weed-strewn cobbles where some neighbours kept their bins. Though he and his wife are close to their immediate neighbours, they knew only two other families in the street. Come lockdown, someone set up a WhatsApp group, and a couple of neighbours asked if anyone was up for tidying the alley. Most of the 14 households in the block turned up to clear their patch. 'It got people quite excited,' says Schofield. 'People began to see how nice the cobbles could look without the weeds.' From there, it snowballed. Someone brought a bench from work, others made a planter out of old pallets; friends donated plants. The alley is now a beautiful space, shared by a group of new friends already making plans for a Christmas grotto. 'I wish this had happened sooner,' says Schofield. 'It's been the highlight of all of our lockdown experience – a moment of goodness that's come out of a bad situation.' Across the country, people who previously shared only a postcode have joined together in pavement aerobics classes, singalongs and physically distanced street discos. Others, less visibly, have texted neighbours, dropped off shopping, or simply shouted good wishes. And this is not just anecdotal. Poll after poll underline the fact that the enormous suffering wrought by COVID-19 in Britain has also provoked a period of unprecedented neighbourly connection. The Office for National Statistics has been tracking the virus's social impacts weekly; figures published last week showed that 71% of Britons were confident that if they needed help during the pandemic, members of their community would support them, while 67% had checked on a neighbour in the past week. 'I think

> it's made us recognise that community is really important. We want to have a sense that there are other people there for us.' Mackay has been shielding due to a health condition and says lockdown has created an 'absolutely astonishing' bond between neighbours who previously stuck to polite if distant hellos but now 'can't do enough to help'. On Tuesday, her 70th birthday, she found that one neighbour had hung bunting in her garden, while at least a dozen more gathered in the street, appropriately distanced, to sing Happy Birthday. 'I just feel that I am part of a village, in a way that I never was. And I hope – I hope – that it doesn't stop.' But its findings, overwhelmingly, show that we are much better at living in a community than we sometimes believe, says Prof Bobby Duffy, director of the Policy Institute at King's College London, which commissioned the research. Almost two-thirds had offered help to friends, family and neighbours in the previous week. Importantly, stresses Duffy, this is not a new thing. Studies before the pandemic show 'we have got this reservoir of helpful behaviour which is there, but just not very visible. The levels we are seeing now are higher but we have an underlying propensity to [help each other]. The crisis has just given us a way to express that'.
>
> ADDLEY, 2020

There was a re-igniting of love and friendship amongst families and friends. COVID-19 showed communal man the way back to his tribe – from his individual self and self-importance. In New Zealand, children were asked to go for walks – to be part of community once again. COVID-19 has demonstrated that Homo sapiens are social animals, that we are part of society, that we do depend on each other, that we need each other, that without each other we become lonely, anxious, depressed and even suicidal. Margaret Thatcher and her ilk must own the loneliness and the consequences of such loneliness of people in the UK and in all parts of the world where her ideology of "there's no such thing as society" was masqueraded as gospel. If capitalism seeks to continually tear man away from his tribe, then COVID-19 in its own strange way sought to rekindle man's relationship with his fellow-human beings:

> Come Thursday evening when we engage in our weekly demonstration of doorstep solidarity with the NHS, we are, of course, a nation united. Last week, the Office for National Statistics (ONS) revealed it had started measuring the way in which people are adapting to the biggest change to lifestyles in living memory – and its first set of findings were cheering. Three weeks into the lockdown, Britons had developed a newfound neighbourliness: more than half of those surveyed said they had checked

> on their neighbours at least once, while a third had done a task for someone who lived nearby, such as shopping or walking a dog. On a wider level, more than half the population said they felt a sense of belonging to their community, and more than two thirds said they thought people were 'doing more to help others since the coronavirus outbreak'. A similar proportion thought they could rely on community support.
>
> WOODS, 2020

COVID-19 had killed man in more ways than one. But in its own strange way, it also enabled the rebirth of man – so long smothered under the heaviness of capitalist ideologies.

4 The Emergence of Socialist Man: Comrades in the Struggle against COVID-19

The concept of "comrades" is usually associated with socialism and communism in order to scare humankind and keep them locked into the capitalist system. It is a powerful ideological tool in the scare-tactics toolbox of capitalism's praise singers. The challenge going forward is to separate the fake news and ideologies built around socialism and communism over the decades – from that of lived realities. We might decide to make a democratic socialist future, but at least a clearheaded understanding and analysis of socialism and communism – instead of fear – should be the reasons for our choice. In the time of COVID-19 we witnessed that Homo sapiens are comrades by nature – and they would go the extra mile to help their fellow human beings. Ninety-nine-year-old Captain Tom Moore raised 32.8 million pounds for the NHS! He once got excellent service from the NHS and wanted to give something back. People came together to help people – even in the smallest of ways. Neoliberal and capitalist marketeers made us believe that I am only capable of helping myself – each man for himself and apparently god for all. But COVID-19 has demonstrated that Homo sapiens help Homo sapiens – even in the presence of all of the gods that we have created for ourselves. In his passion to help others, my brother embarked on helping by collecting food donations and distributing it to the needy. Many others did the same in many parts of the world:

> Elizabeth Edhodaghe, service manager at Solace Women's Aid, said some people who find sanctuary at their multiple-needs refuge are in 'extreme poverty'. 'The Felix Project is essential for us,' she said. 'We were so happy when we knew they were still going to be delivering during the lockdown

> – it was a big relief. A lot of the women struggle with low self-esteem, but the food donations make them feel that there are people out there who care.' 'I knew that if I didn't get out, I would be dead. My children see me as a different woman, not just a punching bag. There is life after domestic abuse – and it's a good one'.
>
> ROACH, 2020

There were those who believed and executed the "we are in this together" principle. In the US, sailors showed solidarity and comradeship with their ship captain after he was fired for speaking out in the Land of the Free. They shouted out his name when he was forced to vacate his vessel by the US state. In the time of COVID-19, the true leaders of society were revealed – not the politicians who chose neoliberal ideology over pragmatism. Seven thousand retired doctors volunteered to go back to service in Italy – they chose to be comrades in arms in the war against COVID-19. The selfish man that was conceived, shaped and formed by capitalist values and ideas was slowly giving way to socialist man. The ideology of self-interest proved weaker – and little or no match for communal and collective interests in the time of COVID-19. People shared information and advice on social media on staying safe and staying alive. The "selfish man" ideology – so prevalent under capitalism – was challenged where possible. Many volunteered in the US. In the UK, the NHS requested 250,000 volunteers – 450,000 turned up! Capitalist-era man began to shed the ideology of "self only" and transformed into a kind and helpful creature:

> We have seen incredible acts of kindness. People stepping forward to help each other – checking in on people who are lonely or isolating by themselves with no family or friends nearby. In the UK and Italy, over 100,000 people have signed up as Red Cross volunteers, supporting vulnerable people in their communities. Throughout our history we have seen that kindness prevails, even in the gravest of times. Now, we must let kindness be the thread that stitches the fabric of society back together, at home, and throughout the world.
>
> ADAMSON ET AL., 2020

But natural caring and kindness amongst the human race will once again disappear when capitalism is allowed to reappear. States, capitalist economic scientists, big businesses and capitalist praise singers are already planning to build back capitalism. Will an ideologically awakened populace allow it? In the time of COVID-19, some wanted to turn their loss and painful experience into helping others. Here and there – elements of socialist man began to develop:

> For Ernest, that journey has meant becoming the sole carer for two very small children – and, recently, a campaigner for expectant couples. Last week he wrote to the prime minister, urging him to make it a legal requirement for employers to allow all pregnant women who pass 20 weeks gestation to work from home or be suspended on full pay.
>
> TOPPING, 2020

Before COVID-19 struck, we went about our lives believing that we are atomised individuals. COVID-19 helped remove the ideological lens that we were forced to wear for so long in the capitalist epoch.

5 Rediscovering Time, Freedom and Happiness

There's a song called *Cats in the Cradle* by Harry Chapin. It's a song about a busy dad that does not have time for his son – not because he does not love his son, but because capitalism has his time and energy welded to his job and capitalist-imposed pressures, strains and values. Spending time with family and friends is not a capitalist value – unless capitalism can profit from this set-up. The son grows up to be just like his dad – not being able to find the time to spend with his dad in his older age. It is a situation in which hundreds of millions around the world find themselves in – there is not enough time to spend with one's family, friends and community. There is not enough time to pursue that hobby. There is not enough time to attend to health issues. We would all like to "stop and smell the roses", but then who is going to keep working – in order to keep capitalism to keep working? In the time of COVID-19, capitalist notions of time became reimagined during lockdowns – as social media did the rounds with the following postings: "until further notice the days of the week are now called thisday, thatday, otherday, someday, yesterday, today and nextday". Creativity flourishes in Homo sapiens when they are not under the tentacles of capitalism and capitalist-imposed time. But under capitalism – time is money! Why spend an hour with your kid – when an hour spent in the boardroom can earn you $1000 or more? Why spend an hour with your kid – when you can spend that hour as a worker at Amazon and earn about $12? In the time of COVID-19 people had lots of time to think about what is important in their lives – as opposed to not having any time during a capitalist working day. Unfulfilling and mundane work takes up most of people's time – in all parts of the world in the capitalist era. COVID-19 reproduced a time for man, woman and child to contemplate life under capitalism. It was a time for consciousness raising. It was a time to confront the false consciousness of capitalist ideologies. For some, time slowed down. For others, time sped up. But for everybody – time was once again precious:

> Time works differently nowadays; it runs faster now that we are mostly in the 'virtual' world. Our words speak louder than our actions, that sometimes we need to spend more time ensuring that our messages are clearly conveyed. Consider extra time and space in your daily activities; allow yourself to appreciate and be more sensitive with others' time.
>
> ROQUE, 2020

People found time to rediscover new ways of moving about – without the societal burden of feeling inferior in capitalist society:

> With COVID-19 cases surging past the million mark in India, more people are shunning buses and trains to travel on what has traditionally been seen in this status-conscious society as the transport of the poor – the bicycle. Everyone is obsessed with boosting their immunity to ward off the virus and exercise is seen as vital. So while some are commuting on their bikes, others are buying them purely for exercise. More Indians are demanding better cycling infrastructure, and this pressure may grow, given the bike boom. Jyoti Pande Lavakare, an environmental activist in Delhi, hopes the trend can cut pollution long term. Subsidising cycles would be an excellent beginning and schools would be a good place to start. Behavioural changes are the hardest to engineer and habits begin at an early age. The fact that it's becoming aspirational will be useful.
>
> DHILLON, 2020

We learnt in the time of COVID-19 that the state of our mental health is influenced predominantly by our socio-economic, cultural, built and natural environments:

> Early intervention is key, so it is important patients continue to report any concerns to their GPs,' says Professor Marshall. 'We can all help to maintain good mental health throughout the crisis by practising good self-care: staying digitally connected to friends and family, and participating in regular outdoor exercise'. John Read, a professor of clinical psychology, adds: 'Being scared at the moment is normal. It is a social problem, not a mental health one'.
>
> NASH, 2020

Family life – different from that under capitalism – took on meaningful shapes and forms during the pandemic:

> Equally, there are others who are thriving, such as friends whose young son is delighted to have the full attention of both his normally frantic professional parents. And my own mother and father who, four weeks into their house arrest in Italy, seem to be happier than I've seen them in years.
>
> VINE, 2020

For the doctor who treated COVID-19 patients in the UK and witnessed some of them die – all he wanted to do was to spend time in his back garden with his wife and children. Everywhere, there was a new awakening – an awakening from the nightmarish life under capitalism, an odd society predicated on speed and consumerism – as an outlet for perceived happiness:

> Even if all this is for but a brief moment in time, it is a critical moment in human history and its memory will abide. For the first time in our lives, we have been allowed a glimpse of what might happen if the machines of human enterprise grind to a halt. Mr S K Chakraborty, in his article 'Rising technology and falling ethics', wrote, 'The march of modern science and technology derived from it coincided with an era when the human race was beginning to snap its ties of personal-feeling-level relationship with earth and nature. From tool to machine to automation to chip, this progression seems to have made the human race increasingly less human. This has happened due to a thoughtless increase in the speed of development and consumerism. Now the pace has slowed, Nature is being purified, and the individual is spending more time with family and loved ones. The warmth of close relationships and living a life of basic necessities has made people see that life can be lived in a way that is not dominated by consumption'. One of the messages circulating on social media in the time of COVID-19 read, 'When you cannot go outside, go inside.' It brings to mind the essence of Bharatiya thought, 'Not just outwards, travel inwards too'.
>
> Joint General Secretary of the RSS, 2020

Everywhere capitalist-supporting ideologies about the propaganda of the "good life" seemed to be falling apart. The Russian Foreign Minister had this to say:

> The pandemic reminds us that we need to stay humble in the face of disasters. Any country or individual, regardless of their geography, fortunes or political ambitions, is equal. The novel coronavirus crisis rips off all fanciful illusions and superficial things and displays the lasting value of human life.
>
> LAVROV, 2020: 7

Everywhere there seemed to be an ideological awakening – from years of deadening under capitalism:

> If we can make sense of the things and people surrounding us, it should help us figure out how we can adapt, respond and evolve as persons – connecting with simple truths and reality in order for us to thoughtfully respond, hopefully adapt and willingly evolve. We're not home alone. We find comfort knowing that like us, everyone is evolving to becoming a better person. Creativity overflows as we see bankers becoming bakers, marketeers becoming their own plumbers and carpenters, fathers becoming storytellers. The ability to build trust in oneself has been remarkable; we have become willing participants in an environment so new to us and yes, we have displayed our true selves comfortably without fear of judgement. We are designed to ease ourselves into the 'new normal.' There may be some distractions along the way, but hey, we keep moving forward and we stay focused on what really matters.
>
> ROQUE, 2020

For those that lost loved ones in the time of COVID-19, they took the steps forward to draw from the love of those passed on – and to make a better world for their children:

> Out of the maelstrom of grief, Ernest is trying to look to the future. He wants to study again, moving into human rights law. He wants to make his children, and Mary, proud. 'I have to make sure I don't disappoint them,' he says. 'I have to come out stronger. And, you know, show the world that we've lost, but we've not lost hope'.
>
> TOPPING, 2020

In the depths of despair, pain and sorrow – Homo sapiens found hope!

6 Pragmatic, Practical and Common-Sense Man Emerges from the Cobwebs of Capitalist Ideologies

For a brief moment in capitalist history, where people were hungry and homeless – the state did not leave it to the free market – the state provided for its citizens. Where people were unemployed – the state put neoliberal ideologies aside – and ensured that the unemployed would receive a monthly income to take care of basic needs. The state finally transformed into a pragmatic institution – attending to the practical needs of its citizens.

Is it civilised to stick to the habit and ideology of shaking hands when we know that our hands can be a magnet for viruses? Is the handshake a symbol of Western dominance and superiority over other forms of greetings? COVID-19 taught us that we do not have to shake hands to demonstrate our human connections – that there are other ways to bring out the social animal in us when greeting our fellow women and men:

> We've long known that for all its convenience and worth, a handshake was a bobbing petri dish of germs and grime. But the ick factor didn't matter because we relied on the handshake to keep Western civilisation humming along. Now, as the novel coronavirus has put a halt on industry, press the-flesh politicking and team athletics, it has also stopped people from shaking hands. Scientists, most notably, Anthony S. Fauci of the National Institute of Allergy and Infectious Diseases, have taken this opportunity to lobby for the handshake's timely death. Ninety-one years later, we are still swapping germs with abandon and indoctrinating children into our nasty habit as a rite of passage into civilised society. It may be that adults will never be able to quit the handshaking habit. But perhaps children can still be reached with a substitute. Scott offers the namaste posture, where you press your palms together in prayer, which recognises that God is in everyone. 'It's a lovely gesture,' he says. But it's doubtful that those Americans who see face masks as unpatriotic, oppressive and a sign of weakness will cotton to 'namaste,' with its roots in Hinduism and association with yoga culture.
>
> GIVHAN, 2020

Talking about god – whilst many religious organisations stuck to dogma and persisted in following ideological behaviours in the face of an invisible enemy waiting to pounce on social, cultural and religious gatherings, there were instances when various religious bodies set aside their practices of collective worship, transformed into pragmatic functioning and found other ways of worshipping in the time of COVID-19. Religious organisations are powerful socialising agents in society. Religion has undergone many transformations during its history. There were some religious organisations who believed that it was the "Christian thing to do" in terms of staying away from churches, etc. during a global pandemic. The most powerful religious leader in contemporary times took time to remind humankind of the stranglehold of capitalist ideologies on humankind:

> Before the pandemic, Pope Francis said, people 'were rushing through life, greedy for profit, undisturbed by wars and injustices and not hearing the cry of the poor or of our ailing planet. We carried on regardless, thinking we would stay healthy in a world that was sick'.
>
> D'EMILIO, 2020

Pope Francis is a poor man's pope. Religion is to the majority of people what food is to the hungry – the one feeds the mind and the other feeds the stomach. Which reminds one of the saying by Archbishop Dom Helder Camara: "when I feed the poor, they call me a saint, but when I ask why the poor are hungry, they call me a communist". There were instances where religious organisations did not allow blind-faith to expose them to the dangers of COVID-19:

> Some religious organisations – ranging from the Jesuit Institute South Africa to the Claremont mosque in Cape Town – urge their congregants to pray behind closed doors during level three of the lockdown. They say their responsibility is not only to protect and guide the faith of their congregants but also to safeguard their lives. 'And whoever saves one – it is as if he had saved humankind entirely,' says the Holy Qur'an'.
>
> Editor, *Mail & Guardian* , 2020: 18

There were instances where religious organisations did stay on the side of public health science in the time of COVID-19:

> It's been broadcast to us specifically, 'please, don't have any more choirs,' Buford Church of God pastor Joey Grizzle told The Washington Times. His church northeast of Atlanta has been taking precautions for weeks. Its large choir started work on an Easter performance in January, but when the big day came, it couldn't join conductor Bob Tabor on stage.
>
> HOWELL, 2020: 4

In the time of COVID-19, practical and pragmatic man emerged gradually from the cobwebs of dogma and ideologies characterising the capitalist way of life. After US aides were infected with COVID-19, many in the White House decided to wear masks: "common sense has finally prevailed, one senior administration official told Reuters" (*The Straits Times*, 2020).

7 The Great Resignation

The term The Great Resignation "was coined last year by Anthony Klotz, a psychologist and professor of business administration at Texas A&M University in the US" (Glover, 2022). COVID-19 provided millions of workers around the world with a window of opportunity to reassess their weddedness to capitalist forms of work. All these years we were made to believe that it is capitalism that provides people with the free choice of working and working loyally for companies. It is under the banner of such ideologies and fake news that Milton Friedman wrote his books *Capitalism and Freedom* (1962) and *Free to Choose* (1980). But with The Great Resignation we learnt that it is not capitalism but COVID-19 that gave people the opportunity to choose. According to Gill (2022), the Great Resignation is "a global movement of people leaving their jobs because it did not suit their lifestyles or priorities". COVID-19 provided people the world over with "an overwhelming pandemic insight that forced people to rethink their careers and life in general" (Ignacio, 2022).

Work is never a valued activity by workers under capitalism. COVID-19 made this quite obvious with The Great Resignation. But more than 170 years ago, Karl Marx wrote about the alienating and estranged nature of work under capitalism. In the *Economic and Philosophical Manuscripts of 1844*, Marx speaks about labour being "shunned like the plague" in capitalist society:

> First, the fact that labor is external to the worker, i.e., it does not belong to his intrinsic nature; that in his work, therefore, he does not affirm himself but denies himself, does not feel content but unhappy, does not develop freely his physical and mental energy but mortifies his body and ruins his mind. The worker therefore only feels himself outside his work, and in his work feels outside himself. He feels at home when he is not working, and when he is working he does not feel at home. His labor is therefore not voluntary, but coerced; it is forced labor. It is therefore not the satisfaction of a need; it is merely a means to satisfy needs external to it. Its alien character emerges clearly in the fact that as soon as no physical or other

> compulsion exists, labor is shunned like the plague. External labor, labor in which man alienates himself, is a labor of self-sacrifice, of mortification. Lastly, the external character of labor for the worker appears in the fact that it is not his own, but someone else's, that it does not belong to him, that in it he belongs, not to himself, but to another.

COVID-19 and the resultant Great Resignation provide material evidence and data for the thought of Karl Heinrich Marx – The Millennium's Greatest Thinker – regarding the unfulfilling nature of work in capitalist society. COVID-19 and The Great Resignation upended the ideology that work is a matter of free choice and freedom in capitalist society. As the many leaders of capitalist countries who demanded that workers "get back to work" in the midst of a global pandemic – and as Marx reminds us in the *Economic and Philosophical Manuscripts of 1844* – work is indeed forced labour under capitalism!

8 And the People Began to Think Differently

People always had a sense of what happiness is – but capitalist ideologies of self only, consumerism, status, power, more money, competition, etc. continually suppressed the gut instinct for the good life. In a study conducted in 2008:

> When people are asked what pleasures contribute most to happiness, the overwhelming majority rate love, intimacy, and social affiliation above wealth or fame, even above physical health.
>
> CACIOPPO and PATRICK, 2008: 5

I think the poem – *And the People Stayed Home* – written by Kitty O'Meara, 2020 – in the time of COVID-19, succinctly captures a global ideological awakening – an awakening from the collective slumber of capitalist brainwashing over the many centuries:

> And the people stayed home. And read books, and listened, and rested, and exercised, and made art, and played games, and learned new ways of being, and were still. And listened more deeply. Some meditated, some prayed, some danced. Some met their shadows. And the people began to think differently.
>
> And the people healed. And, in the absence of people living in ignorant, dangerous, mindless, and heartless ways, the earth began to heal.

And when the danger passed, and the people joined together again, they grieved their losses, and made new choices, and dreamed new images, and created new ways to live and heal the earth fully, as they had been healed.

CHAPTER 8

State Lobbying and Planning for Building-Back Capitalism

> Indeed, if communist central planners could have organised the economy with as much detail, precision, and flexibility as a modern-day Toyota or Wal-Mart, communism would probably still exist!
>
> JIM STANFORD

> Corporations can't exist without a Nanny-State.
>
> NOAM CHOMSKY

1 The Nanny State and Building-Back Capitalism

COVID-19 provided insights of the abnormality of life under capitalism. After the Command Council in South Africa was compelled to side with the enemy of the people and the enemy of nature, the capitalist economy was once again allowed to function and South African society was forced to go back to abnormal life. I went for my morning walk-jog again. The cars were back on the road speeding and spewing poisonous gasses into the air – which I was forced to share. There was no free choice to breathe clean air under capitalism. I did not have the free choice and liberty to not share the poisonous gasses spewed out by the speeding cars. The bird sounds were absent, and nature seemed to have disappeared once again into the background of daily capitalist life. It seemed nothing had changed in our world – except that millions of people were no longer with their loved ones. We were back to abnormal – violence, killings, hoarding of vaccines, self-interest, individualism, profit at all costs, discrimination against South Africa for identifying the Omicron variant, etc. Capitalist or free market ideologues utilised all available ideologies and fear mongering to appeal to the usually despised state – to ensure the continuation of the capitalist system. The state rescued capitalism from its abysmal failure in 2008.

 DOI:10.1163/9789004539808_009

Capitalists and their sycophants expected the same of the state for the post-COVID-19 building back of capitalism. The keen-eyed were quick to observe the importance and workings of the state in the capitalist economy:

> The dangers are clear. Moves to 're-open' the economy and reinstate regimes of accumulation, perhaps with the addition of government payments to help jump-start flailing demand and secure the liquidity of financial markets, seem inevitable.
>
> HEENAN and STURMAN 2020: 194

Capitalist or free marketeers went all out – aggressively influencing the nanny state to kick-start capitalism in the time of COVID-19. Observations of how the state enables capitalism and the free market to once again function were made in the time of COVID-19:

> Alberta is immediately cutting corporate taxes by 20 per cent and adding more than $1billion in infrastructure spending this year as the province attempts to climb out of the economic wreckage of the COVID-19 pandemic and a collapse in world oil prices.
>
> KELLER ET AL., 2020

The impatience to cynically force the state to act on behalf of the capitalist class was glaringly evident:

> Temporary programmes have a horrible tendency to become the new normal, which is why major shocks usually do more to advance socialism than left-wing election victories or the scribbling of ideologues, as FA Hayek once noted. It is incumbent upon libertarians to help devise workable, politically possible, incremental solutions that allow countries to rediscover economic freedom when a calamity ends.
>
> HEATH, 2020

Capitalism itself is the calamity since its arrival into the world of human affairs as a historical system! Some wanted failing capitalism dressed up in different attire – old wine in new bottles:

> Finally, we've ended the era of economic incrementalism. Slow and slight improvements don't cut it right now; 'as good as' isn't good enough. The times demand systemic solutions greater than what we had before. Greater Capitalism. If Friedmanism worshiped profits above all, this

> Greater Capitalism measures return on investment in all facets. Yes, it incorporates a large dose of the stakeholder economy that has slowly made headway over the past few years. But its roots lie not in big companies but in small businesses and entrepreneurs who ask for little more than a fair chance and a level playing field. If practiced correctly, Greater Capitalism will encourage the kind of smart, long-term, accretive actions that create permanent solutions.
>
> LANE, 2020

Good intentions will be the paving on the road to hell for people and planet if capitalism in whatever form is argued to continue. We have had the greatness of capitalism for many centuries. We have been witnesses to the greatness of capitalism's innovation and productivity – but we have also been witnesses to its great devastation and destruction. We have seen the greater number of deaths in the Western world in general – and in the capitalist countries in particular. Greater Capitalism ultimately leads to Greater Exploitation of both man and nature. There is no greater proof of this – than that of the greater changing climate in the time of capitalism's reign. In the time of COVID-19, the praise singers of capitalism did not leave it to the invisible hand, also known as the free market, to lead society to an apparent harmonious and happy future – they demanded state interference in the economy. In country after country, loud capitalist voices were demanding that nanny states kick-start the capitalist economy:

> There's no getting around the fact that any further approach to the IMF will come when we are in a most desperate position and to emerge from it will not be easy. It will require political resolve and a clear focus on structural reforms of SOE's, energy policy reform and labour law changes.
>
> MAVUSO, 2020: 19

By energy policy reforms, the writer actually means using the state's power to allow for greater exploitation of nature's energy. By labour law changes, the writer actually means using state power to devise and implement policies that would allow for the greater exploitation of labour. Even the usually critical component of capitalist society – academia – heavily encouraged the consolidation and continuation of capitalism – the much-loved system:

> The academia has called for active collaboration with free market practitioners to stimulate in-depth discussions on issues that would spur market development.
>
> OJI, 2020

Keenly recognising that society was at a key moment in history – whereby it could consciously choose a preferred economic system for a post-COVID-19 world – capitalism was opportunistically presented as the only socio-economic system known and available to humans: "we're at that same crossroads right now: Toward a Greater Capitalism, or a continued societal fraying, and the sobering alternative that this would all be for naught" (Lane, 2020). Good thing history documents the existence of the hunter-gatherer society, slave society and feudal society. Otherwise praise singers of capitalism would have us believe that in the beginning was only capitalism – and therefore the end should be capitalism! History teaches us that other worlds are possible. All the decades of hearing neoliberal advocates peddle the lie that states are most effective when they stay out of the economy had the effect of such ideology being absorbed by layers of society as fact, truth and gospel. COVID-19 upended ideological heaviness – and exposed the intimate and inextricable link between the nanny state and the free market economy ruled by profit. In many parts of the world, huge appeals were made for the nanny state to once again immerse itself fully in the affairs of the free market economy:

> The government must also undertake reforms to address the longer-term trends undermining growth, including rapid population ageing, structural imbalances and inefficiencies, and slow productivity growth, especially in the services sector. To address its shrinking labour force, South Korea needs reforms to improve labour-market flexibility, strengthen competition, encourage female employment (including through expanded childcare), and deliver life-long education and skills training. To reduce dependence on exports, the government should create a more supportive environment for high-value-added services industries. It should also improve conditions for private investment and research and development.
>
> JONG-WHA, 2020

It is clear that capitalist ideologies bring out the worst in humankind. Homo sapiens – the intelligent species – is relegated to choosing from a list of evil alternatives. *The Economic Times* contained writings with headings such as: "but capitalism is a lesser evil" (Haldar, 2020). That capitalism is among the set of evil choices should be sufficient reason to abandon the system as quickly as possible. We can imagine and create a healthier and happier economic system for humans and the planet. Nowhere in the world did COVID-19 expose the brutality of capitalism – as it did in Mother India. Nowhere in the world did capitalism expose its true and ruthless nature – as it did in Mother India in the time of COVID-19. But capitalism seemingly has to reinvent itself – by whatever means necessary. Planning – especially with the powerful state by its side – is a necessary and fundamental tool in capitalism's arsenal:

> In a world that needs substantial reorienting of production and distribution, Indian capital is resorting to a militant form of moribund neoliberalism to overcome its current crisis. In this pursuit of profit, it is ready and willing to throw into mortal peril millions whom it adjudicates as not worth their means – an admixture of social Darwinism born of capital's avarice and brutalism spawned by Hindutva. The pandemic and the ensuing lockdown has vitiated the conditions of reproduction of capital as a whole. For large capital this has meant that its productive capacity lies idle in the absence of its lifeblood, labour. Capital erodes each day as it is unable to pay for itself or to accumulate for the future. Meanwhile, the future course of the economy becomes ever more uncertain. Each day of economic activity foregone is then both a tangible loss of wealth and a source of great uncertainty, both of which pose an existential threat to capital. Capital confronts the imperative need to restart production immediately and in earnest; but with the daunting, if not impossible, task of rationally planning business in a situation of both deteriorating profitability and historically unprecedented uncertainty. Indian capital is starkly different, especially in the way it has encountered this crisis and intends to tackle it. Almost instinctively, its attempts to mitigate the twin threats of deteriorating profitability and proliferating uncertainty rest on imposing its costs on public ownership, small capital, and labour. Another facet of capital's response relates to its desire to expand operations into profitable avenues that have hitherto been dominated by small or publicly owned capital, such as agricultural supply chains, coal mining, defence equipment, India's space programme, among others. Quite apart from their strategic importance, in itself of significance, these sectors have for long been gainful employers and an important source of revenue for the government. The implication of this expansion of operation of large capital would be a redistribution of wealth away from small capital and public sector undertakings to large corporations.
>
> DEEPAK, 2020

All around the world, the relevance of the nanny state in aiding and abetting capitalism's recovery was made visible and evident in the time of COVID-19. A virus from nature had the effect of peeling off layers of neoliberal ideologies – about the lie of an 'invisible hand' and a passive state in capitalist society. Capitalism has both a passive and an active affair with the state:

> The guiding principle for reform is 'to get Australians back into jobs'. The goals are jobs, investment and growth. Being realistic, item-by-item deals are the best Morrison can hope for. Forget any grand bargain, that's impossible. This crisis poses an immense challenge for the left of politics, notably labour and the unions. What is their role? For a decade they have offered a rigid ideological agenda – no industrial relations reform to create more jobs, greater union statutory power, hefty increases in government spending and higher taxes on virtually every asset class.
>
> KELLY, 2020

Long before COVID-19, the rigid political agenda of the right has been to set-up the state in such a way that it serves the interests of big capital for profit maximisation and capital accumulation. Even when Ronald Reagan and Margaret Thatcher were peddling lies about capitalism's non-dependence on the state, there were those who were able to break through the layers of free market ideologies and reveal the necessity and integral role of the state in the life of capitalism:

> While in Germany we see public indignation when a colliery shuts down one mine or another, year in and year out the management of the American trust determines with great equanimity which enterprises are to be worked and which left idle. In this way capitalism readily creates the economic organisation after its own image: this is shown in location of industry, structure of individual businesses, size and shape of factories, organisation of trade and commerce, and in co-ordination between production and marketing of goods. When one knows that everything has been deliberately made for a rational purpose, one is obliged to conclude from this that everything has been deliberately made to suit capitalist interests.
>
> SOMBART, 1976 [1906]: 5

Just like it required the powerful might of the state to do away with feudalism, embark on colonial conquests and utilise violence and murder to set itself up as a historical system – capitalism once again required the assistance and power of the nanny state to resuscitate the capitalist economy post-COVID-19.

2 State Lobbying and Planning for the Extensive and Intensive Exploitation of Nature

Capitalism is dependent on two fundamental destructive conditions and contradictions for its existence and continuation. The first destructive condition and contradiction of capitalism is the exploitation of the natural environment. This takes place mostly in the developing world – paradises of natural resources. A major part of the history of capitalism has to do with the exploitation and destruction of natural resources. There is no clearer evidence of this exploitation and destruction than that of climate change. Building back capitalism post-COVID-19 therefore means that all laws, rules and regulations seeking to protect the natural environment must be drastically eased, waivered or set aside. Capitalism's nanny state was dependent upon to do its dirty dealings for it. The evidence of this happening was clear in the time of COVID-19. In Australia:

> The environment minister, Sussan Ley, has flagged the government may change Australia's national environment laws before a review is finished later this year. It follows business groups and the government emphasising the need to cut red tape as part of the economic recovery from the coronavirus crisis, and comes as the businessperson Graeme Samuel chairs an independent statutory review of the Environment Protection and Biodiversity Conservation (EPBC) Act. An interim report is due in June, followed by a final report in October.
>
> COX, 2020: 5

Besides access to the natural environment, the resuscitation of capitalism cannot take place without access to cheap forms of abundant energy as well. This also cannot take place without a willing and able nanny state:

> There will be an emphasis on manufacturing with two dominant themes – cheaper energy to boost competitiveness and a more sophisticated agenda for advanced manufacturing relying on research and innovation. Infrastructure will be centre stage. Expect the commission headed by Power to produce ideas on this front.
>
> KELLY, 2020

In the UK:

> Anna McMorrin, Labour's shadow international development minister who is responsible for climate justice, told The Independent: 'There's a lot of rhetoric to end fossil fuels, but within that there are exemptions and loopholes, which means that the government will continue to funnel a vast amount of UK taxpayer money into fossil fuel projects overseas. It would be unacceptable in any year, but in a year where the government is talking up its climate ambitions and hosting Cop26, it shows staggering hypocrisy'.
>
> DUNNE, 2021

In the US:

> A new report from the US based Rainforest Action Network says two of them – Keystone XL and Enbridge Inc.'s Line 3 pipeline – are being 'rammed through' in the final weeks of Donald Trump's presidency. The report points to a long list of prominent international banks it says are lined up to back the projects as evidence they are far from dead.
>
> MCCARTEN, 2020

Nature is the fundamental requirement for the production of commodities. *In Capital* (1867: 30), Marx reminds us of the fundamental role of nature in the production of the commodity:

> If we take away the useful labour expended upon them, a material substratum is always left, which is furnished by Nature without the help of man.

In a system that not only produces use-value but survives primarily on exchange-value, capitalism requires unmitigated and unregulated access to the natural world. With COVID-19 having decimated the capitalist economy, the nanny state was once again heavily lobbied by the capitalist class and its praise singers – to make the exploitation of nature that much easier for the recovery of the failing and ailing capitalist system. The exploitation and destruction of all aspects and forms of nature is one of the pillars upholding the capitalist system. It is why planet earth has been most destroyed in the capitalist age – and hardly ever in the eras of slavery and feudalism. Our ancestors – the hunter-gatherers – lived in harmony with nature – not us intelligent apes under capitalism!

3 State Lobbying and Planning for the Extensive and Intensive Exploitation of Labour

The second fundamental destructive condition and contradiction for capitalism's existence and continuation is the exploitation of labour. This too is aided and abetted by a willing and able nanny state. In the UK, word got out about the plan to roll-back workers' rights since COVID-19 put capitalism on a ventilator:

> Take the issue of workers' rights. Last week the Financial Times reported that they were at risk, with the government considering plans to tear up the EU's labour market rules.
>
> MOORE, 2021

In Indonesia:

> Parliament rushed to pass into law the controversial Omnibus bill on job creation, which government officials say will lure more investments to the country, but protestors argue will promote a 'contemporary form of slavery'. Activists slammed the Job Creation Law (JCL), reasoning that it would trigger job insecurity and deny workers their rights as guaranteed under the 2003 Manpower Law.
>
> PUSPASARI, 2020

In fact, capital and the state were already planning capitalism's build-back, even when the priority was thought to be saving lives in the time of COVID-19:

> The first order of business has been an immediate resumption of production while mitigating any threat to profitability that may arise from labour's bargaining power. In pursuit of this rash adventure, it seeks a complete dismantling of labour laws, which, in effect, will give legal sanctity to suppression of wages, lengthening of the workday, and dramatic curtailing of 'overhead' costs that would have in the current situation provided for workplace safety for workers. The aversion of capital to labour laws is not because they radically affect profitability of capital as such; they barely cover less than a tenth of all workers. Capital's aggressive attempt reflects its desire to snuff out the last whiff of challenge from organised labour that its own vulnerability may have offered labour at this time. This effort to dismantle the last vestiges of formal protection offered to labour, existent only in statutes stacked away in dusty piles in

> government offices, long forgotten by the factory owner and the inspector alike, is essentially a struggle between capital and labour over garnering a larger share in surplus. However, this struggle is paraded, through quackery of hired pens, as measures to tackle 'inefficiencies'. These 'reforms' may in the first instance increase profitability of capital, and that perhaps is its dominant motive. However, while these costs are determined ex-post, their suppression will shift the uncertainty of realisation of profit by capital to wage earners.
>
> DEEPAK, 2020

In the Land of Miracles for the rich – South Africa:

> As the Covid-19 pandemic continues its assault, there is a desire by some to return to a business-as usual, shareholder-first model, but business as usual led us here. Covid-19 sounds a warning bell when this shareholder philosophy infiltrates a sector as crucial as health care. Over the past four years Netcare, Life Healthcare and Mediclinic, the country's three largest private health-care providers with a market share of about 80%, paid out more to shareholders than they made in profits. These payouts amounted to an average of R92m a week and R19bn in four years. During this period health-care workers have suffered increased job insecurity as more nurses are stripped of security, benefits such as medical aid, a minimum number of guaranteed hours, and are outsourced to labour brokers under more precarious working conditions during the pandemic.
>
> BALOYI ET AL., 2020

In capitalist and chaotic India:

> To enable companies to kick-start production, several state governments have announced relaxations in labour and employment laws. These changes are in two broad categories. First, exemptions from provisions of labour laws (Uttar Pradesh, Madhya Pradesh and Gujarat). Second, extension of working hours under the Factories Act, 1948 (Assam, Goa, Himachal Pradesh, Haryana, Odisha, Maharashtra, Uttarakhand and Punjab). Though some of these changes are being reviewed, state governments say flexibility in labour laws will help companies revive production with limited staff and encourage them to invest.
>
> KHETARPAL, 2020

In *Capital* (1867: 179) Marx states:

> Capital is dead labour, that, vampire-like, only lives by sucking living labour, and lives the more, the more labour it sucks. The time during which the labourer works, is the time during which the capitalist consumes the labour-power he has purchased of him.

With COVID-19 putting the capitalist system on pause, the state was subsequently petitioned to make it easy for the capitalist labour market to exploit the labour power or human energy of workers. If freedom to exploit nature is the first condition for the existence and continuation of the capitalist system, then freedom to exploit labour is its second condition. Capitalism devours nature so as to live. Capitalism also – as Marx reminds us – "only lives by sucking living labour, and lives the more, the more labour it sucks".

4 Capitalism – Like Communism or Democratic Socialism – Is a Planned Economy

States in all parts of the world try to manage the economy through a suite of financial tools. It is what the Federal Reserve Bank does in the US. When the US slaps economic sanctions on other countries, its overall plan is to demonstrate hegemony and power over other nations and their economies. Communism was based on a state planned economy in the USSR. The failure of communism also meant – by association – the failure of state planning of the Soviet Union economy. Since the fall of the USSR any talk of a planned economy is viewed as communist ideology and delving in utopianism. When one brings up the topic of planning the economy, the bootlickers of capitalism bring out the bogeyman – the collapse of the Soviet Union and communism. Even in the crucial area of preserving nature from capitalist exploitation – any talk of state planning invoked is castigated as that of communism:

> How could governments heavily regulate, tax, and penalise fossil fuel companies when all such measures were being dismissed as relics of 'command and control' communism?
>
> KLEIN, 2014: 25

Ideologues of capitalism should be taken seriously about the taboos of state planning in and of the economy – but only if capitalism itself did not depend on meticulous planning and execution. After all, Barack Obama called the captains of industry to White House meetings in 2008 – to plan and execute for the continuation and consolidation of capitalism during the Great Crisis of

2008. These were not democratically-elected men – yet they were given tremendous powers to decide the fate of the American people and the peoples of the world! These were the same unelected men who wrecked the economy in the first place through their neoliberal planning! A planned economy is put forward as something akin to a deadly virus by the cheerleaders and spokespersons of neoliberal capitalism. But the world had witnessed how deadly a virus can be – in the absence of a planned economy – left to the vices of the profit market. The neoliberal order is held in place by states favouring capitalism. It is why the West continues to have ideologues with similar thinking to Ronald Reagan, Margaret Thatcher, Donald Trump and Boris Johnson voted into the highest echelons of power. The profit market is supported and held in place by the capitalist state. It is why the struggling middle-classes and the impoverished working classes are impelled to pay taxes proportionate to their incomes. It is why the rich are allowed to pay taxes painfully disproportionate to their income:

> Amazon founder Jeff Bezos paid no income tax in 2007 and 2011. Tesla founder Elon Musk's income tax bill was zero in 2018. And financier George Soros went three straight years without paying federal income tax, according to a report yesterday from the nonprofit investigative journalism organisation ProPublica.
>
> *The Southland Times*, 2021

It is painful for the paying man and woman to be witnesses to such hypocrisy and double standards – but such is the innate nature of capitalism. The state and the free market are not independent isolated entities acting in and of their own accord – and towards opposing goals. They act in concert and in the interests of each other. They support each other. They uphold each other's elevated positions in capitalist society. When the profit market is weakened – through its own doing – a strong state is advocated for – to prop up the ailing and failing free market. In India for example, the state is called upon to strengthen the capitalist free market:

> India's aspiration to become a $5 trillion economy depends critically on strengthening the invisible hand of markets together with the hand of trust that can support markets, according to the Economic Survey 2019–20, authored by Subramanian. The invisible hand needs to be strengthened by promoting pro-business policies to provide equal opportunities for new entrants, enable fair competition and ease doing business, eliminate policies that undermine markets through government intervention even where it is not necessary, it said.
>
> *Millennium Post*, 2020

If the hand of the state in the capitalist economy had been made invisible through decades of ideological overload, then it was made glaringly clear in the time of COVID-19:

> Context and circumstance is critical for policy. In the developed economies – in the European Union and in the United States – central banks are extending and expanding credit. The objectives – to save jobs, protect capital, preserve capacities and promote growth – hold true for India too. The visible hand of the government must invest and fund programmes to enable the invisible hands of enterprise to propel the virtuous cycle of growth.
>
> AIYAR, 2020

China's economy is planned by the state. So are the US's and the UK's economies. In China's economic planning model, the economy has been able to move China from an undeveloped country to a super-power in a matter of decades. In the US's and UK's economic planning model, the economy continues to generate vastly wealthy individuals, struggling middle and working classes – and a plethora of social ills. China's economic planning model is based on the thought of Karl Marx. The US's and UK's planning models are based on the teachings of Adam Smith, Milton Friedman, Ayn Rand, and other capitalist marketeers. If democracy is the seal of civilisation in general – and of Western civilisation in particular – then should not a post-COVID-19 world comprise an economy that is democratically planned? Should not a democratic referendum decide whether there should be full employment in the economy – like was done and accomplished by Franklin Delano Roosevelt? Should not a democratic referendum decide whether the Amazon forest be turned into an industrial zone or be left in its pristine form? Should people in general and workers in particular not plan for participatory democracy in their respective political wards and workplaces? Should not a post-COVID-19 society democratically agree and plan for wealth to be justly and fairly distributed among all who make it? Should not a democratic referendum by people in all countries decide whether fossil fuels should be the energy feedstock for society's functioning – instead of leaving this life and death decision to elites who have attended 26 COP international conferences thus far and the planet is still burning? Should not a democratic referendum in the US decide whether guns should be banned – instead of leaving this decision to an outdated rule in the constitution?

It makes sense to plan one's day, one's week, one's holiday, etc. It makes sense to embark on family planning. It makes sense to plan for one's career. It makes sense to plan for a future that is not characterised by continued fossil-fuels usage, mass shootings in the US and elsewhere, constant anxieties and fears of unemployment, debt and poverty, etc. It makes sense to plan for the next pandemic that may arrive. It makes sense to democratically plan and make a better world – than the one we currently inhabit. As an intelligent species, we possess the experiences, capacities and resources to plan and make the best of all possible worlds! We could start by achieving global consensus that capitalism is a failed system for all of humanity and the natural environment – and that it should be eradicated within the shortest and earliest possible time-frame in the 21st century. People in all parts of the world should work towards ending capitalism – a remarkably productive but a remarkably destructive system as well!

CHAPTER 9

Talk of a New World Order in the Time of COVID-19

> No society can surely be flourishing and happy, of which the far greater part of the members are poor and miserable.
>
> ADAM SMITH

•••

> Then the world will be for the common people, and the sounds of happiness will reach the deepest springs. Ah! Come! People of every land, how can you not be roused.
>
> KARL MARX

1 Talk of a New World Order

Whilst in the West in general, and in capitalist countries in particular, capitalism was hastily being resuscitated by the powerful and elite in capitalist society, many in all corners of the globe thought and spoke about a new world order post-COVID-19. It seems that they have had enough of capitalism. They have spoken in all parts of the world. There are those who want the abhorrent capitalist system to remain – and there are those who want a new world order. There are those who want to merely reform capitalism – and then there are those who want to completely get rid of capitalism. In Russia the following sentiment was expressed by the Foreign Minister:

> It's time to give up conventional thinking based on stereotypes and finally start acting from a moral perspective. After all, our best bet is a happy future for all who live on Earth, our common home. The pandemic has once again debunked the long-held myth in the West about the 'end of history,' an all-powerful model of hyper-liberal development, based on the principles of individualism, and a firm belief in the ability to solve all problems through the market alone.
>
> LAVROV, 2020: 7

 DOI:10.1163/9789004539808_010

In India, media carried headlines such as: "Bharat can help shape a new world order" (*The New Indian Express*, 2020). Based on what was happening in India, voices called for an end to the existing world order that produces and reproduces the poor, the vulnerable and the destitute:

> These masses of workers left Delhi. These migrant workers did not suddenly fall from the sky. They have existed on the peripheries of the cities, in the ghettos and the slums; they are deliberately kept invisible and unnoticed by the elite. A hasty show of compassion for them as they form long lines on the roads that leave the cities is not enough; the system that uses them, keeps them barely alive, and then throws them out must be struggled against, another system put in its place. The hideousness of social inequality produces a heap of sorrow and anger amongst the damned of the earth.
>
> YADAV, 2020

In Italy, Giuseppe Conte, the Italian prime minister stated: "it's an opportunity for us to design a better Italy" (*Gulf News*, 2020). In South Africa the following were the headlines among the many others: "this is the moment that we need to awaken and demand an alternative future" (Jonas, 2020: 19). The minister of public enterprises in South Africa, Pravin Gordhan, argued for the humanising of the free market – and for the state to take a more central role in distributing the good life to all:

> The restructuring and reform programme for the SOEs is pragmatic and devoid of any ideological fundamentalism. It has been proven time and time again that the free market system is not a panacea for resolving economic and institutional challenges. Much of the world has moved on and new, more equitable options, are being sought to the chronic challenges of inequality, poverty and jobs. In moments of crisis, well-run SOEs are important for economic growth and contribute to the prosperity of countries. States are playing an important role in nurturing innovation capabilities for the benefit of the people and states.
>
> GORDHAN, 2021

In Australia, Greens leader, Adam Bandt, argued for the state to lead society to a post-COVID-19 world:

> The government should spend big on the infrastructure and services we need to address the jobs crisis, the economic crisis and the climate crisis.

> We need government-led investment in renewable energy, manufacturing, public housing and public transport, as well as expanding the education and training system needed to skill up the workforce.
>
> FARRER, 2020

In the US, where the ideology of the state being a problem is as strong as citizens' views on the second amendment and religion, voices sought to chip away at the myth of little or no state involvement – towards ensuring the good life for all:

> Government is not and cannot be the only solution, but competent government can be part of that solution. A government that believes in its ability to address society's problems has a chance to be successful compared to one that believes that government is the problem.
>
> MCKINNEY, 2021

But for those who benefit tremendously from how the world currently functions, they will use all their power, might and capitalist ideologies to ensure that the status quo remains – that capitalism remains – that free markets favouring profit and not people and planet – rule. Those who wish to exit the current make-up of the world – to some imagined socialism, communism, eco-socialism, post-capitalism, etc. – have a long and hard battle to fight on all fronts. People who come to mind that wish for the status quo to remain are the Republicans in the US – many of whom are still in the White House, the Tories in the UK, the BJP in India and the Royal Family in Saudi Arabia. There are many others like them – big businesses and economic scientists included – who wish for the status quo to remain. But there are many who wish for capitalism to be abolished. People and organisations with a view toward creating a socialist world that come to mind are: Bernie Sanders, Jeremy Corbyn and Antifa – the 'organisation' that the right in the US accused of hijacking the Black Lives Matter movement in the time of COVID-19. Then, there are people like myself who wish to see the end of capitalism. And there are many millions of others who are intent on making a socialist, communist or a democratic socialist world. COVID-19 has provided a window of opportunity to transform the current make-up of the world to imagined futures. Appeals were made for states – by a former head of state – to set aside ideology and continue with supporting the elderly and creating environmental jobs for the youth post-COVID-19:

> But the part-holiday from standard party politics won't last. Once battle resumes, for the center right there should be less dogma about the size of government and more of an appeal to the strength of our country and the quality of its citizens. While subsidies to business can be readily enough withdrawn, personal benefits such as the double-dole will be harder, especially when recipients will be able to say it was government policy that threw them out of work. Instead of just withdrawing the payment – on the grounds the immediate crisis has passed and it's no longer affordable – I'd be inclined to turn it into a wage subsidy for older people and a part time environmental job with local government for younger people.
>
> ABBOTT, 2020

A call was made for political leaders to move beyond just caring for the economy – to caring directly for the people:

> I'd make it about improving society rather than about improving the budget. Eventually, the budget will improve because people will earn their pay (and won't need subsidies) and people will choose their job (and won't just stay where they were allocated). But the successful political leaders will be those who make it less about economics and more about ensuring people have purpose in their lives.
>
> ABBOTT, 2020

The former head of state acknowledges the importance of a strong and vibrant economy. But more than that, he appeals for the economy to serve the needs of the people – and not for the people to be the servants of the economy, as is the case with the capitalist economy:

> It's true that governments can't give to some what they don't get from others, hence the need to be prudent and frugal. But it's a moral vision of self-reliant individuals and cohesive communities that will win the political argument, not a Scrooge-like concern over dollars and cents. Of course, you can't have healthy communities without a strong economy to sustain them, but economics is a means to that goal of human flourishing, not an end in itself. It's the strength of our commitment to those communities and to the society they make up that will be the key to political success in the new world ahead. To adapt Bill Clinton, it's society, stupid!.
>
> ABBOTT, 2020

There were those who envisioned a new way of working in a post-COVID-19 world:

> He [Stephen Rue] believed the post-coronavirus world would see many more people choosing to work from home consistently, which would enhance diversity and inclusion in the workplace by increasing the availability of flexible working arrangements.
>
> KITNEY, 2020

It seems that if we are going to be successful in democratically planning a post-COVID-19 world, then ideologies that are prevalent under capitalism must be abandoned. This is the view of one writer:

> Three principles govern the Morrison-Frydenberg approach. First, an open mind and 'fresh eyes' on the agenda – this is fundamental. Returning to the Coalition's pre-crisis ideological nostrums won't work.
>
> KELLY, 2020

Voices were calling for a new way of distributing value, a new way of expending our labour and a new economy:

> At present the purpose of all of this labour, essential or otherwise, is to create surplus value, and resulting profit for the capitalist class. Any account of a post-COVID-19 economic recovery must deal with the centrality of the surplus extraction for the capitalist class, and the ways they are compelled to restructure the economy in light of the crisis. This private investment, which seeks as its ultimate aim not the satisfaction of needs or social good, but profit, directs what kind of labour we engage in, the conditions we do it under, and the resulting products.
>
> HEENAN and STURMAN 2020: 195

The authors continue:

> A new labour ecology is not only about the conditions determining labour but how we direct our collective labour to provide what is necessary for a good life. COVID-19 has reemphasised the fatal weaknesses in delivering access to food, shelter and other basic goods and services via the invisible hand of the market. In volume three of Capital, Marx distinguished between the 'realm of necessity' and the 'realm of freedom' to argue that only by satisfying our basic needs through democratic and collective production, could we have access to more time for 'what we will', and therefore true human flourishing. How do we replace the cold logic of the market with collective provisioning, the commoning of spaces and

> activities for core social reproduction, and coordinated planning of production, as determined by what is socially necessary?
>
> HEENAN and STURMAN, 2020: 197–198

Headlines crying out for an alternate to capitalism were plentiful in the time of COVID-19: "A return to socialist approach is needed" (*The Chronicle*, 2020). In New Zealand, negative sentiments on the free market economy were articulated: "Famously, during the 2017 election campaign Jacinda Ardern agreed neoliberalism 'had failed' and suggested New Zealand was better served with an interventionist government" (Dickson, 2020). Twaij (2020) states that the: "Coronavirus has presented us with a prime opportunity to start anew and implement positive, progressive change for society – a clean slate if you will … we must take this rare opportunity to redefine how we live and promote greater equality." In the UK, the all-party parliamentary group (APPG) on loneliness called for:

> More public toilets, better street lighting, ramps and quiet safe spaces, so that everyone from all ages and all backgrounds has the facilities they need to make valuable friendships in their area.
>
> CAMPBELL, 2021

There was talk about finally taxing the rich – people who have loads of monies to pay their fair share of tax:

> The Biden administration is planning a sweeping overhaul of the US tax system to make wealthier individuals and big companies pay more in tax, tackling inequality and helping to foot the bill for the president's economic agenda.
>
> PARTINGTON, 2021

Twaij (2020) states that:

> In the same way that the Black Death helped end the feudal system and redistribute wealth, coronavirus has given us the potential to once more have a 'great leveller' in our society.

If the Black Death was the bridge from feudalism to capitalism – then COVID-19 may just be the bridge to a post-capitalist world.

2 COVID-19: The Bridge to a Post-capitalist World

COVID-19 has exposed the many weaknesses and fault lines of our world under the iron-fist of capitalism. We deserve better as a human race. All other species and creatures that are continually at the mercy of capitalism deserve better. The climate deserves better. The rhinos in South Africa deserve better. The oceans deserve better. Rainforests like the Amazon deserve better. Indigenous peoples together with their lands deserve better. The planet deserves better. Our children deserve better. The future generations deserve better. The democratic planning of a world alternate to capitalism can only truly come about when people in all parts of the world are factually aware of the ways that capitalism really functions. The democratic planning of a world alternate to capitalism can only truly come about when people in all parts of the world are no longer under the spell of capitalist ideologies. To imagine a democratic socialist future may seem utopic, but what COVID-19 has revealed is that living under capitalism is hell for the vast majority of humankind. Ask the many doctors, nurses and other frontline workers living in capitalist countries about their experiences in the time of COVID-19. Ask the millions of workers who were left unemployed and fearful of their future and their children's future – because only a minority own the means of production in capitalist society. Ask the tens of millions of migrant workers who were left stranded to walk back to their villages in India. Ask the millions of people who lost loved ones to a virus that was allowed free rein to infect and kill in a world saturated with money, resources, life-saving technologies and boundless amounts of knowledge and science. If thinking that humanity will come out the other end of COVID-19 much stronger is utopian thinking – then we must be utopic in our thinking. If thinking that all wars will one day be a thing of the past – then we must be utopian in our thinking. If thinking that we can plan and create the best of all possible worlds is utopian thinking – then we must be utopian in our thinking. We in South Africa may not yet be living in our hoped-for-paradise, heaven, or utopia since 1994, but we are surely not living in an evil and a crime-against-humanity system – as was the case under apartheid. The Jews may not be living peacefully in their dreamland in Israel, but they are surely not hated and dying in concentration camps – as was the case in Germany under the evil of Adolf Hitler. The Palestinians believe that they live in an apartheid state – but just like South Africans that finally overcame the evils of apartheid – they too must be enabled and supported to overcome the evil apartheid system that imprisons them so that they too can seek their utopia. Capitalist society must surely be utopia – when compared to feudal society – and feudal society must surely be utopia when compared to slave society. But COVID-19 has revealed that if this is the way capitalism functions, then it is time we imagine, forge, shape and democratically make and construct a truly utopian society. COVID-19 has demonstrated why it is time to untangle and free ourselves of capitalist ideologies – which have kept and continue to keep so many billions in servitude and in subjection to the god of profit. COVID-19 has shown that it cannot be business as usual – whereby the capitalist economy is master of all the meek and the subservient – but a safe and secure provider for the rich and powerful. The world and its people's survival must no longer be premised on Darwinian style competition viz. only the fittest survives! If anything, we have seen that survival depends on cooperation and collaboration – and not on outright ruthless competition. Competition can be left to the sporting field – and to democratic elections in both public as well as workplaces. In all other matters of human affairs – especially in the life and death spheres of health and economics – cooperation and collaboration should be the fundamental guiding principles and societal values shaping a post-COVID-19 world. The problem with capitalism is that our lives and livelihoods are in the hands of calculating investors and career politicians. COVID-19 has shown that workers in all countries were worse affected – compared to moneyed people. Any socio-economic system is supposed to protect people – no matter the threats – whether the threats be fires, floods, wars, pandemics, etc. We were all witnesses to the fact that the capitalist economy has a life of its own – independent of the lives of people. The logic of profit dominated – no matter the practical challenges which confronted humankind. Imagining, recreating the future and transitioning away from the current world disorder requires an integrated and holistic approach. It requires, first of all, the acknowledgement that capitalism is a failed system for humankind and the natural environment. Our present, our future and our children's future require the democratic planning and making of the best of all possible worlds. To leave the future to an "invisible hand" – or a minority capitalist class to plan and implement – is to lead us on the road to the end of the world. Climate change is showing us how we are doing so on a daily basis under capitalism. It is time for humanity to go on the search for REAL FREEDOM! COVID-19 has provided the data – albeit through painful means – for humankind to imagine, plan and create a new world order. WE HUMANS have made capitalism. WE HUMANS can unmake capitalism and remake a better world suitable for all of humanity and the planet!

CHAPTER 10

Democratically Planning a New World Order

> The measure of the restoration lies in the extent to which we apply social values more noble than mere monetary profit.
>
> FRANKLIN D. ROOSEVELT

•••

> Nothing is as powerful as an idea whose time has come.
>
> VICTOR HUGO

1 Exploring Ideas and Spheres of Influence for a Post-capitalist World

Ideas and ideologies are an inextricable part of human history. As humankind continues its historical march toward a post-capitalist society, it is heavy with the ideas of the old society – and burdened with the responsibility of creating ideas for a new society. Which ideas do we leave behind and which ideas do we carry with us into a post-capitalist world? Is co-operation amongst peoples and countries a better idea than outright and ruthless competition – like we have seen with vaccine apartheid? What about ideas and values of inclusivity and equality – instead of exclusion and large-scale inequality? Is unity a better idea than divisiveness? Instead of the idea of blind economic growth, how about the ideas of growth in employment, growth in housing for the homeless, growth in literacy levels, growth in healthy people, growth in the number of hospitals, growth in the number of places and spaces for children to play, growth in the number of green spaces, growth in the number of vaccine manufacturing plants, growth in wind farms in the oceans, growth in solar power farms in the oceans, growth in selflessness, growth in kindness, growth in family and community time, growth in accountability, growth in transparency – especially where public funds are concerned, growth in democratic functioning in both the public and the private spheres, growth in equality, growth in peace, growth in tolerance, etc.? Homo sapiens create history. Homo sapiens

 | DOI:10.1163/9789004539808_011

create socio-economic and political life too. Homo sapiens create things and markets for such things. COVID-19 has thrown up immense pain and suffering. COVID-19 has also thrown up ideas in so many spheres of life and living. Ideas are real. Ideas are contested. Ideas are born. Ideas are what are required for making a new world – a world different to that of capitalism:

> In other words, ideas and ideologies count in history. They enable us to imagine new worlds and different types of society. Many paths are possible.
>
> PIKETTY, 2020: 7

In imagining and dreaming up new ideas for a new society and a new human being, we also have to dispense with the old ideas that have caused the planet and its people to travel on a destructive journey for so long. We have to undo the colossal damage done by the ideas and ideologies of the Milton Friedmans, the Ludwig von Mises, the Ayn Rands, The Friedrich von Hayeks, the Margaret Thatchers, the Ronald Reagans, etc. of the world and the fanatical and ardent followers of such scholars and leaders. In the main, we have to cull their ideas and ideologies from our social, economic, cultural, political and natural lives. These ideas and ideologies – just like the ideas and ideologies of Adolf Hitler, Mussolini, Hendrik Verwoerd etc. – must belong in history books only – as ideas and ideologies never to be applied to human and planet earth's affairs ever again. We need the ideas and ideologies of the Mahatma Gandhis, the Martin Luther Kings, the Pope Franciss, the Mother Theresas, the Greta Thunbergs, the Naomi Kleins, the Nelson Mandelas, the Berni Sanderss, the Jeremy Corbyns, the John Lennons, and the ideas of the millions of common men and women of the world who really know what life is like under capitalism. We need the ideas of the workers of the world to save the world from capitalism – as we needed their immense help in the time of COVID-19. The capitalist system and the capitalist state were ill-prepared to respond appropriately and effectively to COVID-19, in the same way that it is ill-prepared to respond effectively, efficiently and timeously to the global social pandemics of unemployment, poverty, inequality, environmental catastrophes, crime, gender-based violence, mass shootings, opioid deaths, climate change, wars, etc. In fact, the capitalist system – underpinned by the free market and the capitalist state – is the key enabler of these social and environmental ills – the long-standing global social pandemics of our time. COVID-19 revealed to the world that sicknesses and diseases are not only a medical challenge, but are social, cultural, political, economic and scientific challenges as well. Capitalist societies in the main have been treating it as an economic challenge and opportunity i.e., one in which to stop profit from falling and one from which to profit and accumulate. We witnessed the huge profits generated by the health care industry in the time of COVID-19. We also witnessed the profits lost in the time of COVID-19, when visits to hospitals for other illnesses and diseases were at an all-time low. Those countries that left health care to the free market fared much worse in staving off COVID-19, than states with good, humane, effective and efficient public health care systems. Cancer, HIV/AIDS, heart diseases, diabetes, obesity, mental health illnesses, etc. are also global challenges – and require a unified global response as well. COVID-19 may not have clearly and confidently shown us the way to a future society just yet – but it has certainly awoken us to the fact that we need to abandon capitalism and the neo-liberal free market – and we need to abandon these inhumane man-made institutions fast. Even for a brief moment, we witnessed how effective an efficient state can be – in responding to a national crisis, in keeping people safe, in acting in the interests of the common good – instead of selfish individualism, rights devoid of contexts, relativity and responsibility, and an economy predicated on profit-making and wealth accumulation. This historical moment cries out for the deconstruction and dissolution of the profit economy – and in its place the reconstruction and building of the citizens' economy. This historical moment calls for building an economy that will have a symbiotic and mutualistic relationship with nature – instead of a parasitic one – as is the case under the capitalist mode of production, consumption and destruction. Responding to the world's challenges means first sweeping aside capitalist and neo-liberal ideologies that seek to place profit before – and most times at the expense of – people and planet. We need a practical philosophy and outlook to deal with the problems and challenges of the world and planet. Unemployment is practical in nature – and hence its response should also be practical in nature. It should not and cannot only depend on foreign direct investment, for example. Nature and people primarily make and build the economy – not solely foreign direct investment. In fact, foreign direct investment profits from this teamwork of nature and people. COVID-19 tore capitalism's rulebook and policy to shreds – how to work, how to shop, how to sustain livelihoods, how to create employment, how to socialise, how to greet one another, etc. Capitalism is anti-human and anti-nature. Individual capitalists – like the Rupert Murdochs, the Harry Oppenheimers, the Mark Zuckerbergs, the Elon Musks, the Jeff Bezoss, the Bill Gatess, or many of the other big-, medium- and small-sized capitalists of the world are not the problems per se; the problem is capitalism itself – as an exploitative historical system. In the words of Marx, the capitalist economy:

> Can less than any other make the individual responsible for relations whose creature he socially remains, however much he may subjectively raise himself above them.
>
> MARX, 1867: 7

In other words, it is the job of the capitalist to make money – and it is the task of the worker to look for work and earn a wage. They have no free choice but to perform their respective historical roles – in the similar manner that a white person had no or limited choice but to be superior – and a black person to be inferior – in a country which had apartheid as the overarching ideology and politico-legal system. The capitalists of the world are merely doing what capitalism expects them to do – to make money and to make lots of it. The workers of the world are merely doing what capitalism expects them to do – to work and to work long and hard. The unemployed are doing what capitalism expects them to do – to continue looking for work. There is no free choice within the system. You cannot have a debate with a capitalist as to why he is a capitalist. He did not choose the capitalist way of life. The capitalist way of life chose him. His choice to be a capitalist then followed. The logic of capitalism is the survival of the fittest. It is this ruthless logic that transforms men and women – made good by nature – into beasts of profit and selfish individualism. The problem with capitalism is that it is under the auspices of maximum profit at all costs and – if need be – at the cost of lives as well, as was evident in the absence of a democratic and citizens' economy in the time of COVID-19. COVID-19 demonstrated to the world how hopelessly dependent and enslaved the human race is to the capitalist economy. The challenge for Homo sapiens is to ensure that the post-COVID-19 economy is under the deliberate and conscious democratic governance of humankind (women, men and youth). Humankind and the planet must never again be under the governance and dictatorship of the economy. In the time of COVID-19 we witnessed the goodness of humankind – not because of capitalism – but in spite of it. COVID-19 gave us a glimpse as to what a post-capitalist world could be like. It could be a future comprising of caring states – and rid of non-caring ones. It could be a future comprising states that will enable the feeding of the poor when they are hungry, enable the provision of shelters to the homeless, medicine and hospital beds for the sick, care homes for the elderly, safe houses for the abused, help for the mentally ill, jobs for the jobless, etc. Will we continue to stand aside and leave lives and livelihoods to the neoliberal free market? The future can comprise states which will work tirelessly toward a gun-free society. The rich in Nigeria, who usually go overseas for health issues, were forced to seek treatment for health challenges at local hospitals – lest they get infected overseas (Al Jazeera, 2020).

Boris Johnson thanked the NHS for saving his life. It is possible for the rich and the elites of the world to argue strongly for formidable public health systems in all countries of the world – not only in preparation for future pandemics, but for the many other preventable diseases as well – that afflict large swathes of the human race. The future is not only that which we work towards; the future also begins from that which we need – and long to exit from. Just like most of the world finally agreed that apartheid was bad, most of the world must first agree that capitalism is bad for humanity and nature. Only then, can we meaningfully transition to a post-capitalist society.

2 Placing Humans Back in Nature and Nature Back in Humans: Toward a Global Environmental Movement

Are we going to continue subscribing to the dominant ideology that man was made by a yet-to be proven deity – living somewhere high up in the carbon-filled sky? What we do know is that the sky has satellites hovering about – and much debris, as a result of man's vanity for continued rocket send-offs. What we do know through the development of natural science is that man had come from nature. Man is nature. Man needs nature. Nature does not need man. But the scale and speed at which capitalist man is destroying nature seems to suggest that man does not need nature. Man will return to nature. Planetary science has discovered many galaxies, planets, stars, black holes, etc. but has not discovered places called heaven and hell. Since there is no planetary science proof for such ideas, we should accept that planet earth is man's only abode – both when alive and when dead? In the same way that trees, insects, animals, viruses etc. are part of the ecosystem alive or dead, man is subject to the same law of "ashes to ashes, dust to dust". The archaeological science records prove this to be the case. The starting point of any and all democratic planning should be nature and the natural environment. Homo sapiens are an inextricable part of nature: we do not exist outside or independent of nature. As far as livelihoods, profits, wages, commodities, capitalists, workers, etc. are concerned, all economic activities are embedded in and dependent on the natural environment. The economy is not an abstract entity as made out to be – by neoliberal economic science and scientists. In the era of climate change and colossal environmental destruction, nature can no longer and should no longer be tossed onto the conveyor belt of profit-making and wealth accumulation. Since its inception and during its existence, capitalism has eaten away at the natural environment – and harmfully transformed the planet – our only home. It has done this under the ideological banners of exchange-value, profit and supposed free markets. Ideologies upholding the free market, profit-maximisation and wealth accumulation have been given immense freedom to degrade the planet. Use-value is never the aim of capitalism or the capitalist. A large part of the history of environmentalism has been one of indigenous communities and citizens attempting to stop capitalism from eating away at nature, thoughtlessly transforming planet earth, destroying livelihoods and eradicating any prospects for a sustainable future. Democratic planning for a post-COVID-19 future should entail consulting and listening to people in communities – before any agreements are reached on development projects. Development has to steer away from being profit-centred – to being people and nature-centred. In this regard, it was heartening to see the democratically elected president of the US – Joe Biden – stopping the oil pipeline from Canada. Canada is notorious for its oil derived from tar sands. Whilst there was talk of a new world order, there was also action as well. Old and destructive ideologies can be let go of. Oil as our only energy source need not be taken as fact any longer. Positive changes are possible – even in capitalist USA!

Man's place in nature, as well as in the built environment, is as a tribal animal – much like the other apes that exist in nature – and sometimes in cities. He may try speaking to a tree. He may do okay speaking to other animals like a dog, cat or chameleon – like I had done during the lockdown. But he is really at home when he speaks with and to his own kind. Communication is the hallmark of a tribal animal. It is why WhatsApp, Face Book, Instagram, Twitter etc. are such busy and popular platforms – as witnessed during the lockdown – when human contact was non-existent. Like in the real world, man longs to be part of society; so, in the virtual world, he seeks to be part of chat groups as well. Man is a tribal animal – a social animal – part of the collective. Even when he breaks away from his 'original' tribe, he seeks to join another tribe. In the hunter-gatherer society he is part of the hunting tribe or the gathering tribe or the broader family tribe. In capitalist society, he is either part of the capitalist tribe – or the tribe of workers. Even in Margaret Thatcher's "no such thing as society" ideological fantasy, she was a member of the conservative tribe or society – not of the labour tribe or society. Independent candidates do not usually do well in electoral politics. Tribes do. Even in Ronald Reagan's "no government" ideological fantasy, man is either part of the governing tribe – or the governed tribe. In the economy, man belongs to the tribe of producers – and to the tribe of consumers. Man is a tribe of the human-race. The only time that man transforms fleetingly into an individual is the distance and time between him leaving one tribe to join another. Can man continue to believe that he can be the owner of a planet that is home to all species? Should not the perspective be that planet earth owns man – instead of the other way around? Is it not time to place humans back into nature and nature back into humans? As an intelligent species – and in the words of Naomi Klein – we need to:

> Think big, go deep, and move the ideological pole far away from the stifling market fundamentalism that has become the greatest enemy to planetary health.
>
> KLEIN, 2014: 30

A good starting point would be to accept the fact that we are an earthly and a natural species – and not the unequal and desperate children of the many gods that we have imaginatively and creatively created for ourselves over the ages on planet earth. We can try hard to search for the attributes of gods in each other, in ourselves and in nature. It is only humans that can help uplift the entire of humanity and stop the destruction of the natural environment. No other creature can do this – either real or imagined!

3 Exploring an O-shaped or Use-Value Economy and Society

Planet earth is a blue spec from space. I do not think that earth as a planet grows. What we do know is that life on planet earth grows and then dies off. It is sometimes referred to as the cycle of life. However, there is an economic system that wishes to grow incessantly and linearly on planet earth – capitalism. In the time of COVID-19 we often heard about whether the economic recovery post-COVID-19 would be V-shaped, L-shaped and W-shaped. Can society consider instead an O-shaped economy – an economy that works according to nature's limits? Can society move away from an economy that focuses on producing exchange-value towards producing use-value? There have been instances of this happening:

> In the early 1970s in Sydney, members of the NSW Builders Labourers Federation (BLF), led by the late Jack Mundey, concerned themselves with these questions. Their 'Green Bans' remain a world-historic example of the social responsibility of labour, achieved by connecting industrial issues to the experience of everyday life in the city. Construction bans were placed on sites by the builders' labourers union, and members refused to work on projects that were deemed socially or ecologically harmful by the community. By demanding a say over the purpose of their labour, the BLF called into question a core part of capitalism itself, rejecting the premise that all investment should be directed by the profit

> motive. Instead they wanted to build things according to communities' needs. Their understanding of labour conditions included the specific alienation that results from performing work that is destructive, rather than socially useful.
>
> HEENAN and STURMAN, 2020: 196

Affordable health care and affordable hospitals are useful to society – so are schools, fresh air, clean environments, ample play spaces for children, housing, etc. These all should be part of a use-value society – and not be subjected to exchange-value. Work should contribute directly to a use-value society – and not be subjected to exchange-value. Work should be for work and use-value sake – and not for the purposes of accumulation and economic growth. A fundamental requirement for such a transformation would be the democratisation of the economy. When all women, men and youth have collective ownership of the economy, then all women, men and youth will have opinions, inputs and decisions to make on what commodities and which industries are best for humankind, planet earth, our children and future generations.

4 Freedom, Democracy, Free Choice, Human Rights and Privacy in a Post-capitalist World

The Universal Declaration of Human Rights was proclaimed and adopted by the United Nations General Assembly in 1948 (UN, 2015). It was the same year that the neo-Nazi Apartheid state proclaimed its power over the majority of South Africa's peoples. To add insult to injury, the authoritarian white Afrikaner party that captured the state and the country was named the National Party. The black majority in South Africa had to fight for another 46 years before we could taste any form of rights, freedoms and nationhood. We in South Africa cherish our democracy because we have never known democracy for 350 years since colonial and apartheid rule imposed by the West. It took the European Union and the UK about 3 years to implement the democratic vote of the citizens of the UK to exit the European Union. Can the West be trusted to pronounce on the important subjects and principles of democracy? This is not an argument for less or no democracy. This is an argument for more democracy. Liberals, democrats and a freedom-loving people cannot be satisfied with the current quantity and quality of democracy in the 21st century in all parts of the world. Let there be discussions, debates and democratic votes in each country as to whether the coal industries should be abolished or not. The world is about to host its 28th climate change conference (COP28) and countries are still building coal-fired powered stations! We need more democracy – not less. Obviously, China, Cuba, North Korea, Saudi Arabia, etc. cannot be held up as models for a post-COVID-19 society – in terms of democracy, human rights, freedoms and liberties. But so can't the Western world! Let there be a democratic vote or referendum – as to whether a country should have nuclear power or not. Let there be a democratic vote or referendum – as to whether a country should go to war or not. New Zealand's prime minister proposed a 4-day week when the world experienced COVID-19. Let there be a democratic vote or referendum – as to whether the working week should be 3 days, 4 days or 5 days? Let there be a democratic vote or referendum – as to whether society should have 100% employment. Children once used to work – but child labour is no longer legal. Let there be a democratic vote or referendum – as to whether children should be religiously institutionalised from a young age. Let there be a democratic vote or referendum – as to whether a person should own more than one car. Why didn't democratic Japan call for an online referendum to decide whether the Olympic Games should take place during a global pandemic – when the polls showed that more than 70% of Japanese did not think it was a good idea! COVID-19 has shown us that all things are possible and can be beyond ideologies – if we will it – and if citizens compel the state to act in the best interest of society and the natural environment. Is it not the realisation of all possibilities being possible – a good guideline and principle if such possibilities help create a better, safer and just world? Let a post-COVID-19 society extend the democratic processes and principles to all economic sectors of society – like energy, food, water, housing, etc. Freedom to choose must be the cornerstone of any society. The quantity and quality of our freedoms should be measured up against the freedoms of the Chinese – but it must also be measured up against the freedoms in one's own country as well. How much freedom do citizens, in general, and workers, in particular, in the US and UK have to discuss and debate the impacts of guns and weapons manufacturing on society – and to democratically decide on what is to be done? If freedom is to be truly valued, then other countries with no democracy – like Saudi Arabia – must also be shouted down with the same strength and vigour – like is done with China. Only then can the West be taken seriously on the very important matters of freedom, human rights, liberty, choice and democracy. COVID-19 has, in the main, demonstrated that the majority of people all over the world are willing to forgo some of their freedoms if this will save their lives and the lives of their loved ones and their fellow humans. But the true test of the West's commitment to freedom, human rights, liberty, fraternity, democracy, etc. is whether such societies will enable these cherished, hard-won and valued ideals to be implemented and practiced in the workplace – and not only in the public sphere:

> How we build a truly just, ecological society begins with the struggle for democratic control over our labour, so that we can collectively decide the conditions under which we produce and reproduce the world.
>
> HEENAN and STURMAN, 2020: 195

Two of the many posters at the protest against the lockdown in the US were: "Give me liberty or give me death!" and "I prefer dangerous freedom over peaceful slavery". Fair enough! Let there be freedom and liberty in the workplaces, factories, coal mines, gold mines, Amazon warehouses as well – in the Land of the Free and everywhere else in the world. Are those in the Free World willing to make their lands freer – and much more democratic – or do they intend to continue to remain a schizophrenic society when it comes to the important matters of democracy, freedom and liberty? In capitalist society, political freedom does not necessarily entail economic freedom. We see material evidence of this in countries like South Africa – the last country on the African continent to achieve political freedom and to put in place a democratic government. Yet, 29 years after attaining political freedom, the majority of South Africa's population is in economic bondage tantamount to economic slavery. Democracy is less than complete in the Western world. It needs upgrading and perfecting:

> Marx argues that there is a gap in liberal capitalist society between the political sphere and what he calls 'civil society', meaning social and economic existence. In the former – at the ballot box, for example – men and women appear equal and autonomous, each of them counting as one; but this simply serves to mask the actual divisions, inequalities and dependencies of everyday life. It is as though the political dimension abstracts from these conditions, so that citizens become pale simulacra of themselves. Only if democratic self-government were extended to civil society itself – in, for example, workers' self-management – would this gap be closed.
>
> EAGLETON, 2018: ix

The deepening and strengthening of democracy should be work in progress. We must continue this progress in democratic functioning and evolution. For example, in South Africa:

> Our constitution had given us one person, one vote, but did not give us the right to know vital information about the finances of the parties on the ballot paper. Now, voters will know whose money is behind the

> party they vote for. Therefore, this fundamental right becomes one person, one informed vote. This law also requires political parties to do what has long been normal for everyone else – keep proper books of account; produce independently audited financial statements annually; refuse to take money from known crooks; etc. Another brick has been added to our already solid constitutional foundation.
>
> MOOSA, 2021: 18

Transparency is a fundamental pillar of the democratic process. Taxpayers' monies and the projects and programmes that they are funnelled into should be made transparent. The internet and digitally connected world make such transparency possible. Which company or firm gets what and for what – from taxpayers' monies – should be made transparent and known to the public at large.

Scientists are a special people among Homo sapiens. They know more about the world than the ordinary masses. But scientists are only as good as the questions put to them by the masses. We have seen proof of this in the time of COVID-19. The intelligent scientists became even more intelligent after taking questions from citizens. Citizens themselves became more intelligent after listening to the scientists – and had a little bit of a scientist in them after such interactions:

> As people become better educated and informed, economic and financial issues can no longer be left to a small group of experts whose competence is, in any case, dubious. It is only natural for more and more citizens to want to form their own opinions and participate in public debate. The economy is at the heart of politics; responsibility for it cannot be delegated, any more than democracy itself can.
>
> PIKETTY, 2020: 13

Zoom significantly pushed open the democratic door in the time of COVID-19. People in all parts of the world are now able to share common spaces – as they discuss and debate the many challenges of the world – as well as the opportunities at our disposal to make a better the world. The infrastructure and scaffolding for consolidating, deepening and strengthening democratic processes in society are present. A post-capitalist society should make full use of this hard-won social tool – to enable the further development and social evolution of democracy in a post-COVID-19 society.

5 Making the Free Market Serve People and Planet – Instead of the People and Planet Serving the Free Market

> Free markets provide incentives for innovation. They enforce pragmatism at the expense of ideology. They fit production to needs and desires of consumers and they lower the price of goods. But free markets can also cause problems. Some of these stem from the pre-eminence of the short term. This endangers long-term prosperity.
>
> FRIEDMAN, 2003: 4

Anyone knows after being bombarded by companies to purchase their products that the free market is not factually free, that it is not really a free choice that customers have; customers are pressured into purchasing products in the so-called free market. This is not free choice – this is economic harassment and coercion. This is citizens being elbowed and pressured into purchasing stuff – that one may not really want – and that one may not really need. Never again should it be a case of the people versus the free market – as has happened in the time of COVID-19. The free market is in reality the anarchy market. Climate change and mass unemployment characterises such anarchy. The US state removed bureaucratic red tape to respond to the pandemic by buying ventilators. It did not depend entirely on the free market to respond to the crisis. Where possible, states took control of the free market. They regulated the free market. They scolded the free market. They reprimanded the free market. They praised the free market. They guided the free market. They made the free market serve the people and not the other way around. When the free market was left free to mediate the affairs of humans and the planet – it did a bad job. It destroyed the natural environment. It produced killing machines. It failed humanity when humanity most needed it to step up to the plate. Instead, it exposed its ruthless nature in the time of COVID-19. Making the free market serve the people and planet also means taking "back ownership of essential services like energy" (Klein, 2014: 14). The free market has to be governed in the interest of broader society and the natural environment. For example, on 26 May 2021:

> A court in The Hague has ordered Royal Dutch Shell to cut its global carbon emissions by 45% by the end of 2030 compared with 2019 levels, in a landmark case brought by Friends of the Earth and more than 17,000 co-plaintiffs.

With this ruling, the people, together with the courts, made the free market serve the people and the planet – and not the other way around, as is the case under capitalism. One would have thought that Shell would be thrilled that it was being assisted by concerned citizens and the courts to save millions of species and future generations from harm and possible extinction. Instead, its response was that it was "disappointed by the ruling and plans to appeal the ruling"! By stopping the 2000 km pipeline from Canada to the US, President Biden made the free market serve the people and the planet. A central idea of a post-COVID-19 world is for the free market to serve the people and the planet – not for the people and planet to serve the free market. Citizens – through democratic means – should guide and at times instruct the free market on how to conduct its affairs, what to produce, how to produce, how much to produce, etc. The 2008 Great Crisis, climate change, the massive inequality, unemployment and poverty that is so pervasive in capitalist society, and the observations of the failure of the capitalist world to protect its citizens in the time of COVID-19 are screaming out that the invisible hand operating in the free market must now be replaced by the democratic hand of a free and democratic society. It is a historical moment for democratic and free societies to decide and inform the workings of the free market. Democratic man – the intelligent ape – must now take centre stage in guiding the free market. It is therefore noteworthy to take a cue from the Nobel prize winner for economics, Joseph Stiglitz (2020: xii):

> My study of economics had taught me that the ideology of many conservatives was wrong: their almost religious belief in the power of markets – so great that we could largely simply rely on unfettered markets for running the economy – had no basis in theory or evidence.

Society witnessed the huge benefits when society proclaimed that the free market should not decide on whether children should work, whether humans should be sold as slaves, whether smoking should be left to individual choices, etc. The current crisis is also demonstrating that fossil-fuels use should not be decided by the free market – but by democratic society. COVID-19 has produced the historical window of opportunity for democratic society to govern and manage the free market – instead of allowing the free market to continue to govern and decide what is best for democratic society. When the visible hand of democratic society governs the free market, humans can once again become masters of the universe – this time in a positive and non-destructive way.

6 Declaring War on Global Enemies and Flattening Their Curves

The language of war was initially invoked to fight the COVID-19 pandemic, and rightly so. We have other known enemies in the world which are a "clear and present danger". We have known visible 'pandemics' in the globalised world such as unemployment, poverty, inequality, etc. Let us wage all-out wars on these forever 'pandemics' under capitalism. Let us flatten the unemployment curve. Let us flatten the poverty curve. Let us flatten the inequality curve. Let us flatten the war curve. Let us flatten the climate change curve. Let us flatten the mental health challenges curve. Let us flatten the domestic violence curve. Let us flatten the racism curve. Let us flatten the pollution curve. Let us flatten the corruption curve. Let us flatten the sexism curve. Let us flatten the patriarchal curve. Let us flatten the alcohol and drug abuse curve. Let us flatten the high suicide rate curve. Let us flatten the modern slavery curve. Let us flatten the human trafficking curve. Let us flatten the mass shootings curve in the US. Let us flatten the deforestation curve. Let us flatten the migrant deaths curve. Let us flatten the consumerism curve. Let us flatten the North-South and West-East divide curves. Let us measure these various curves – and provide feedback on a regular basis on how the state is leading the way towards flattening all of these social pandemic curves. Let us use global statistics for unemployment, mental illnesses, environmental destruction, modern slavery, etc. – in the same way that states around the world did for COVID-19. War should be declared on all the present ills of society. State and society should set goals and timeframes to win the war on the many 'pandemics' which still characterise the early part of our 21st century world.

7 Planetary and People Well-Being Side-by-Side with the Health of the Economy

If there is one thing that was most concerning to politicians, capitalists and economic scientists in all parts of the world in the time of COVID-19, it was the health of the economy. In fact, this is the one thing that preoccupied their minds in all the years and decades before COVID-19. It has always been about the health of the economy. Never has the national and international paradigm and priority been about the health of the people – even though a healthy people make for a healthy economy. Never has the national and international paradigm and priority been about the health of the natural environment – even though a healthy natural environment means a healthy people – and a sustainable and healthy economy. The trouble with the economy under capitalism is that it has become an end in and of itself. COVID-19 has revealed that the capitalist economy exists only for its bottom line – maximum profit – and not for addressing the needs of people. In fact, under capitalism, people are instruments for capitalism's bottom line. For example, in Japan, the state is encouraging the young to drink more in order to boost the economy. The *Evening Standard* carried the following headlines: "Young people in Japan urged to drink more to help economy" (Howie, 2022). This is the absurdity of life under capitalism! Who cares about the physical and mental health of the young of Japan – as long as the Japanese economy is healthy! COVID-19 has taught us that if the capitalist economy does not meet the needs of people, then life and livelihood-centred states must make the economy meet the needs of people. The economy should come under democratic and collective ownership – if we are to live comfortably, harmoniously and happily in the days, weeks, months, years, decades, centuries and millennia ahead of us. The economy must come under democratic and collective ownership – if we are to not lose so many millions of lives if the next pandemic comes along. A post-capitalist society requires caring states to plan and distribute resources – in conjunction with a democratically-governed free market. We also have to ask some tough and uncomfortable questions. One such question is what sacrifices does the demand side of society have to make to ensure that energy is used sustainably, so that future generations will not have to ask: What happened to the bountiful energy that was once part of planet earth? If we are to survive as a species, then we must first and foremost ensure the survival of planet earth. It is absurd to embark on infinite economic growth whilst at the same time aiding and abetting the heating-up and destruction of the planet. The obsession with the economy must occur side-by-side with the obsession for planetary and people well-being. This is only possible if the economy is governed democratically and collectively. When the economy is owned and governed by a tiny minority in society, then the current sick state of human and planetary affairs is what we will always get – and worse.

8 Toward a Global Workers Movement

The world is ripe for change. The health care workers in the UK experienced the similar negative impacts of COVID-19 as that of health care workers in other parts of the world. The meat workers in the US had to go to work in the midst of a pandemic – so too did the mine workers in South Africa. In South Africa, the Congress of South African Trade Union (COSATU) spokesperson stated on national television that workers are selling labour – and not lives! Businesses are global in the capitalist world. Big tech companies are global. Nothing is more globalised than finance. Labour-power or human energy is also globalised as migrant workers are essential for the workings of the global economy. We produce co-operatively in the workplace – but the major portion of such proceeds of this co-operation goes to a minority of people in the world. Capitalists are innovators because man is by nature an innovator. Workers are also innovators – and this, believe it or not, is the thinking of Adam Smith, the author of *The Wealth of Nations* and capitalism's pioneer advocate:

> A great part of the machines made use of in those manufactures in which labour is most subdivided, were originally the inventions of common workmen, who, being each of them employed in some very simple operation, naturally turned their thoughts towards finding out easier and readier methods of performing it.
>
> SMITH, 1776: 23

Smith goes on to relate the story – not of an innovative capitalist, but of a child worker's natural ability to innovate when the Industrial Revolution was picking up speed:

> In the first fire-engines, a boy was constantly employed to open and shut alternately the communication between the boiler and the cylinder, according as the piston either ascended or descended. One of those boys, who loved to play with his companions, observed that, by tying a string from the handle of the valve which opened this communication to another part of the machine, the valve would open and shut without his assistance, and leave him at liberty to divert himself with his playfellows. One of the greatest improvements that has been made upon this machine, since it was first invented, was in this manner the discovery of a boy who wanted to save his own labour.
>
> SMITH, 1776: 24–25

Workers' skill and human energy create the many commodities that we need. If machines replace workers – then workers make the machines that make the commodities. Amazon workers in the US should seek solidarity with Amazon workers in Europe. Uber workers in other parts of the world should seek solidarity with Uber workers in the UK. McDonald's workers in all parts of the world should seek solidarity with each other. Workers of Starbucks in Europe should seek solidarity with Starbucks workers in the US and other parts of the world.

Teachers in all parts of the world should seek solidarity with each other. Miners in all parts of the world should seek solidarity with one another. In the same way that there should be a global environmental movement, so too should there be a global workers' movement that will act in solidarity with workers of all specialisations in any part of the world. Zoom and other advanced technologies make this convenient and easy to do. A united global workers movement is a fundamental requirement for the transition to a post-capitalist world. Workers of the world should shed their superficial national, race, political party, etc. identities and mobilise around their real identity as workers. Karl Marx was of the view that workers of the world should unite towards ensuring the end of capitalism.

9 Deepening, Strengthening, Consolidating and Trusting the People's State in Transitioning to a Post-capitalist World

In Ronald Reagan's and Margaret Thatcher's world – and the world that was made in their names – all states are bad, evil, no-good doers, anti-freedom, anti-people, etc. I was born in the 60s – the time of drugs, sex and rock and roll. It was the time of so-called flower power – love, not war. It was the time that capitalist 'Goliath' USA was bombing the daylights out of communist 'David' Vietnam. We in South Africa were living under an apartheid state. Since 1994, South Africa has a democratic state which – demographically speaking – is predominantly black. It is a relatively new state – about 29 years young. It came into being through decades of struggle – under the leadership of the ANC and Nelson Mandela. Prior to the ANC-governed state, the apartheid state – made up of the white race – came into being in 1948. The then South African state was both heavenly and evil. It was heavenly for the white minority – and evil for the black majority. The apartheid state was a powerful state – but a powerful state that was both moral and sinful. It held up the mores and values of white supremacy – and treated whites as saints. It crushed indigenous ways of living – and treated the oppressed black majority as sinners. The state in apartheid South Africa was both an enabling and a caring state – as well as a totalitarian police state. It served as a protective and nanny state for the white minority – but as a monster state which destroyed the lives and livelihoods of the black majority. The apartheid state used its military power, might and white supremacist ideology to hand over the best of South Africa to the white minority – and the worst to the black majority. The state transformed a bountiful South Africa into a Bantustan South Africa for blacks.

The legacy of the apartheid state's ideology and actions are for all to see and experience. Twenty-nine years after the demise of apartheid, the country is the most unequal in the world – thanks to the apartheid-state then – and the

ANC-governed democratic state at present. The state is not a neutral player in society – it takes sides. The German state during the first half of the 20th century was both heavenly and evil. It was heavenly for the Germans – and evil for the Jews. The Red Army under a socialist state was able to obliterate the evil nature of the German state. The German state is now one of the most respected and efficient states in the world. Just like the apartheid and Nazi states that took the side of the powerful in society, in capitalist society the state always takes the side of the powerful class – the capitalist class. We cannot wish away the state. We can only transform it – in the similar manner that the apartheid and Nazi states were transformed. Broader society must decide the shape, form and functions of the state for a post-COVID-19 world. COVID-19 shone the lights on states in all parts of the world. The most recent 'country' of freedom loving individuals – CHOP (Capitol Hill Organized Protest) or CHAZ (Capitol Hill Autonomous Zone) in the US – lasted less than one month! Because it did not have a nanny state to protect its citizens – three killings took place in three weeks. The Mayor, who pulled the state out of CHAZ or CHOP three weeks earlier – with the aim of creating a "summer of love" 'country' – sent the mother state back in – and crushed the ideals and utopianism of freedom loving individuals of life, liberty and the pursuit of happiness.

Like the umpire on the sports field, the judge in the courtroom, the speaker in parliament, the dad overseeing a dispute between his kids, the marriage counsellor mediating a marital discord – the state is the overseer of society and its operations. As to whether all these mediators and overseers will judge fairly is a matter based on experience and open to discussion and debate. With the aim of envisioning a post-COVID-19 world, we should ask the following such questions: Do we want a state like that of the US, or like that of New Zealand? Do we want a state like that of China, or like that of Saudi Arabia? Do we want a state like that of Israel, or like that of South Africa? Do we want a state like that of Sweden, or like that of Norway? Do we want a state that is better than all these states? Do we want a state that will do everything it its power to save lives during the next pandemic – and the one that may come after? Do we want a state that will be informed by economic and religious ideologies – or by science, pragmatism and common-sense?

The state is the most powerful institution in society. It has the power to go to war with another country – under false pretext – as was done under the reign of George W. Bush and Tony Blair. Or the state can use state power to build a hospital in 10 days – and command all available resources to save lives, as was demonstrated by the communist state of China. The state can steal from its people during a global pandemic – as was the case in South Africa during COVID-19, or the state can motivate its doctors to be at the service of humanity during crisis and disasters, as was demonstrated by the socialist state of Cuba in the time of COVID-19. For now, we accept the fact that states – like oxygen for life – are necessary for any country that wishes to count itself as being in the civilised world. According to Worldometer (2020):

> There are 195 countries in the world today. This total comprises 193 countries that are member states of the United Nations and 2 countries that are non-member observer states: The Holy See and the State of Palestine.

Had CHAZ/CHOP survived as an independent 'country', then it would have been the 196th 'country' in the world. It did not even have a chance at surviving as the 51st state of the United States of America! Countries may come and go, but states or governments are part and parcel of man's social and cultural fabric since the dawn of civilisation. It is clear that the state is not going to vanish anytime soon from the life of man – more so since the entry of COVID-19. In fact, the empirical evidence is showing that an efficient, effective and caring state that can secure both lives and livelihoods is the best choice for humankind – than the state that is frantically scratching its head over whether to choose lives or the profit-economy. States – like mothers, fathers, teachers, judges, bus drivers, etc. – have a job to do. One of its many tasks is to distribute resources in society: "all states, even the most primitive ones, are intimately involved in the redistribution of resources" (Cohn, 2008: 27).

If the free market is still left to an invisible hand, it will still lead to all sorts of economic crimes. Ironically, none stated this better than the father of free markets himself – Adam Smith. Ironically, none advocated for state intervention in the economy more so than Adam Smith himself (well except Karl Marx that is). Nothing is more central to the economy than money. Money binds the state and the free market at the hip. If given half a chance, the free market will corrupt money – so as to literally squeeze out more profit. Many witnessed what happened during the 2008 financial crisis, after the state left too much of the control of money in the hands of the free market. The state, according to Adam Smith, is therefore necessary in order to rein in the free market:

> Before the institution of coined money, however, unless they went through this tedious and difficult operation, people must always have been liable to the grossest frauds and impositions, and instead of a pound weight of pure silver, or pure copper, might receive in exchange for their goods an adulterated composition of the coarsest and cheapest materials, which had, however, in their outward appearance, been made to resemble those metals. To prevent such abuses, to facilitate exchanges, and thereby to

> encourage all sorts of industry and commerce, it has been found necessary, in all countries that have made any considerable advances towards improvement, to affix a public stamp upon certain quantities of such particular metals as were in those countries commonly made use of to purchase goods. Hence the origin of coined money, and of those public offices called mints; institutions exactly of the same nature with those of the aulnagers and stamp-masters of woollen and linen cloth. All of them are equally meant to ascertain, by means of a public stamp, the quantity and uniform goodness of those different commodities when brought to market.
>
> SMITH, 1776: 44–45

Like Zoom and porn – the state is here to stay. The state is only as strong or weak as its strongest or weakest constituencies in society. In capitalist society, the constituency that exerts the most power over the state is the capitalist class. Second to the capitalist class are the dominant ideological entities – such as religion, law, educational system, etc. – that help preserve the status quo that favours the capitalist class over the rest of capitalist society. Any phenomena – such as the fall of the Berlin Wall, or a global pandemic– tests the allegiances of the state in marked ways. The South African democratic state of 1994 was nudged and elbowed from the left to the right of centre with the fall of the Berlin Wall. In the time of COVID-19, the South African state of 2020 first demonstrated command and control over the pandemic – until there was push-back from capitalist forces deeply entrenched in the country since the arrival of colonialism to its shores. Others with ideological power and influence over the South African state – such as religious organisations – also lobbied and elbowed the state to allow it to go back to its usual business of empty promises of the good life for the unsuspecting masses. Capitalist and religious ideologies finally won the day over science and pragmatism. Individuals in South Africa had little or no agency to lobby the state in order to ensure that both lives and livelihoods were secured. Free market ideologies – under the disguise of good economic science – seemed to have had the greatest push-back impact on the state. Even the all-powerful Congress of South African Trade Union (COSATU) demonstrated little or ineffective agency in influencing the state to protect its constituency during the time of a global pandemic. However, teacher unions – like teacher unions in the UK – managed to teach the state a thing or two about the dangers of community transmissions – and were successful in closing down schools once again. Jonas (2020: 19) states: "those countries that had done well with their pandemic responses have the qualities of state capacity, social trust, and leadership". Free market ideologues have for decades been successful in demonising the state – but history and facts tell another story altogether:

> In our enthusiasm for the dogma that any government interference is necessarily bad, we forget it was government action that ended child labour. It was government action that outlawed slavery, despite its profitability. It was government action that ended the Great Depression, after years of failure of non-intervention. It was government action that curbed the most virulent expressions of racism, that provided an education for the great majority, that created a large stable middle class. The free market did not achieve any of these goods, and there is no indication that it ever would have done so.
>
> FRIEDMAN, 2003: 2

What COVID-19 has proven is that:

> It's now possible to imagine levels of state intervention in the economy, and of government debt, that would have been unthinkable under a Labour government, never mind under previous Conservative governments.
>
> WALKER, 2020

COVID-19 has demonstrated that the state has the capability and potential to be a force for good in society. Scholars were aware of this force for good – even before the COVID-19 pandemic struck:

> Just as the government is the most efficient provider of policing and national defence, it is often the most efficient provider of other social and administrative services. There are sectors where the advantages of a single centralised system can lead to large economies of scale. In such cases, it is more efficient to have a service (e.g. Medicare and Social Security) provided by the government, instead of having a large number of competing firms.
>
> BAKER, 2006: 12

During the Great Depression in the 1920s, the US state transformed itself into serving people – and not profit. COVID-19 has demonstrated that in order to save lives and rescue both businesses and workers from bankruptcy, we required efficient and responsive states – not unstable and complacent ones. COVID-19 has shown us that when people are afraid, anxious and worried, they can look to states to protect them – not only from foreign attacks in times of war, but also from unemployment, hunger, homelessness and sicknesses. The state is the most powerful and structured institution in society – but only if the people will it. There was political will – and ideologies did give way to pragmatism in the time of COVID-19. The state is here to stay – for a very long time. It is the citizens of the world that should discipline the state – if or when it steers off-course from mandates democratically decided upon. We live in an age whereby the people can – but not without a fight – hold the state accountable. In South Africa it was the state under the ANC that enabled a handful of blacks to become extremely wealthy. The free market did not do this on its own accord. In fact, the free market in South Africa is continually seeking to exclude the black majority from participating meaningfully in the economy. The state is the creation of society. Like money – it can become a power onto itself. It is therefore the responsibility of broader society to hold states accountable – even if citizens have to do so with their lives, if need be, as has happened under apartheid – and in many revolutions in world history. State intervention should be democratically agreed upon. For example, even though the South African constitution allows for land expropriation without compensation, the state ensured that input is made by all and sundry on the important matter of land expropriation. Nature provides – workers produce – and the state should distribute evenly and equitably to its citizens. It is therefore the responsibility of the state to enable and oversee that nature provides sustainably – and to create conditions for the workers to produce, without debt and distress. It is then the responsibility of the people to ensure that the state distributes according to the needs and abilities of society and citizens. From ancient times, states have had immense power to better society:

> When Solon ruled Athens, he acted to reduce inequality between rich and poor. He abolished certain debts, refused to allow enslavement as a penalty for the inability to pay debts, changed the tax system to benefit the middle class, and modified the electoral process to give the lower economic classes an audible political voice. This political action helped create a broad-based prosperity that fostered the Golden Age of Athens.
>
> FRIEDMAN, 2003: 40

Like responsible states had done in the time of COVID-19, when they had the power to do so, or when they chose to do so, responsible states must continue in their roles to be the overseers of economic security, physical and mental health, and social security for its citizens. Like responsible states had done in the time of COVID-19, states must lead in their role in providing shelter for the homeless. Where unemployment exists through no fault of the powerless and less-than-powerful individuals, states must continue to ensure the survival of the unemployed – like responsible states had done in the time of COVID-19. In this regard there are many ideas floating about like the Universal or Basic Income Grant. COVID-19 has taught us that challenges are practical in nature – and that solutions are practical in nature as well. State and society can put in place a formidable infrastructure that will be able to withstand the next pandemic since: "other viruses will inevitably follow" (Naish, 2020). That infrastructure should be the iron dome against the next pandemic. States in the US, UK, India, Brazil, etc. should learn from China, Vietnam, New Zealand, etc. on how to save the lives of their citizens when the next pandemic strikes. The colonial states of the past have led us into the historical era called capitalism. The states of the present can lead us out of the harsh, ruthless and brutal capitalist system to a humane and planetary friendly economic system. We should embrace the state – but we should also force it to exit the capitalist era. It is time for citizens around the world to force the state to kick open the door to a better world that awaits us all!

10 Toward Advancing, Deepening and Consolidating the Economic Sciences

In *Capital* Marx tells us: "every beginning is difficult, holds in all sciences" (Marx, 1867: 6). We saw this with public health scientists at the beginning of COVID-19, as they were grappling to understand the nature of the coronavirus and ways to defeat it. The virus had instituted a formidable battle in the field of science. The vaccine rollout may be the weapon that finally beats COVID-19, but we've seen that science in capitalist society serves mainly the developed world and the rich in developing societies. However, with all of its ideological biases, baggage and analytical weaknesses, economic science since its inception has given humankind the scientific tools with which to understand the economic world that it has thus far created for itself. The scholars of yesteryear have written about the economy in the best way they knew how – and in the best way they chose to do so. Adam Smith's *The Wealth of Nations* has given us a treasure trove in the field of economic science that humankind must cherish – but critically engage with – in order to understand and analyse our economic lives. But there are other economic scientists that have built on Smith's, and other classical economic scientists' work, thereby giving us better understandings of how the economy in general – and the capitalist economy in particular – works. One economic scientist that stands out – and stands tall – is Karl

Marx, who wrote *Capital* in 1867, almost a century after Adam Smith wrote *The Wealth of Nations*. In fact, he stands so tall among other scientists that a BBC poll carried out in 1999 found that Karl Marx is the world's greatest thinker for the last 1000 years! Imagine that! Albert Einstein came second and Isaac Newton third, followed by Charles Darwin in fourth place (Mirchandani, 2018). Marx – the economic and social scientist – was voted way ahead of the world's most renowned and respected scientists. Often despised in the circle of free market economic scientists, he does have very important things to say about the capitalist economy. It is why almost 150 years after Marx wrote *Capital,* Terry Eagleton wrote *Why Marx was Right* in 2011. Many usually associate Karl Marx with the labour theory of value. However, it is the much-admired Adam Smith – and not the much-despised Karl Marx – that first gave the world the labour theory of value: "labour, therefore, is the real measure of the exchangeable value of all commodities" (Smith, 1776: 50). Marx was an admirer of Smith's work. But he was also an ardent critic of Smith's brand of economic science, as he was a critic of so many other economic scientists of his time and before. Marx was a critic par excellence. There could be a hypothetical argument that Marx would not have been able to write *Capital* had Smith not written *The Wealth of Nations* (1776) – but that is a hypothetical argument for a hypothetical day.

Friedrich Engels, Marx's friend and financial supporter for 40 years, oversaw the English translation of *Capital* (1867) a few years after the author had passed on. In it, Engels states:

> Every new aspect of a science involves a revolution in the technical terms of that science. This is best shown by chemistry, where the whole of the terminology is radically changed about once in twenty years, and where you will hardly find a single organic compound that has not gone through a whole series of different names.
>
> 1888: 19

Science evolves. Following in the tradition of the evolving nature of science, I wish to put forward the suggestion that the commodity called *labour* by Adam Smith – and which Marx argued is actually *labour-power* – be reconceptualised as the economic science category of *human-energy*. A post-COVID-19 economic science should consider viewing human-energy as the 'material' commodity which the worker sells in the labour market. Marx was the first to discover the two-fold nature of labour in capitalist society – its qualitative nature on the one hand, and its quantitative nature on the other. For example, the labour used to make a cloth mask is different from the labour used to make the cloth.

Such labour is qualitatively different from each other. The one is as a result of tailoring – the other of weaving. But in so far as the cloth mask could be exchangeable with the cloth, then the labour of both commodities is the same viz. it falls within Marx's economic science category known as the quantitative nature of labour. The latter is what Marx referred to as *abstract labour*. I wish to put forward the suggestion that abstract labour be viewed as human-energy by a post-COVID-19 economic science. I put forward the theory that it is human-energy that the labourer or worker sells to the capitalist. According to Marx, labour-power: "exists in the organism of every ordinary individual" (1867: 31). Labour-power is human-energy that exists in the organism of every ordinary individual. Man – and therefore the worker – is an embodiment of human-energy. He is a mechanical entity in factories, firms and on farms. He exudes his human-energy during the creation of commodities such as masks, protective gowns, ventilators, etc. If economic science accepts that labour-power is the labour that Adam Smith referred to – and that human-energy is the labour-power that Karl Marx referred to – then society could consider human-energy as a renewable energy source – and one that could aid in the fight against climate change. It could therefore take care of the unemployment problem so pervasive in capitalist society. If human-energy is accepted as a scientifically-updated concept for the commodity sold in the labour market, then this could be a leap forward for economic science – and for a society caught in the grip of an incomplete and most times an ideological economic science – which overwhelmingly favours the capitalist mode of production. Scholars have alluded to the energy basis of labour and labour power: "as labour-power is precisely energy, even 'tension'" (1867 *Capital* 1, p. 583) in (Brennan, 1993: 125). And: "If labour can stand in for another energy source more cheaply and more effectively, it will be the source chosen" (Brennan, 1993: 125).

Other areas of the economy where economic science requires major advancement is in the role that nature and energy play in the production of commodities and the increase in wealth. Using the commodity examples of coat and linen, Marx demonstrates the integral role that nature plays in the creation of material wealth:

> The use values, coat, linen, &c., i.e., the bodies of commodities, are combinations of two elements – matter and labour. If we take away the useful labour expended upon them, a material substratum is always left, which is furnished by Nature without the help of man. The latter can work only as Nature does, that is by changing the form of matter. Nay more, in this work of changing the form he is constantly helped by natural forces. We see, then, that labour is not the only source of material wealth, of use

> values produced by labour. As William Petty puts it, labour is its father and the earth its mother.
>
> 1867: 30

Marx continues: "an increase in the quantity of use values is an increase of material wealth" (Marx, 1867: 32). The questions for economic science are: What role does nature play in the creation of value? Does nature create use-value or exchange-value or both? If nature results in an increase in material wealth, does it mean that increased wealth leads in the final analysis to degraded and depreciated nature? All the signs point in this direction. The scientific consensus needs to demonstrate if this is – or is not – indeed the case. If there is a key constituent and variable of the economy that capitalist-biased economic scientists have intentionally or unintentionally ignored in their economic science, it is that of energy:

> How can someone write a book about economics without mentioning energy? How can economists ignore what might be the most important issue in economics? In the standard economic model, energy and matter are ignored or, at best, completely subsumed under the term 'land', or more recently 'capital', without any explicit treatment other than, occasionally, their price.
>
> HALL and KLITGAARD, 2018: vi

The 2008 Great Crisis and COVID-19 are compelling us to cancel economic scientists like Friedrich von Hayek, Milton Friedman, Ayn Rand, Ludwig von Mises, etc. from our current economic policies, plans and implementations. Their brand of economic science belongs in libraries – but should never again be applied to human and planetary affairs. A post-COVID-19 society requires a post-COVID-19 economic science. Like capitalist society, economic science too needs to be transformed at its roots. COVID-19 has made us all public health scientist to varying degrees. COVID-19 has also revealed the cracks in the scientific scaffolding upholding contemporary society. If capitalist society is required to undergo a transformation or revolution, then it is also required of its economic science to undergo a transformation or revolution.

11 Knowing Capitalism

One of the sure ways to get rid of capitalism is when the majority of the world's citizens, if not all, know what capitalism really is – instead of unquestioningly believing the mainstream narrative or views about capitalism. To know capitalism means to separate the propaganda about capitalism from the facts of the capitalist system. To uncover capitalism is to uncover the lies protecting capitalism. To comprehend capitalism is to comprehend the fake news ring-fencing capitalism. Exposing capitalism means exposing the ideological scaffolding that upholds the capitalist system. To recognise capitalism is to open one's eyes and recognise the miserable state of the world in the 21st century. In the same way that the mainstream narrative about climate change not being caused by humans was slowly but surely challenged, the mainstream narrative about capitalism being good for humankind and the planet must also be challenged. In the same way that the youth – who were once thought to be inactive citizens regarding climate change – the youth have to be made aware of the many dangers of capitalism too. The Great Crisis of 2008 and COVID-19 have accelerated humankind's consciousness of the real and dreadful world that we live in. Social media has really flourished in recent times regarding common citizens' yearning and inclination to give their views on the many challenges facing humankind and the planet. Many are sharing their views in general and their unhappiness in particular on the capitalist system. For example, if one types in "evils of capitalism" on the YouTube webpage, the following are some of the many videos that are viewable: "Capitalism (the rich man's choice) vs socialism (the poor man's choice)"; "The dirty secret of capitalism and a new way forward"; "The evils of capitalism"; "Three evils of capitalism"; " How you are being exploited"; "Disaster capitalism"; " Capitalism is evil", etc. If one types in "is capitalism ending" on the YouTube webpage, the following are some of the many videos that are accessible to learn about the repulsive system called capitalism: "Is this the end of capitalism?"; "Is capitalism dying?"; "What comes after capitalism?"; "Will we see the end of capitalism?"; "Capitalism will end – what is a better system?"; "How to Abandon Capitalism"; "Recession – Capitalism's Failure Invites System Change", etc.

Only because the many were able to identify and know fascism in Europe was fascism destroyed in the main. Only because we in South Africa, and the supporters of South Africa's freedom worldwide, knew what apartheid was, were we able to destroy the evil apartheid system. Capitalism being a world system, it is only when the majority in the world know and understand the exploitative and unjust DNA of capitalism can and will capitalism be formidably challenged and finally obliterated from the affairs of humankind and the planet.

12 14 March: End-Capitalism Day

One of the most famous days in the capitalist era is that of Christmas Day. It is the day when much of the world celebrate the birth of Jesus Christ – the revolutionary who was put to death in the time of the Roman Empire. May 1st every year is International Workers' Day or Labour Day, except in the US and Canada. It is also known as May Day. The world is reminded of the plight of workers, the gains that they have made over the centuries and the struggles that they still have to overcome – whilst capitalism rules. International Women's Day is celebrated each year on 8 March. It is also a day when the world is made to focus on the history of women's oppression, the daily struggles that women endure and still have to overcome. Earth Day is an annual event on the 22nd of April. World Environment Day is celebrated each year on the 5th of June. Both these days are set aside during the year to make us busy humans sit-up and take notice of how we have trashed the planet. Mandela Day is celebrated each year on 18 July.

14 March is the day that Karl Marx died. At Marx's graveside on 17 March 1883, Friedrich Engels read out the following eulogy:

> On the 14th of March, at a quarter to three in the afternoon, the greatest living thinker ceased to think. He had been left alone for scarcely two minutes, and when we came back we found him in his armchair, peacefully gone to sleep, but forever. An immeasurable loss has been sustained both by the militant proletariat of Europe and America, and by historical science, in the death of this man. The gap that has been left by the departure of this mighty spirit will soon enough make itself felt .... His real mission in life was to contribute, in one way or another, to the overthrow of capitalist society and of the state institutions which it had brought into being, to contribute to the liberation of the modern proletariat, which he was the first to make conscious of its own position and its needs, conscious of the conditions of its emancipation. ... His name will endure through the ages, and so also will his work.

Barring Marx, the capitalist system has proven and is proving to be detrimental to both humankind and the planet. If for no other reason but the devastation caused and that is being caused, the world needs an annual day – like Workers' Day, Women's Day, Earth Day, etc. – to be reminded of the anti-human and anti-planet nature of the capitalist system. But as a fitting tribute to the man who has sacrificed so much of his and his family's lives for making the world conscious of the true nature of capitalism, 14 March every year should be *End-Capitalism Day*!

13 Marching and Protesting against the Capitalist System

The rallying call in the time of COVID-19 was "we are all in this together". Whilst there was no evidence of this in deed – as witnessed by vaccine apartheid – it is hoped that this powerful motivating cry will hold true – for democratically making and creating a better post-COVID-19 world. But if it turns out to be the case that we are not all in it together in making a future that is certainly not in the image of capitalism, then – just like the workers on the frontline of COVID-19 – the burden will once again fall on the workers, the downtrodden, the middle classes, etc. of the world to imagine, democratically plan and unite in making that future. Through the centuries, workers have marched and protested. It is why workers in many countries now have an 8-hour working day, sick leave, annual leave, etc. Women have marched since the beginning of the 20th century. Women in many countries now have the right to vote – like their male counterparts. Blacks in America marched and protested for decades – before they were granted equal rights in the US. We in South Africa marched and protested against apartheid for decades – before apartheid was finally destroyed. The youth in many parts of the world are marching and protesting against the inaction against climate change. Ineffective leaders are starting to take notice.

In the US, many protestors went out and marched when COVID-19 was still a clear and present danger – and freely held up placards that read: "Stop the Tyranny", "Don't Use Fear to Steal our Freedom", "Don't Tread on my Rights", "Pro Common Sense", "America – The Land of the Free", "Let my People Go", "Those who would give up essential Liberty to purchase a little temporary Safety, deserve neither Liberty nor Safety", "Fauci Lied, The Economy Died", "Work Matters" (BBC). If COVID-19 is the pandemic for the past few years, capitalism has been the pandemic for many centuries and continues to be so. If COVID-19 was a clear and present danger for a few years, capitalism was a clear and present danger for many centuries – and will continue to be a clear and present danger for all of humanity and planet earth – unless capitalism is seriously challenged by all in all parts of the world. COVID-19 has made the world ripe for marches and protests. People the world over are marching and protesting against high food prices, high energy costs, low wages, poverty, etc. Such marches and protests must finally transcend into marches and protests against the capitalist system itself. Persistent marching and protesting against injustices of various sorts in the past – finally achieves the desired result. Persistent marching and protesting against the capitalist system – will finally achieve the desired result. A definite way to significantly and formidably challenge capitalism is for citizens in all parts of the world to plan and embark on marches and protests calling for the end of the capitalist system. The infrastructure of social media at the global level is in place to mobilise citizens at a global level against the capitalist system. The majority who suffer under capitalism must take ownership of the streets against the minority that bizarrely benefit from the capitalist system. The capitalist system cannot and will not be changed from within – change has to start from without. The following are some of the sayings, maxims or thoughts that could adorn such marches and protests against capitalism: "For the Many – Not the Few"; "Capitalism is the legitimate racket of the ruling class" (Al Capone); "Capitalism is the extraordinary belief that the nastiest of men, for the nastiest of reasons, will somehow work for the benefit of us all" (John Maynard Keynes); "As capitalist, he is only capital personified. His soul is the soul of capital" (Karl Marx); "The evils of capitalism are as real as the evils of militarism and evils of racism" (Martin Luther King, Jr.); "Call it democracy, or call it democratic socialism, but there must be a better distribution of wealth within this country for all God's children" (Martin Luther King, Jr.); "The paradise of the rich is made out of the hell of the poor" (Victor Hugo); "Every day I wake up on the wrong side of capitalism" (Sun Rise); "They got money for war, but can't feed the poor" (Tupac Shakur); "Capitalism cannot reform itself; it is doomed to self-destruction" (W.E.B. Du Bois); "Capitalism has not always existed in the world and will not always exist in the world" (Alexandria Ocasio-Cortez); "Capitalism is war; socialism is peace" (Karl Liebknecht); "We want capitalism and market forces to be the slave of democracy rather than the opposite" (Thomas Piketty); "We have two evils to fight, capitalism and racism. We must destroy both racism and capitalism" (Huey Newton); "Capitalism is a stupid system, a backward system" (Stokely Carmichael); "Capitalism offers you freedom, but far from giving people freedom, it enslaves them" (Ian Mckellen); "Capitalism is an evil, and you cannot regulate evil. You have to eliminate it and replace it with something that is good for all people and that something is democracy" (Michael Moore); "Capitalism has destroyed our belief in any effective power but that of self-interest backed by force" (George Bernard Shaw); "I have said it already, I am convinced that the way to build a new and better world is not capitalism. Capitalism leads us straight to hell" (Hugo Chavez); "Unbridled capitalism is the dung of the devil" (Pope Francis); "I ask you to ensure that humanity is served by wealth and not ruled by it" (Pope Francis); "I should tie myself to no particular system of society other than of socialism" (Nelson Mandela); "There is a sufficiency in the world for man's need but not for man's greed" (Mahatma

Gandhi); "World-wide capitalism kills more people everyday then Hitler did. And he was crazy" (Ken Livingstone).

Humans are creative. Whilst capitalism suppresses the creativity of humans, the crisis of capitalism will also unleash the creativity of humans. We can therefore look forward to seeing many interesting and creative slogans denouncing the capitalist system – in hundreds of marches against capitalism worldwide in the years and decades to come.

14 A Willing and Peaceful Transformation or an Inevitable Violent Revolution?

It was John F. Kennedy who, in March of 1962, said: "those who make peaceful revolution impossible will make violent revolution inevitable." He was assassinated the following year! Violent revolutions have been part and parcel of human history. History uncomfortably demonstrates that revolution is the mid-wife for a better life – from the one revolted against. South Africa's 1994 democratic transition has been termed a negotiated revolution – it did result in a better life – from that lived under apartheid. It was a minimalist violent revolution, but one that has also delivered the 3 social ills – poverty, unemployment and inequality. In the time of COVID-19, we witnessed breakouts of protests and revolts in different parts of the world. Violence was part of these protests and revolts. Are we to conclude that those in and with power are making peaceful revolutions impossible? Are we to conclude that only violent revolutions can lead to a better society? These are difficult questions for a 21st century society to ponder upon. If politicians will not declare capitalism a disastrous system, then maybe it is time for citizens globally to do so: "politicians aren't the only ones with the power to declare a crisis. Mass movements of regular people can declare one too" (Klein, 2014: 13). Millions have died as a result of the violence heaped on people by the capitalist system. COVID-19 was merely the trigger that set off the death and destruction inherent in capitalism. A post-COVID-19 world cannot ignore such violence piled on people – that set it off on a transition course. To expose people to an enemy is the first step of any violent chain reaction. It is what capitalism had done. By not having capable states to help in the war against COVID-19, people the world over were left to themselves – to fight the virus in their homes and on their hospital beds. The doctors and nurses did their best with the meagre resources that capitalism grudgingly handed over to them. For the millions that lost their lives – the violence of the virus was overwhelming.

A new society was born in Russia after 1917 through violence –first by violence against the people by the Romanovs and subsequently by violence against the Romanovs. A new society was born in France through violence – first by violence against the people and then through violence against the state. That capitalist-continued greed, plunder and looting from the masses is what will enable revolution, was opined by Friedrich Engels:

> Hence also the deep wrath of the whole working-class, from Glasgow to London, against the rich, by whom they are systematically plundered and mercilessly left to their fate, a wrath which before too long a time goes by, a time almost within the power of man to predict, must break out into a revolution in comparison with which the French Revolution, and the year 1794, will prove to have been child's play.
>
> ENGELS, 1845: 17

It is hoped that science, democratic principles and processes and peaceful marches and protests – and not violent rebellion and revolution – will be the midwives for shaping and forming a post-capitalist society. A civilised society must use all of its resources, historical experiences of violence and intelligence to avoid a violent transition to a post-capitalist world. Those in power in society are the ones who carry this historical burden. After J.F. Kennedy, the powerful in society can either make a peaceful revolution possible – or make a violent revolution inevitable. Just like the powerful in global society finally acknowledged that apartheid in South Africa had to go – it is hoped that the powerful in society can start by acknowledging that global capitalism needs to go.

15 Capitalism – This Too Shall Pass!

Planet Earth is about 4.5 billion years old. Life on planet Earth is about 3.8 billion years old. The use of fire by man is about 300,000 years old. The agricultural revolution is about 12,000 years old. Money is about 5,000 years old. Buddhism is about 2,500 years old. Christianity is about 2,000 years old. Islam is about 1,400 years old (Harari, 2014). And Capitalism is only about 500 years old (Heller, 2011: xi)! Capitalism is a latecomer in the life of nature and man. Just like the invention of money and religion – capitalism is also an invention of man. In its very brief history, capitalism has delivered to humankind the Industrial Revolution and the British Empire. In its brief history, capitalism has also forced onto humankind: colonialism, two destructive World Wars, Nazism, nuclear fear, apartheid in the global south and in the middle-east, climate change the world over, a life of debt and guaranteed death during a pandemic. We have lived through 500 years of capitalism. We have witnessed the chaotic nature of capitalist societies in the time of COVID-19. The capitalist West, India and Brazil have shown the world how this historical system has failed and continues to fail humankind. Judging from its history, capitalism has always been complex, chaotic, contradictory and conflictual. With five hundred years of innovation and unimaginable productivity, capitalism has not been able to protect women, children and men when they most needed that protection. It has delivered on its material genius, but it has not delivered the good and happy life for all. It has delivered on its brilliance of profit-making, but the people and planet have paid too high a price for this strange exchange and trade-off. Like COVID-19, capitalism has spread to all four corners of the globe since its inception. And like COVID-19, it has killed off people in places where it had settled itself. If the break-up of the Soviet Union made it appear that capitalism was The End of History, then the Great Crisis of 2008 once again showed capitalism to be a socio-economic system in decline. Capitalism is struggling to sustain its expansionist tendencies. COVID-19 dealt a further blow to the failing and ailing capitalist system. Capitalism, after fulfilling its destiny of increasing the productive nature of the worker and the means of production, has no other alternative but to reach a dead end – in the same way that feudalism did. This is the hypothesis of Karl Marx – one that is proving to be true the world over. The economic ideologies of Milton Friedman, Friedrich Hayek, Ayn Rand, etc. have thus far served to keep the extractive system of capitalism in place – in the same way that the ideology of loyalty to the king and the ideology of fear, sin and hell had served to keep the extractive feudal system in place. Capitalism's rot has expanded. Its devastation has intensified. It is a system in major disequilibrium. Its contradictions have become unmanageable and an eyesore. Just like slavery and feudalism – capitalism is doomed to fail. The 500-year-old economic system is no longer able to function on free market ideologies. COVID-19 has exposed all of the ideologies that have upheld and protected capitalism for so long. If capitalism is to continue to survive, it will require the intervention of the nanny state and socialist principles for the rich. Modern Man is about 300 000 years old. In that time, man went from a hunter-gatherer to a slave and master, to a peasant and lord and then to a worker and a boss. Capitalism is just 500 years old – about 0.17% of mankind's time on planet earth! Man is 600 times older than capitalism! How did we allow capitalism to overpower the majority of humankind! How did we allow capitalism to take people away from their means of livelihoods – their land! How did we allow capitalism to take away the means of production from the majority of people in all parts of the world! How did we allow capitalism to take away our humanity! How did we allow capitalism to remove man from nature – and nature from man! How did we allow capitalism to atomise the human race into nationalities, races, ethnicities, etc. How did we allow capitalism to infect tens of millions in the time of COVID-19 and kill millions of our fellow human beings as well! How did we allow the capitalist system – that is only 500 years old – to rule over man who is 300 000 years old! Surely *this too must pass*!

CHAPTER 11

Imagine

A Better World Is Waiting to Be Born

Life isn't about finding yourself. Life is about creating yourself.

GEORGE BERNARD SHAW

•••

Anything you can imagine, you can create.

OPRAH WINFREY

Imagine there's no heaven
It's easy if you try
No hell below us
Above us only sky
Imagine all the people
Living for today .... Aha-ah ....

Imagine there's no countries
It isn't hard to do
Nothing to kill or die for
And no religion, too
Imagine all the people
Living life in peace .... You ....

You may say I'm a dreamer
But I'm not the only one
I hope someday you'll join us
And the world will be as one

Imagine no possessions
I wonder if you can

 | DOI:10.1163/9789004539808_012

No need for greed or hunger
A brotherhood of man
Imagine all the people
Sharing all the world .... You ....

You may say I'm a dreamer
But I'm not the only one
I hope someday you'll join us
And the world will live as one

JOHN LENNON (1940–1980)

I guess Homo sapiens have the capacity to be both romantic dreamers and evolving scientists! Besides *"Workers of all Lands Unite"*, there is another maxim engraved on Karl Marx's tombstone in Highgate Cemetery in London: *"Philosophers have only interpreted the world – the point however is to change it".*

Bibliography

Abbott, T., 2020. We need a strong economy, but people come first. The path ahead should be about a better society rather than just dollars and cents. *The Australian*. 24 April 2020.

Abernathy, G., 2021. I hope mask-wearing won't outlast the pandemic. *Winnipeg Sun*. 2 January 2021.

Adams, R., Stewart, H., and Brooks, L., 2020. Reopening schools on 1 June is too dangerous, say doctors. *The Guardian*. 16 May 2020.

Adamson, M. and Rocca, F., In this pandemic, none of us are safe until we are all safe. *The Independent*. 7 Jun 2020.

Addley, E., 2020. 'I feel as if I'm part of a village'. How COVID-19 has transformed neighbours into communities. *The Guardian*. 6 June 2020–15.

Adler, Moshe. 2009. *Economics for the rest of us – debunking the science that makes life dismal*. London: The New Press.

Africa, S., 2022. Our own 'Arab Spring'? *Cape Argus*. 28 July 2022.

Aiyar, S., Fund brick and Mortar to Construct growth. *Sunday Express*. 5 July 2020.

Al Jazeera Television Network. 2020. COVID-19 coverage.

Alden, T., 2020. Why nobody can agree on anything. *The Malta Independent on Sunday*. 7 June 2020.

Anderssen, E., 2020. 'No One Should Die Alone'. *The Globe and Mail (Ontario Edition)*. 21 November 2020.

Andress, D., 2020. A tale of two revolutions. *BBC History Magazine*. 9 July 2020.

Andrews, E., Who Were the Luddites? https://www.history.com/news/who-were-the-luddites. accessed on Tuesday 11 May 2021 at 2.18pm.

Ansari, T., 2020. US virus death toll tops 100,000. *The Australian*. 29 May 2020.

Aratani, L., 2021. Long overdue step or censorship? US split on tweets ban. *The Observer*. 10 January 2021.

Armus, T. 2020. 'Every day it's getting worse': Bodies of coronavirus victims are left on the streets in Ecuador's largest city. *The Washington Post*. 3rd April 2020.

Baker, D., 2006. *The Conservative Nanny State: How the wealthy use the government*. Published by the Center for Economic and Policy Research. Washington, DC.

Baloyi, B., and Mhlanga, R., 2020. Time to put the welfare of health workers before profits: Private health-care providers pay dividends but neglect frontline staff. *Sunday Times*. 8 November 2020.

Bankole, M., 2020. The Tories are ignoring the root cause of BAME deaths. *The Independent*. 4 June 2020.

Bay, 2021. Kim Jong Un-Reliable North Korea Intersects Amazon Servers. *Ridgway Record*. 22 January 2021.

BBC, 2016. Backlash after Barack Obama EU referendum intervention https://www.bbc.com/news/uk-politics-36117907 accessed on Wednesday 19 May 2021 at 4.01am.

Billeck, S., and Snell, J., 2021. Face Plant. Demonstrators topple Legislature statues: *Winnipeg Sunday*. 2 July 2021.

Bob, Y.J. 2021. Free speech with no checks is death blow to democracy. *The Jerusalem Post*. 8 January 2021.

Boffey, D., 2021. Court orders Royal Dutch Shell to cut carbon emissions by 45% by 2030. *The Guardian*. 26 May 2021.

Booth, R., 2020. Covid-bereaved suffer more grief and isolation than those mourning cancer deaths, finds study. *The Guardian*. 27 November 2020.

Bowles, S., and Gintis, H., 1985. *Democracy and Capitalism – Property, Community and the Contradictions of modern social thought.* London: Routledge and Kegan Paul.

Brennan, T., 1993. *Feminism for Today – History after Lacan*, London: Routledge.

Bruce, P. 2020. Ancient culture of domination spawns another murder. *Sunday Times*. 07 June 2020.

Bruce, P. 2020. Cabinet is dangerously off the rails of good sense. *Sunday Times*. 16 May 2020.

Business Mirror, Philippines, 2020, https://www.pressreader.com/article/281513638489605 *COVID-19 News*. 2 August 2020.

Cacioppo, J.T. and Patrick, W., 2008. *Loneliness – Human Nature and the need for social connection*. New York: W. W Norton & Company.

Campbell, D., 2020. People dying alone often left for up to two weeks. *The Guardian*. 8 June 2020.

Campbell, D., 2020. First-time cases on the rise. *The Guardian*. 16 May 2020.

Campbell, D., 2021. Action needed to help tackle aftermath of lockdown. *The Guardian*. 24 March 2021.

Carroll, R., Lorenzo Todo, L., Connolly, K., Jones, S., Gillet, K., 2020. Need for migrant farm workers across EU increasing tensions. *The Guardian*. 11 May 2020.

Chiu, A., 2020. The coronavirus ravaged a Michigan convent, killing 13 nuns and infecting 18 others. *The Washington Post*. 25 July 2020.

Chomsky, 1992. What uncle Sam really wants in *How the world works*. Soft Skull Press.

Chulu, B., Govt must clarify pricing policy. *The Zimbabwe Independent*. 22 January 2021.

Clark, R., 2020. .... Are totally divided over "the science". *The Week*. 24 April 2020.

Cohen, J., Cornforth, M., Dobb, M., Hobsbawm, E.J., Klugmann, J., Mynatt, M., Allen, J.S., Foner, P.S., Struik, D.J., Weinstone, W.W., Karmanova, N.P., Pavlov, V.N., Shcheglova, M.K., Solovyova, T.Y., Yeremin, Y.V., Fedoseyev, P.N., Golman, L.I., Malysh, A.I., Yegorov, A.G., and Zevin, V.Y., 2010. *Karl Marx and Frederick Engels, Volume 8. Marx and Engels 1848–49.* UK: Lawrence & Wishart. Electric Book.

Cohn, S.K., 2008: *Lust for liberty : the politics of social revolt in medieval Europe, 1200–1425 : Italy, France, and Flanders*. London: Harvard University Press.

Corcoran, T., 2021. Markets. In praise of shareholder capitalism. *National Post* (Latest Edition). 23 January 2021.

COVID-19 News. 2020. Mayor sends teams to address "breathtaking" number of cases in Chicago's Latino community. *COVID-19 News*. 8 May 2020.

Cox, L., 2020. Coalition is aiming to change Australia's environment laws before review is finished. *The Guardian* Australia. 24 April 2020.

Daley, J., 2020. Yet again, the radical Left has infiltrated a protest and ruined it. *The Sunday Telegraph*. 5 July 2020.

Dawson, T., 2021.'Deplatforming' And Free Speech. *National Post* (*Latest Edition*). 11 January 2021.

D'Emilio, F., 2020. Plague reminder looms over Pope's prayer. *New York Daily News*. 28 March 2020.

Dearden, L., 2020. Black and Asian people fined disproportionately under coronavirus laws. *The Independent*. 4 June 2020.

Deepak, K., 2020. Capital's Malthusian moment. *FrontLine*. 5 June 2020.

Dehler, G. Ludlow Massacre. United States history [1914]. https://www.britannica.com /event/Ludlow-Massacre accessed on Tuesday 11 May 2021 at 14.40.

Delaibatiki, N. 2021. Assault Democracy .... What Kind Of Democracy Do We Want? ' We must guard against the rise in extremism'. *Fiji Sun*. 10 January 2021.

Devlin, H., 2020. Growing exasperation among experts over politicians who claim they 'follow the science'. *The Guardian*. 24 April 2020.

Dhillon, A., 2020. Indians swap bus travel for bikes as virus cases surge. *The Guardian*. 25 July 2020.

Dickson, A., 2020. ACC: A confused neoliberal fairy tale. *Manawatu Standard*. 5 October 2020.

Dixon, H., 2020. Teaching unions 'celebrating shutdown' Child health expert says youngsters' lives have been put on hold to protect the middle-aged and elderly. *The Daily Telegraph*. 12 June 2020.

Dlamini, K., 2021. Vaccine nationalism should be made a crime against humanity. *The Sunday Times*. January 23 2021.

Dudden, A. and Marks, A. 2020. South Korea took rapid, intrusive measures against COVID-19 – and they worked, *The Guardian – International Edition*. Friday 20 March 2020.

Duffy, A., and Gillis, M., 2021: A Canada day like no other: A peaceful day of reckoning on Parliament Hill. *Ottawa Citizen*. 2 July 2021.

Dunlap, A., and Correa-Cabrera, G., 2020. Documentary reveals flaws with renewables. *Houston Chronicle*. 28 May 2020.

Dunne, D., 2021. Pledge on fossil fuels full of loopholes, say campaigners. *The Independent*. 25 April 2021.

Eagleton, T., 2018. *Why Marx was Right*. London: Yale University Press.

Edgerton, D., Where Brexit and Covid collide. *The New European*. 30 April 2020.

Editor, 2020. Advice ignored by Trump helps Vietnam fight virus. *COVID-19 News*. 2 August 2020.

Editor, 2020. Eco Survey calls for pro-business policies, strengthening invisible hand of market. *Millennium Post*. 1 February 2020.

Editor, 2020. Improve the world: Stop buying from China. *Santa Fe New Mexican*. 12 July 2020.

Editor, 2020. Mask opponents claim to be fighting "tyranny." Instead, they're surrendering. Foes drag on our misery. The *Philadelphia Inquirer*. 1 July 2020.

Editor, 2020. Meghan will make millions but Camilla will make a difference. *Daily Mail*. 5 September 2020.

Editor, 2020. Modi govt should focus on real task over Covid. *The Asian Age*. 23 June 2020.

Editor, 2020. More protests in Jakarta. *The Straits Times*. 9 October 2020.

Editor, 2020. Move to limit Trump, Pence's exposure to virus comes after 2 aides get Covid-19. *The Straits Times*. 13 May 2020.

Editor, 2020. Sharing stories: COVID survivors find solace in support group. *DT Next*. 12 July 2020.

Editor, 2020. Today in quotes. *Gulf News*. 18 June 2020.

Editor, 2020. US virus death toll a new stain on its human rights record and politics. *Global Times*. 29 May 2020.

Editor, 2020. For the virus, Canada is two countries. *The Globe and Mail* (Alberta Edition). 11 May 2020.

Editor, 2020. Vietnam records 1st death in virus rebound. *New Straits Times*. 1 August 2020.

Editor, 2021. Capital change. How to ensure economics leaves no one behind. *New Straits Times*. 31 March 2020.

Editor, 2021. In emphasising the role of institutions in their economic analysis, Gunnar Myrdal and Friedrich von Hayek paved the way for later research in institutional economics. *Millennium Post*. 17 January 2021.

Editor, 2021. Vaccine access: Think of others before profits. *Daily Camera (Boulder)*. 26 January 2021.

Editor, 2021. WHO Warns of Mass Trauma Caused by COVID-19. *Pandemic. Fiji Sun*. 7 March 2021.

Editor, The faithful too have a duty of care. *Mail & Guardian*. 29 May 2020.

Editor, War against the Covid-19 pandemic is far from over. *Daily Dispatch*. 19 June 2020.

Editor. Bezos, Musk among list of Uber-rich tax avoiders. *The Southland Times*. 10 June 2021.

Editor, 2020. A return to socialist approach is needed. *The Chronicle*. 29 September 2020.

Editor, 2020. Blockade: Protests over poor service delivery, costly electricity. *The Citizen* (*KZN*). 2 August 2022.

Editor, 2021. Huge vaccine divide threatens global economic recovery. *Sunday Times.* 7 February 2021.

Editorial. 2020. US government should stand with Minnesota people. *Global Times – Weekend.* 30 May 2020.

Elliot, L., 2020. Mass unemployment heralds an explosion of anxiety and despair. *The Guardian.* 11 May 2020.

Ellis-Petersen, H. and Hassan, A., Violent clashes as Indian farmers storm Delhi's Red Fort. *The Guardian Australia.* 27 January 2021.

Ellis-Petersen, H. and Rahman, S.A., 2020. H.E. West Bengal Muslims count cost of violence. *The Guardian.* 8 Jun 2020.

Engels, F., 1845. *The Condition of the Working-Class in England in 1844.* Translated by Florence Kelley Wischnewetzky. London: George Allen & Unwin Ltd.

Evans, D., A date to remember … or to forget? *Westside Eagle-Observer.* 13 January 2021.

Evans, R., Garside, J., and Smith, J., 2020. £1bn in state contracts given to companies without public tender. *The Guardian.* 16 May 2020.

Farhi, P., 2020. Pence's staff targets reporter over tweet on masks. *The Washington Post.* 2 May 2020.

Farrer, M., 2020. 'Who cares about the AAA rating?': the Covid financial crisis calls for reset, not recovery. *The Guardian. Australia.* 15 June 2020.

Fasan, O., 2021. What behavioural economics tells us about Nigeria's elusive change. *Business Day* (Nigeria). 25 January 2021.

Fikeni, S., 2021. Poverty, Unemployment, Inequaity: A better life for all remains elusive for millions in SA's democracy project. *The Sunday Independent.* 1 August 2021.

Friedman, K., S. 2003. *Myths Of The Capitalist Market.* New York: Algora Publishing.

Friedman, M., and Friedman, R., 1980. *Free to Choose.* New York: Harcourt Brace Jovanovich.

Fukuyama, F., 1992. *The End of History and the Last Man.* New York: The Free Press, Macmillan Inc.

Gearan, A., Chiu, A. and Wagner, J., 2020. Trump skips mask in plant visit, defying Ford's request and Michigan law. *The Washington Post.* 22 May 2020.

Gemeda, A., 2014. https://www.academia.edu/7159193/Marx_and_Human_Rights. Accessed on 5 September 2022.

Gerard, L., 2020. Journalism's Jeopardy. *The New European.* 30 April 2020.

Gill, S., 2022. In search for a better life: Lecturer joins 'great resignation'. *Manawatu Standard.* 2 July 2022.

Gillits, T.B., 2020. Tweak narrative on black lives to forge racial unity. *Daily News.* 11 June 2020.

Givhan, 2020. Handshakes are petri dishes for germs, but possible replacements aren't up to the task. *The Washington Post*. 19 May 2020.

Glover, F., 2022. Three in 10 employees in Middle East plan to look for a new job this year – The 'Great Resignation' trend is continuing, as workers prioritise flexibility and wellbeing, survey finds. *The National News*. 23 June 2022.

Gordhan, P., 2021. State is tackling the problems of SOEs'. *Sunday Times*. March 7 2021.

Gordon, B., 2020. 'War' is far from over. *The Expositor (Brantford)*. 17 June 2020.

Goswami, K. and Luthra, S., 2020. Commissions of Omission. *The Sunday Guardian*. 7 June 2020.

Govender, N. 2020. WhatsApp family communication. 29 April 2020.

Govender, P. 2020. New Schools Timetable – Teacher unions insist Angie halt all classes until late next month, pleasding Covid risk. *Sunday Times*. South Africa. 20 July 2020.

Grattan, S., and Faiola, A., 2021. Fears grow over escalating violence in Colombia. *The Washington Post*. 5 May 2021.

Greenhill, S., 2008. It's awful–Why did nobody see it coming?: The Queen gives her verdict on global credit crunch. *The Daily Mail*. 6 November 2008.

Haldar, N., But Capitalism Is a Lesser Evil. *The Economic Times*. 16 October 2020.

Hall, C.A.S., and Klitgaard, K., 2018. *Energy and the Wealth of Nations – An Introduction to Biophysical Economics* Second Edition. Switzerland: Springer International Publishing.

Hanna, M. 2021 Does it violate President Trump's right to free speech? Trump and backers cried foul, but while this is not government censorship, there are other issues. *The Philadelphia Inquirer*. 10 January 2021.

Harari, Y.N., 2014. *Sapiens: A Brief History of Humankind*. UK: Harper.

Harford, T., 2021. Lead by Example. Tim Harford writes in praise of the pencil and other low-key feats of engineering. *The Expositor (Brantford)*. 16 January 2021.

Harper, P., 2020. Save us from a deadly mistake, *Mail & Guardian*, 29 May 2020.

Hazra, A.I. 2021. Democracy's Discontents Lessons From Investing All Capitol Carnage In a Messiah Red Herring. *The Economic Times*. 8 January 2021.

Heath, A., 2020. The Chancellor wants to replace central control with policies that harness the power of the market. *The Daily Telegraph*. 9 July 2020.

Heenan, N. and A. Sturman (2020) 'Labour, Nature, Capitalism and COVID-19' *Journal of Australian Political Economy* No. 85, pp. 193–9.

Heller, H., 2011. *The Birth of Capitalism A Twenty-First-Century Perspective*. London: Pluto Press.

Henley, J., Jones, S., Giuffrida, A., Oltermann, P., Smith, H., and Carroll, R., 2020., UK handling of crisis gets short shrift overseas. *The Guardian*. 7 May 2020.

Hogbin, G., 2008. Legacy of free-market thinker pinpoints government failure. *The Weekend Australian*. 23 August 2008.

Horne, D.N., 2020. Dead-end policy. *The New Zealand Herald*. 20 May 2020.

Hosken, G., 2021. Obligatory workplace jabs debated. *Sunday Times*. 14 February 2021.

Hosken, G., and Nair, N., 2020. Nighmare at hospitals as alcohol takes its toll – booze-based trauma surges in overworked ERs after ban is lifted. *Sunday Times*. 07 June 2020.

Howell, T., 2020. Virus clusters traced back to members of choirs. Singers breathe in others' infections. *The Washington Times Weekly*. 11 May 2020.

Howie, M., 2022. Young people in Japan urged to drink more to help economy. *Evening Standard*. 18 Aug 2022.

Ignacio, C.K.P., 2022. Understanding the metaverse and the Great Resignation. *Business World*. 6 June 2022.

Islam, Y., [Cat Stevens]. 1970. *Where do the children play?* https://www.lyrics.com/lyric/919514/Cat+Stevens/Where+Do+the+Children+Play%3F Accessed on 23 May 2022.

Jamison, P., 2020. After Mardi Gras ministry, he never made it home. *The Washington Post*. 28 Apr 2020.

Javed, A., 2020. War against the Invisible enemy viz-a-viz COVID-19. *Times of India*. 30 March 2020.

Johns, C., 2021. Now would be a good time for unusual candour. *The Irish Times*. 25 January 2021.

Johnstone, C., and Taylor, P., 2020. PM schools teachers: go back to class. 'Bus Drivers are Showing up for Work'. *The Weekend Australian*. 25 April 2020.

Joint General Secretary of the RSS. 2020. Bharat can help shape a new world order. *The New Indian Express*. 8 June 2020.

Jonas, M., 2020. This is the moment that we need to awaken and demand an alternative future. *Sunday Times*. 07 June 2020. South Africa.

Jong-Wha, L., 2020. Building South Korea's post-pandemic economy. *Bangkok Post*. 15 June 2020.

Kampfner, J., 2020. The suffering of poorer nations will be felt by us all. *The New European*. 30 April 2020.

Kari, P., 2020. Amazon executive resigns over company's 'chickenshit' firings of employee activists. *The Guardian* (USA). 5 May 2020.

Keller, J., Cryderman, K., Graney, E., 2020. Government estimates corporate tax cut will result in up to $300-million in forgone revenue this fiscal year. *The Globe and Mail* (*BC Edition*). 30 June 2020.

Kelly, P., 2020. Morrison Needs To Find His Finest Hour. Political capital built during the crisis must be spent on reform. *The Weekend Australian*. 25 April 2020.

Kelly, W.J., 2020. At the mercy of the invisible hand. *National Post* (*Latest Edition*). 23 September 2008.

Kgosana, C., and Hosken G., 2020. We can't pay R5bn sin taxes, says alcohol industry. *Sunday Times*. 19 July 2020.

Khetarpal, S., 2020. The Labour Law Conundrum. States have proposed radical changes in labour laws post lockdown. But those cannot trigger an economic revival. *Business Today* 28 June 2020.

Kings, S., 2020. COVID-19 brings South Africa's daily carbon emissions down by 20%. *Mail & Guardian.* 22 May 2020.

Kirchgaessner, S., 2020. The tiny team spying on hacking giants. *The Guardian.* 13 May 2020.

Kishtainy, N., Abbot, G., Farndon, J., Kennedy, F., Meadway, J., Wallace, C. and Weeks, M. (2012). *The Economics Book.* Dorling Kindersley Ltd. Great Britain.

Kitney, D., 2020. Virus has transformed society: NBN chief. *The Australian.* 24 April 2020.

Klein, N., 2014. *This changes everything – capitalism versus the climate.* New York: Simon & Schuster.

Kommenda, N., 2021. Rich use business jets to seek winter sun and escape Covid lockdown. *The Guardian.* 22 January 2021.

Kovel, J., 2007. *The Enemy of Nature – The End of Capitalism or the End of the World?* London: Zed Books.

Lane, R., 2020. Greater Capitalism: The coronavirus pandemic is transforming the economic system day by day, hour by hour What's emerging is something better, fairer, smarter – and it's happening right now. *Forbes.* 21 June 2020.

Lau, M., 2020. Betting billions on economic ignorance. *Calgary Sun.* 10 September 2020.

Lavrov, S., 2020. Conclusion and mission on COVID-19. *Global Times.* 29 May 2020.

Lebedev, E., 2020. While the world reels from the coronavirus, the next pandemic is not far away. *The Independent.* 19 April 2020.

Lehohla, P. 2020. Finding solutions beyond the virus. *Sunday Tribune.* 15 April 2020.

Lin II, R.G., Greene, S., and Vega, P., 2020., As virus surges, so does its toll's disparity. *Los Angeles Times.* 25 July 2020.

Lovett, S., 2021. Labour: Punish UK firms working with PPE suppliers accused of modern slavery. *The Independent.* 24 March 2021.

Macharis, O., and Farajalla, N., 2020. COVID-19 clarifies climate crisis – Unlike the virus, there is no treatment for global warming except to immediately abandon economic activities that cause it. *Mail & Guardian.* 15 May 2020.

Mandela, N. "I am prepared to die". https://www.nelsonmandela.org/news/entry/i-am-prepared-to-die. Accessed on Wednesday 24 May 2022 at 5.02.

Mannheim, K., 1953. *Ideology and utopia: an introduction to the sociology of knowledge: 1893–1947.* London: Routledge and Kegan Paul Ltd.

Marshall, A., 2013 [1890]. *Principles of Economics.* New York: Palgrave Macmillan.

Marshall, E., 2020. A nation adrift under a president still in denial. With his country now at the centre of the Covid-19 pandemic, Brazil's Jair Bolsonaro is in deep water. *The Daily Telegraph.* 25 May 2020.

Marx, K., 1959. *Economic and Philosophical Manuscripts of 1844*. Moscow: Progress Publishers.

Marx, K. 1845 [1998]. *The German Ideology*. New York: Prometheus Books.

Marx, K. 2011 [1867]. *Capital Vol 1-A Critique of Political Economy.* Translated by Samuel Moore and Edward Aveling, edited by Friedrich Engels. New York: Dover Publications Inc.

Marx, K. and Engels, F., 1848. *Manifesto of the Communist Party*. Moscow: Progress Publishers.

Mason, G., 2020. Most of us agree that violence against women is a blight on our culture – so why are we doing so little about it? There are not enough shelter spaces for women to turn to when fearing danger at home. *The Globe and Mail*. (*Ontario Edition*). 22 May 2020.

Mason, R., and Devlin, H., 2020. 'One in 400 has COVID-19'. Data from ONS survey gives first snapshot of virus rates outside care homes and hospitals. *The Guardian*. 15 May 2020.

Mavuso, B., 2020. We must take the medicine before IMF forces it down our throats. *Sunday Times*. 07 June 2020. South Africa.

Mawson, A.K., 2008. PM should not misrepresent Friedrich Hayek's views. *The Australian*. 5 August 2008.

McCarten, J., 2020. Trump rushing pipeline approvals: report. *The Globe and Mail* (*Ontario Edition*). 9 December 2020.

McCausland, N., Why every black life matters. *Belfast Telegraph*. 11 June 2020.

McKinney, F., 2021. On Biden and the role of government in life. *The Norwalk Hour.* 23 January 2021.

McKinnon, J.D., 2021. PM should not misrepresent Friedrich Hayek's views. *The Australian*. 5 August 2008.

McPhee, P., 2002. *The French Revolution – 1789–1799*. UK: Oxford University Press.

Meaker, M. 2021. Leader of the free world silenced online. *The Daily Telegraph*. 8 January 2021.

Merrick, R., 2020. Independent scientists say new rules are 'dangerous'. *The Independent*. 13 May 2020.

Milman, O., 2020. Trump ignores warning of 'death sentence' to press on with 'getting our country open'. *The Guardian*. 7 May 2020.

Milman, O., 2020. US warned of 'darkest winter' due to Trump's virus failures. *The Guardian*. 15 May 2020.

Mirchandani, A., 2018. Karl Marx- The Revolutionary Thinker. *The Policy Voice*. By March 22, 2018.

Moffat, J., 2021. Need to see Dunedin grow and reduce debt before plan. *Otago Daily Times*. 30 January 2021.

Monbiot, G., 2021. Misinformation kills and we have a duty to suppress it. *The Guardian.* 27 January 2021.

Monroe, S., and Monroe, L., 2020. Wear masks. *The Union Democrat.* 20 June 2020.

Moore, J., 2021. Blinkered Tories keep the Trump fires burning with review of workers' rights. *The Independent.* 21 January 2021.

Moore, O., 2020. Suicides on TTC have spiked during COVID-19: data. *The Globe and Mail (Ontario Edition).* 9 December 2020.

Moore, T., and Feis, A., 2020. Would-be bombers wind-up and pitch. *New York Post.* 1 June 2020.

Moore, W.J., Ed. 2016. *Anthropocene or Capitalocene? Nature, History, and the Crisis of Capitalism.* USA: PM Press.

Moosa, V., 2021. The political party funding act is finally here. *Sunday Times.* 24 Jan 2021.

Morris, D., 1967. *The Naked Ape – A Zoologist's Study of the Human Animal.* New York: Delta, Dell Publishing.

Morris, S., 2020. 'Lockdown has been so lonely – I can't wait to finally see my grandchildren'. *The Daily Telegraph.* 12 June 2020.

Morrow, A., 2020. Why is there a resurgence of COVID-19 cases across the US.? *The Globe and Mail (Alberta Edition).* 11 July 2020.

Morss, A., 2020. Drop in noise pollution used to map world's dawn chorus. *The Guardian.* 30 May 2020.

Mthombothi, B., 2020. Some ministers a bit too happy to wield total control without the nuisance of a bill of rights. *Sunday Times.* 07 June 2020.

Mulcahy, S., Shah, A. and Jacobs, J. 2020. Nursing-home staffs lay lives on the line to keep working: More than four months into the outbreak, caregivers feel largely left to fend for themselves. *The Washington Post.* 4 July 2020.

Murnaghan, D., 2020. After the Pandemic – Our New World. *Sky News Television Network.*

Naidoo, B., 2021. "We are chasing destinations". Conversation with my friend in South Africa.

Naish, J., 2020. From bat to snake to humans – it's a real life sci-fi nightmare. *Daily Mail.* 27 Jan 2020.

Nash, J., 2020. Will drug firms cash in on COVID ANXIETY? *Irish Daily Mail.* 30 June 2020.

Ning, Yu., 2020. US virus death toll a new stain on its human rights record and politics. *Global Times.* 29 May 2020.

Njilo, N., 2020. Mkhize urges young people to fight 'unseen enemy'. *The Herald (South Africa).* 17 June 2020.

Nolen, S., and Singh, K.D., 2022. India stalling global report on COVID toll. *Houston Chronicle* Sunday. 17 April 2022.

Norris, M.L., 2020. The 'us and them' pandemic. *The Washington Post.* 22 May 2020.

Norton, J., Stevens, J., Keogh, G., Sultan, K., Sears, N., and Joseph, C., 2020. Ministers say get back to the office. So why won't their own staff turn up? *Daily Mail.* 1 August 2020.

O'Caroll, D., Interview on CNN (12 May 2020).

O'Connell, O. 2020. Coronavirus: US doctors warned they will be fired if they complain to media about lack of resources. *Independent.* 31 March 2020.

O'Grady, S., and Berger, M., 2020. A tangled history of Hong Kong geopolitics. *The Washington Post.* 22 May 2020.

O'Meara, K., 2020. *And the people stayed home.* Miami: Tra Publishing.

Oji, H., 2020. Academics seek capital market collaboration to stimulate economic growth. *The Guardian (Nigeria).* 21 Oct 2020.

Oomkes, R., 2014. November 9, 1848: The Execution of Robert Blum on the German Revolution and the execution of Robert Blum. https://www.slowtravelberlin.com/nov-9-1848-the-execution-of-robert-blum/. Accessed on Thursday 13 May 2021 at 2.54.

Osama, K., 2020. What planet does Johnson live on to think our virus response has been a success? *The Independent.* 1 May 2020.

Packham, B., UK seeks help in resettling refugees from Hong Kong – More was lost than innocent lives in the appalling massacre at Tiananmen Square. *The Australian.* 04 June 2020.

Parashar, A., Those left behind. *Drum.* https://www.news24.com/drum/News/Local/recovery-and-death-3-people-whove-been-affected-by-covid-19-on-their-harrowing-experience-20200626. Accessed on 4 September 2022.

Park, R., 2021. PM should not misrepresent Friedrich Hayek's views. *The Australian.* 5 August 2008.

Partington, R., 2021. Bitcoin tumbles after reports that Biden plans tax rises for the rich. *The Guardian.* 24 April 2021.

Petrucci, J., 2021. Pope's grand vision. *The Times-Tribune.* 14 February 2021.

Pheto, B., and Wicks, J., 2020. Church massacre blamed on fight for leadership resources. *Sunday Times*, South Africa. 20 July 2020.

Phillips, D., 2020. 'Totalitarian' government halts release of Brazil's virus figures and wipes data. *The Guardian.* 8 June 2020.

Picard, A., The coronavirus mess in the US. will only get worse. *The Globe and Mail (Ontario Edition).* 4 July 2020.

Picard, A., The coronavirus mess in the US. will only get worse. *The Globe and Mail (Ontario Edition).* 4 July 2020.

Piketty, T., 2020. *Capital and Ideology.* London: The Belknap Press of Harvard University Press.

Pilkington, E., 2020. Blow for Trump's image of control over virus as top doctor self-isolates. *The Guardian.* 11 May 2020.

Pinker, S., 2018. *Enlightment Now: The case for Reason, Science, Humanism and Progress.* New York: Viking.

Pollard, S., 2020. The tracing app has got lawyers howling about human rights, but what about the rights of people like me to stay alive! *Daily Mail.* 7 May 2020.

Pope Francis' coronavirus prayer: 'Save us, O Lord, from illness'. *The Oregonian.* https://www.oregonlive.com/coronavirus/2020/03/pope-francis-coronavirus-pray-save-us-o-lord-from-illness.html. Accessed on 9 May 2020.

Prashad, V. 2020. The Three Apartheids of Our Times (Money, Medicine, Food): *The Sixth Newsletter* . Tricontinental: Institute for Social Research.

Prashad, V. 2021.The Country Where Liberty Is a Statue: *The Second Newsletter.* Tricontinental: Institute for Social Research.

Proctor, K., 2020. Government must learn from its 'terrible mistakes', MPs are warned. *The Guardian.* 25 July 2020.

Public Health Online. A guide to careers in epidemiology. Public Health Online. https://www.publichealthonline.org/epidemiology/ Accessed on 12 August 2020.

Puspasari, S.E., 2020. Indonesian protesters push repeal of Job Creation Law. *Arab News.* 7 October 2020.

Rankin, J., 'Corona bubble' poses problems in Belgium. *The Guardian.* 11 May 2020.

Rhan, W., 2021. Tracking the cruelest tax-Raising the minimum wage puts a prohibitive tax on the ability to get a job. *The Washington Times Daily.* 26 January 2021.

Roach, A., 2020. Women are suffering during lockdown with 'no escape'. *The Independent.* 4 June 2020.

Romm, T, 2020., Return to work or risk jobless aid, states warn. *The Washington Post.* 1 May 2020.

Ronquillo, M., 2021 wish list of PH Big Business is all for business. *The Manila Times.* 10 January 2021.

Roque, 2020. A New Work-Life Balance. Form follows function – and creativity overflows. *Philippine Daily Inquirer.* 7 June 2020.

Rose, D.G., 2020. Beirut burns again as furious crowds demand revolution. *The Mail on Sunday.* 9 August 2020.

Rupar, A., 2020. Trump says 200,000 Americans could die from coronavirus, because he's done "a very good job". https://www.vox.com/2020/3/30/21199586/us-coronavirus-deaths-trump-200000-good-job. Accessed 30 March 2020 at 10pm.

Ryan, M., 2020. Executive Director, WHO Health Emergencies Programme. Interview on Aljazeera Television Network.

Sadike, M., 2022. Four killed as Tembisa burns: Death, destruction and mayhem erupts as angry residents take to the streets over service delivery, exorbitant rates, taxes and electricity bills. *The Star Late Edition.* 2 August 2022.

Sartorius, K., 2021. Covid articles could confuse. Letters to the editor. *Sunday Times.* 28 February 2021.

Schram, S.F and Pavlovskaya, M. (Ed). 2018. *Rethinking Neoliberalism – Resisting the Disciplinary Regime.* New York: Routledge.

Service, R., 2000. *Lenin – A Biography*. London: MacMillan Publishers.

Sherman, C., The Cost of Ventilators Just Skyrocketed – And New York Needs Thousands More. https://www.vice.com/en_us/article/m7qnx3/the-cost-of-ventilators-just-skyrocketed-and-new-york-needs-thousands-more. Accessed on 22nd June 2020.

Sherwood, H., 2020. Call for early reopenings for Catholics. *The Guardian*. 15 May 2020.

Shipton, M., 2021. Genteel Swiss origins of an intellectual movement that helped create Trump. *Western Mail.* 11 January 2021.

Shukla, S., 2021. Fix the underlying first – it is broken. *Business Standard.* 7 Jan 2021.

Siddique, H., 2020. Equality Khan calls for inquiry into impact on BAME people. *The Guardian*. 11 May 2020.

Simkins, P., Jukes, G. and Hickey, M. 2013. *The First World War – The War to End all Wars.* UK: Osprey Publishing Limited.

Sircar, O., 2020. The Paradox of Liberty. *The Sunday Guardian*. 7 June 2020.

Smart, T., 1996. *Children's Encylopedia of British History*. London: Kingfisher.

Smil, V., 2017. *Energy and Civilization – A History*, London: The MIT Press.

Smiley, T., and West, C., 2012. *The Rich and the Rest of US – A Poverty Manifesto.* US: Third World Press.

Smith, A. 1759 [1984]: Ed. Raphael, D.D., and MacFie, A.L. *The Theory of Moral Sentiments*. Indianapolis: Liberty Fund.

Smith, A., 2003 [1776]. *An inquiry into the nature and causes of the wealth of nations.* New York: Bantam Dell.

Smith, R., 2011. Green capitalism: the god that failed. *Real-world economics review, issue no. 56.*

Sombart, W., 1976. *Why is there no socialism in the US*. London: The Macmillan Press Ltd.

Speer, S., 2021. Government will never be the same. *National Post (National Edition).* 21 January 2021.

Ssemogerere, K., 2020. How COVID-19 has disrupted the international economy. *Daily Monitor*. Accessed on 27 March 2020.

Stiglitz, J.E., 2020. *People, Power and Profits: Progressive Capitalism for an Age of Discontent.* UK: Penguin Random House.

Stubley, P. 2020. Coronavirus: Boy, 13, 'dies alone' in UK hospital after testing positive. *Independent*. March 2020.

Swoyer, A. and Munñoz, G., 2020. Strict stay-at-home orders put violence victims in tougher situation. *The Washington Times Weekly*. 11 May 2020.

Taylor, A., 2021. Hundreds join Detroit car rally in support of farmers in India. *The Detroit News.* 25 January 2021.

Taylor, G. 2020. Crisis lets Beijing get more debtors under its Belt. *The Washington Times Weekly*. 11 May 2020.

Taylor, G. 2021. Adversaries blast US. for clash at Capitol. *The Washington Times Weekly.* 11 January 2021.

Taylor, H.K., 2020. How the other half locks down. *Scottish Daily Mail.* 19 June 2020.

Taylor, M. 2020. Cycling into the future. *The Guardian.* 16 May 2020.

Thapar, K., 2020. The Intersection of Politics and Science. *Hindustan Times (Delhi)*. 5 July 2020.

The Freedom Charter. https://www.sahistory.org.za/article/congress-people-and-freedom-charter accessed on Wednesday 24 May 2022 at 4.58.

Thomson, D., 2013. Why Economics Is Really Called 'the Dismal Science'. The (not-so-dismal) origin myth of a ubiquitous term. The Atlantic. https://www.theatlantic.com/business/archive/2013/12/why-economics-is-really-called-the-dismal-science/282454/. Accessed on 12 Augsut 2020.

Tianliang, L., 2020. Anti-China attacks spike in Australia. *Global Times.* 29 May 2020.

Topping, A., 2020. 'I can't fail Mary'. A grieving husband's fight for new Covid maternity rules. *The Guardian.* 14 November 2020.

Twaij, A., 2020. Can the coronavirus crisis bring about real change? *The Independent.* 21 October 2020.

United Nations (UN). 2015. Universal Declaration of Human Rights.

Vine, S. 2020. Lockdown stasi are coming for YOU. *Daily Mail.* UK. Wednesday 15 April 2020.

Walker, J., Has the left won the argument? *Birmingham Post.* 9 July 2020.

Walker, P., 2020. 'We did not understand virus,' says Johnson *The Guardian.* 25 July 2020.

Web 1. Power, Politics and Protest. The growth of political rights in Britain in the 19th century. What was Chartism? https://www.nationalarchives.gov.uk/education/politics/g7/. Accessed on Tuesday 11 May 2021 at 13.54.

Werner, A., 2020. "Walking Dead" actor Daniel Newman's coronavirus test wasn't processed, but he got billed $9,000. https://www.cbsnews.com/news/coronavirus-test-cost-hospital-bill-insurance-daniel-newman/. Accessed on 22 June 2020.

Wikipedia. *Luddite.* https://en.wikipedia.org/wiki/Luddite. Accessed on 2 August 2021.

Wintour, P., 2020. United Nations 'Emergency used to breach human rights'. *The Guardian.* 24 April 2020.

Woods, 2020. Will lockdown push us into war with our neighbours? *The Sunday Telegraph.* 19 April 2020.

Woodyatt, A., Hollingsworth, J., Westcott, B., Renton, A., Wagner, M. and Hayes, M., CNN. New York governor says ventilator prices went from $20,000 to $50,000 in a matter of weeks. CNN webpage.

Wootton, D., 2015. *The Invention of Science – A new History of the Scientific Revolution.* UK: Harper Collins Publishers.

Worldometer. 2022. https://www.worldometers.info/geography/how-many-countries-are-there-in-the-world/. Accessed on 05 December 2020.

Wyatt, T., 2020. Church leaders challenge lockdown ban on services. *The Independent.* 15 November 2020.

Wyld, A., 2021. COVID-19 magnified discrimination against Indigenous women: minister. *Times Colonist.* 9 March 2021.

Yadav, U. 2020. These Migrant Workers Did Not Suddenly Fall From the Sky: *The Fourteenth Newsletter (2020).* Tricontinental: Institute for Social Research.

Yang, J., 2020. He lost his mother to COVID-19. Now he's starting school year without his fiercest ally. *Toronto Star.* 5 September 2020.

Zavala, E., 2021. Funeral home sued over man's mistaken burial. *San Antonio Express-News.* 8 March 2021.

Index

Printed in the United States
by Baker & Taylor Publisher Services